1764

Basic Economics
A dictionary of terms, concepts and ideas

Arrow Reference Series

General Editor: Chris Cook

Basic Economics
A dictionary of terms, concepts and ideas

Tim Congdon and Douglas McWilliams

Arrow Books

Arrow Books Ltd
3 Fitzroy Square, London W1

An imprint of the Hutchinson Publishing Group

London Melbourne Sydney Auckland
Wellington Johannesburg and agencies
throughout the world

First published 1976
© Tim Congdon and Douglas McWilliams 1976

Set in Monotype Times

Made and printed in Great Britain
by The Anchor Press Ltd
Tiptree, Essex

ISBN 0 09 913020 3

Authors' Note

Someone once said that books on economics can be divided into two categories – those which try to make complicated things simple and those which try to make simple things complicated. We hope this dictionary will join the first category.

The emphasis throughout has been on comprehensibility. We have tried to convey meanings in simple and straightforward language. We have not tried to capture refinements. At times this may have resulted in infidelity to scientifically recognized definitions. We apologize, but hope that the loss of precision has been compensated by a gain in clarity.

The dictionary should be useful to the interested general reader. Most of the terms he finds in the business and financial pages of newspapers are covered. But the greatest appeal of the dictionary should be to students in sixth forms, technical colleges and polytechnics, who find the dictionaries intended for universities rather hard going.

One of the difficulties in economics, as in most subjects, is that it is often impossible to grasp the meaning of a term without knowing its role in the subject. For example, the idea of 'marginal cost pricing' only becomes intelligible when the theory of resource allocation has been understood. We thought that it might be helpful, therefore, to outline the nature and objectives of economics in an introduction. Our account must necessarily be brief, but it should enable the reader to acquire a sense of direction and to develop a feel for the subject. The definitions which then follow should fall into place more easily.

Tim Congdon
Douglas McWilliams

Introduction

Economics was defined by Alfred Marshall, the famous Cambridge economist who lived between 1842 and 1924, as 'on the one side a study of wealth, and on the other, and more important side, a part of the study of man.' Although this definition tells us how economics differs from, say, politics or chemistry, it tells us very little about the objectives of the subject. Perhaps, to get a better idea of the nature of economic study, it would be more rewarding to consider the questions which economics tries to answer.

One of the aims of economic activity is clearly the satisfaction of wants. The more wants are satisfied, the higher are levels of *utility*. But the ability of any society to satisfy wants is limited because it has only a given quantity of *resources*, of raw materials, manpower and equipment, available. The problem, therefore, is to use resources in the most effective way and to achieve the highest possible levels of utility. In the words of Lord Robbins in his classic work, *An Essay on the Nature and Significance of Economic Science* (Macmillan, 2nd edition, 1960), economics can be regarded as 'the relation between ends and scarce means which have alternative uses.' The question to be answered is 'Which *allocation of resources* maximizes society's utility and what rules have to be followed to achieve this *optimal* allocation?'

But this question is by no means the only one which economics considers. Indeed, it tends to be the concern of a particular branch of the subject known as *microeconomics*. Microeconomics deals with the behaviour of individual persons and individuals within an economy, such as companies, banks and consumers. The function of microeconomics is partly to describe the real world and partly to suggest rules for conduct. These rules form the core of *welfare economics*.

Two other questions considered by economics are 'What determines *the distribution of income*?' and 'What determines the level of *national income* and *employment*?'

Some economists believe that the first of these questions can be adequately handled with the tools of microeconomics. They think that individuals seek the job where they are most well paid and that their reward (or *income*) depends on their effort (or how much they have produced, their *output*). The allocation of workers between employments and of *inputs* (of labour, raw materials and so on) between industries is an aspect of the original problem, the satisfaction of wants. It is not really a separate question. Production and distribution, these economists insist, cannot be considered in isolation.

Other economists believe that the distribution of income is not determined by productivity, but by power. They think that the rich have become wealthy by exploiting the poor, often by the use of force or the threat of force. Production and distribution are distinct, they claim. These economists are usually Marxist or socialist and believe that the existing pattern of income distribution is unjust.

The second question, 'What determines the level of national income and employment?', is, however, generally understood to be quite distinct from microeconomics. It has to be answered with ideas generated by *macroeconomics*, the study of the economy as a whole and of its most important corporate features, or *aggregates*, such as aggregate *consumption* and aggregate *investment*. Aggregate consumption is the consumption of all individuals in an economy; it is not concerned with the choices made by a consumer between particular *goods* and *services*. Similarly, aggregate investment is the investment of all the companies in an economy, not the choices made by a particular saver between different assets, like bank deposits or property.

In macroeconomics it is not always assumed, as it is in microeconomics, that resources are scarce. Indeed, this branch of the subject grew up in the 1930s when the existence of mass *unemployment* and considerable spare capacity in industry suggested that large quantities of resources were unused and that the problem of allocating them to the best industries was secondary to that of obtaining any output at all.

The foundations of modern macroeconomics were laid by Lord Keynes in a book called *The General Theory of Employment, Interest and Money* (Macmillan) which was published in 1936. Keynes argued that the government could manipulate aggregate *demand* to maintain a high level of national income. If demand was high, he suggested, companies would be able to sell their output easily and production would be increased to the best possible levels. This would involve employing as many people as wanted to find a job and would result in the eradication of unemployment.

The contrast between macro- and microeconomics can occasionally be a nuisance, particularly to the relatively inexperienced reader, because some terms tend to be used in different ways in the two branches of the subject. For example, in microeconomics 'demand' normally refers to the demand of an individual for a particular product. In macroeconomics it usually refers to the community's desire to spend money on output at the prevailing price level. A statement that 'demand is too high' is taken to imply that the community wishes to buy more goods than it is able to produce and that either prices must rise, causing *inflation*, or that imports must exceed exports.

Clearly these two usages are distinct. In this dictionary we have tried to alert the reader to difficulties of this sort, but only long familiarity with economic language and thinking will overcome them.

Using this Dictionary

Not all the terms defined in this dictionary are cross-referenced to one another every time they occur. Only when the understanding of a term used in an entry adds to the student's comprehension of the particular area under discussion will the term be marked in small capitals, thus:

Futures. Contracts made in a FORWARD MARKET to sell certain specified goods in the future.

A single arrow has been used for 'See'; double arrows for 'See also'.

A list of books for further reading can be found at the back of the book.

Abbreviations

The Bank	Bank of England
BIS	Bank for International Settlements
CAP	Common Agricultural Policy
CBI	Confederation of British Industry
CED	Consumer expenditure deflator
c.i.f.	Commission, insurance and freight/charged in full
Comecon	Council for Mutual Economic Aid
CSO	Central Statistical Office
CTT	Capital transfer tax
DCE	Domestic credit expansion
DCF	Discounted cash flow
DEA	Department of Economic Affairs
ECGD	Export Credit Guarantee Department
ECSC	European Coal and Steel Community
EEC	European Economic Community
EFTA	European Free Trade Association
EMA	European Monetary Agreement
EPU	European Payments Union
FAO	Food and Agriculture Organization
f.o.b.	Free on board
GATT	General Agreement on Tariffs and Trade
GDP	Gross domestic product
GNP	Gross national product
IBRD	International Bank for Reconstruction and Development (World Bank)
ICOR	Incremental capital–output ratio
IMF	International Monetary Fund
IRR	Internal rate of return
LDC	Less developed country

Abbreviations

NBFI	Non-bank financial intermediaries
NBPI	National Board for Prices and Incomes
NEB	National Enterprise Board
NEDC ⎫ **Neddy** ⎬	National Economic Development Council
OECD	Organization for Economic Cooperation and Development
OEEC	Organization for European Economic Cooperation
OPEC	Organization of Petroleum Exporting Countries
PDI	Personal disposable income
P/E ratio	Price/earnings ratio
REP	Regional employment premium
RPDI	Real personal disposable income
RPI	Retail price index
RPM	Resale-price maintenance
SDRs	Special drawing rights
SET	Selective employment tax
UA	European unit of account
UN	United Nations
Unctad	United Nations Conference on Trade and Development
VAT	Value added tax

A

'A' shares. ▷EQUITY.

Accelerated depreciation. ▷COMPANY TAXATION.

Acceleration coefficient. ▷ACCELERATION PRINCIPLE.

Acceleration principle. When the demand for a company's products increases its machinery and equipment are put under pressure. More machines have to be used and the point may be reached where it is only possible to increase output further by undertaking investment. This link between output and investment changes is known as the acceleration principle.

The number of units of capital required for a unit change in output is measured by the acceleration coefficient.

The accelerator theory of investment plays an important role in macroeconomics. It shows how investment responds to changes in output and then itself causes further changes in output by adding to demand. This theory has been integrated with the multiplier model of national incomes determination and has generated important insights into cyclical fluctuations in output and employment. These models, which are mathematically complicated, are known as multiplier-accelerator models.

The link between output and investment changes is also sometimes termed 'the relation'.

Accelerator-multiplier model. More commonly known as the multiplier-accelerator model. ▷ACCELERATION PRINCIPLE.

Accelerator theory of investment. ▷ACCELERATION PRINCIPLE.

Accepting house. ▷BILL OF EXCHANGE; MERCHANT BANKS.

Accessions tax. ▷PERSONAL TAXATION.

Account (1). A record of purchases and sales required by law for companies and certain other institutions.

Account (2). The period, usually a fortnight, between settlement days on the London Stock Exchange. On settlement days the purchase or sales of shares is finalized as money changes hands and shares are passed on to new owners. The account period is important to speculators because they can buy shares without having the money and then sell them again at a profit before the next settlement day.

Account day; also known as settlement day. The day on which transactions on the Stock Exchange are settled. (◊ACCOUNT (2).)

Activity rate. Although most people in a country are of working age and could do a job if they had to, only a proportion are actively employed. This proportion, expressed as a percentage of those who are of working age (normally defined as those between the ages of sixteen and sixty-five for men, and sixteen and sixty for women), is known as the activity rate.

Ad valorem **tax.** A tax which is proportional to the price of a good. For example, value added tax is *ad valorem* because it is expressed as a percentage of the value added in production. The amount of tax to be paid increases as the price of the good increases. An *ad valorem* tax may be contrasted with a specific tax which is levied as a fixed sum regardless of the price of the good. (◊INDIRECT TAXATION.)

Adjustment process. The process by which an economy adjusts to a change in some economic variable and reaches a new state of balance or equilibrium. A notable example is the adjustment of an economy to a surplus or deficit on the balance of payments.

Administered prices. Prices set by an administrative body, such as the government, or by a monopoly seller, rather than by the interaction between consumers and suppliers in a competitive market.

Aggregate demand and supply. In any economy people want to spend money to buy goods and services. The total amount that they want to spend is called aggregate demand. It is generally divided into four categories: demand for consumption goods, demand for investment goods, demand for goods and services provided by the government, and demand for foreign goods or imports.

However, the ability of the economy to meet these demands is limited by its capacity to produce goods. The total value of production in an economy is called aggregate supply. Like aggregate demand, it is divided into four categories: supply of consumption goods, supply of investment goods, supply of goods and services for the government, and the supply of goods for foreign markets or exports.

A distinction may be drawn between planned aggregate demand and supply and actual aggregate demand and supply. Planned aggregate demand may be considered as the amount people want to spend on goods at present prices and actual aggregate demand as the amount they eventually do spend. These may differ because, before purchases are completed, prices may change, forcing people to revise their plans. Similarly, planned aggregate supply may be considered as the amount producers want to supply at present prices and actual aggregate supply as the amount they finally decide it is worthwhile to supply.

The difference between planned and actual magnitudes is sometimes referred to as the difference between *ex ante* and *ex post* magnitudes.

If planned aggregate demand exceeds planned aggregate supply there is said to be an inflationary gap. People want to buy more goods at the prevailing price level than producers are willing to supply. The gap between the economy's spending power and its ability to produce can be removed in several ways, but the main one is an increase in prices. This reduces the number of goods which can be bought with a particular amount of spending power and thereby brings aggregate demand and supply into balance.

If planned aggregate supply exceeds planned aggregate demand there is said to be slack in the economy. This is the opposite of an inflationary gap and is eliminated by a fall in the price level. Slack is sometimes used more loosely to describe an economy with high unemployment and low utilization of machinery and equipment.

In any economy, as these examples show, there are forces which equate aggregate demand and supply even if the plans of consumers and producers are inconsistent. The consequence is that actual aggregate demand is always equal to actual aggregate supply. The equivalence of the two is central to an understanding of Keynesian macroeconomics and is particularly important for the relationship between savings and investment. (⇨KEYNESIAN ECONOMICS.)

Aggregate supply. ⇨AGGREGATE DEMAND AND SUPPLY.

Aid. The world is often said to be divided into rich and poor countries. The rich countries try to give help to the poor by making grants (in effect, gifts of goods and services) or providing loans at low rates of interest. These forms of assistance are known as aid. Aid is channelled either through international organizations, such as the WORLD BANK, in which case it is called multilateral aid, or through agreements between the country which gives and the country which receives help, in which case it is called bilateral aid. Multilateral aid is usually thought to be preferable to bilateral aid because it has fewer political strings attached.

Another drawback of bilateral aid is that it is often 'tied' to a particular donor country. For example, France may decide to lend money at a low rate of interest to India but only if India uses the money to buy goods from France. But India may want to spend the money elsewhere because the sort of goods it needs are not obtainable in France. Tied aid is therefore less helpful than aid where no restrictions are placed on the way it is used.

The United Nations has recommended that rich countries give at least 0.7 per cent of their total output to the poor countries in aid, but few countries give so much.

Allocation, Resource. ◊ECONOMIC EFFICIENCY.

Allocative efficiency. ◊ECONOMIC EFFICIENCY.

Amalgamation. ◊MERGER.

Amortization. When a company has incurred a debt it has to set aside money each year to meet its repayment schedule. The amount set aside is known as amortization. If the debt is to be repaid in a lump sum some years in the future the company may establish a SINKING FUND, into which regular amortization provisions are paid until there is enough to cancel the debt.

Amortization is sometimes used as a synonym for DEPRECIATION.

Amplitude of cycle. ◊TRADE CYCLE.

Annuity. An asset which entitles the owner to a regular annual income of a specified amount. It is possible to buy annuities from insurance companies and certain other financial institutions. For example, an individual might pay an insurance company £20 000 if the insurance company agrees to pay him an income of £2000 every year until he dies.

Appreciation. An increase in the value of an asset. For example, if an antique bought in 1960 for £150 is sold in 1970 for £500 it is said to have appreciated. The £350 gain in value is its appreciation.

Arbitrage. Most commodities and financial assets can be bought and sold in several places at the same time. Apart from unavoidable cost differences due to distance or risk, the prices should be identical everywhere. If this is not true it is worthwhile for a merchant to buy goods in a place where they are cheap and to sell them where they are expensive. This process, which eliminates price differences between markets, is known as arbitrage.

The most important cases of arbitrage are found in international financial markets. For example, if dollars are cheaper in New York than in London it is profitable for a currency operator to purchase them in New York and sell them at a higher price in London. The price of dollars in the two financial centres should then become the same.

Arithmetic mean. ⊳AVERAGE.

Asset. One of the most widely used terms in economics, but also one of the most difficult to define. Considered most generally, it is anything owned by a company or individual.

However, the usage of the term is slightly more restricted than this might suggest. A good which is owned with the intention to consume is not normally regarded as an asset. Instead, assets are considered to be durable and permanent; they can be saved and accumulated. A further defining feature is that assets yield an income or can be easily converted into other assets which do yield an income.

Assets are of two main kinds, fixed and floating. Fixed assets include land, buildings, plant and machinery. Floating assets include bank balances and stocks of raw materials and finished goods. The distinction between fixed and floating assets is determined by convention and does not depend on an important theoretical difference.

Current assets are assets which can be readily turned into cash. These include holdings of liquid assets such as gilts and certificates of deposit, and also stocks and outstanding trade credit.

A liability is the opposite of an asset, because it is obligation to pay something to another individual or company. The net assets of a company are calculated by deducting its liabilities from all the assets at its disposal. For example, a company may have a large debt to a bank. To find out its net asset position an accountant would have to subtract the value of this debt from the value placed on its land, buildings and so on.

Company law requires certain types of asset to be distinguished. Part of any company's profit is distributed to its shareholders as dividends and part is retained in the business where it is added to reserves. Under the Companies Acts reserves have to be divided into revenue reserves and capital reserves. Sums committed to revenue reserves may be paid out in dividends later on; sums in capital reserves may not.

Asset stripping. A business tactic which became common in the late 1960s. Unprofitable companies often own valuable assets such as land or buildings, but are still given a low valuation on the Stock Exchange because they are not making money. It can be worthwhile for a businessman to buy up the shares of such a company, close down its operations and sell off the land and other assets. The proceeds from the sale of land may exceed the cost of the shares. The tactic, which has been widely criticized as ruthless and antisocial, is known as asset stripping.

Atomistic competition. ⇔PERFECT COMPETITION.

Austrian School. A school of economic thought which developed in Vienna in the late nineteenth century. Its most important contributions came in the theory of capital.

Most products are made partly by labour and partly by machinery. One way of considering the production process is to compare the quantities of labour and machinery, or capital, which are used. Another way, emphasized by the Austrian School, is to look at the number of production stages involved. For example, a car is produced as a result of several stages of manufacture. Iron and steel have to be produced in a blast furnace; then transported to a components factory; in the components factory a number of parts are made; and in the car factory itself the parts are assembled into the finished product. The Austrian School realized that all these stages of production take time. The school therefore became involved in questions like 'what determines the rate of interest?' and 'what is the economic significance of "ROUNDABOUT" METHODS OF PRODUCTION?'

The most famous capital theorist in the school was Eugen von Böhm-Bawerk (1851–1914). The later members of the school, notably Ludwig von Mises (1881–1974) and Friedrich von Hayek (1899–   ), have been interested in problems of political philosophy and have been noted defenders of the free enterprise system.

Authorized capital. The amount of share capital registered when a company is set up under the Companies Acts. Authorized capital is to be distinguished from ISSUED CAPITAL. (⇔EQUITY.)

Autonomous investment. A distinction is drawn in economic theory between INDUCED INVESTMENT and autonomous investment. Induced investment is undertaken in response to changes in output or to replace worn-out machinery. But other types of investment, prompted by, for example, changes in the rate of interest or in profitability, are known as autonomous investment. There is more scope for discretion in businessmen's decisions over autonomous investment.

The distinction is slightly artificial and has been of most use to economists in multiplier-accelerator models (⇔ACCELERATION PRINCIPLE).

Average. A single number which is representative of the size of numbers in a group. Its main use is to describe a characteristic of the group. For example, if a country has a low average income it is said to be poor. An average enables an economist to make statements about large populations without repeating every single number in the population.

There are four main concepts of the 'average':

(a) The arithmetic mean. The most commonly used average. It is calculated by adding up all the numbers in a series and dividing the total by however many numbers there are. For example, if the results of a test are 5, 10, 15, 20 and 20, the arithmetic mean is $(5 + 10 + 15 + 20 + 20) \div 5 = 14$.

(b) The geometric mean. This is calculated by multiplying all the numbers in a series together and taking a root of the total. The power of the root is determined by how many numbers there are in the series. In the example, the geometric mean is $5\sqrt{(5 \times 10 \times 15 \times 20 \times 20)} = 12.46$ (roughly). The geometric mean is used for calculating the *Financial Times* Industrial Ordinary Index. ($\Diamond$FINANCIAL TIMES STOCK INDICES.)

(c) The median. The central number in a group. There are as many numbers above it as there are beneath it. In the example, 15 is the median because two numbers (5 and 10) are beneath it and two are above it (20 and 20). The median is unaffected by extreme values.

(d) The mode. The number in a series which occurs most often. In the example, the mode is 20 because it occurs twice whereas all the other numbers occur once. The mode is the number one would be most likely to pick if a sample were being conducted at random.

No one concept is 'better' than the others. The merits of each concept depend on the purposes for which it is required. For some purposes the arithmetic mean is better than the median and vice versa. However, the arithmetic mean is used so often that it can be regarded almost as a synonym for 'average'. When average is referred to without further qualification it is almost certainly the arithmetic mean which is under consideration.

A further concept is a moving average. A TIME SERIES may be marked by a variety of random fluctuations which disguise the underlying TREND. A moving average is the arithmetic mean of the value of a variable in a particular period and of its values in a fixed number of preceding and subsequent periods. Using a moving average 'smooths out' the series.

Average propensity to consume (APC). The proportion of all income consumed (or not saved) by an economy or individual. The average propensity to consume is calculated by dividing total consumption by income.

The concept of the propensity to consume was developed by Lord Keynes in *The General Theory of Employment, Interest and Money*. He conjectured that, in wealthy societies, people will increase their consumption by less than their increase in income. Some economists have interpreted this as meaning that the average propensity to consume should fall through time. However, the average propensity to consume has in practice been remarkably stable from decade to decade and most studies have instead examined the reasons for the different propensities to consume of different classes in a society. The rich, it seems, always save more than the poor.

The average propensity to save is the proportion of all income saved. As income is either saved or consumed, the average propensity to save and the average propensity to consume add up to 1.

Average propensity to save. ▷AVERAGE PROPENSITY TO CONSUME.

B

Backwardation. In financial and commodity markets contracts can be made to deliver goods or assets at some agreed point in the future rather than immediately. The price if the purchase were completed immediately is known as the 'spot price' (SPOT MARKET) and the price at the agreed future date as the 'forward price' (FUTURES). The spot price is normally, but not always, above the forward price. The difference between the two prices is known as the backwardation.

Balance of payments. Most countries have economic relations with other countries. They buy and sell goods abroad and they invest money elsewhere or are hosts to foreign investment. All these transactions have to be recorded to ensure that a country is not running heavily into debt with the rest of the world.

The balance of payments is the set of accounts which records a country's international transactions. Such accounts are prepared in accordance with conventional accounting principles: the purchase of goods and services from other countries is treated as a debit and the sale of goods and services to other countries as a credit. But, as in conventional accounts, the distinction between different kinds of transaction can become complicated.

There are two main accounts in the balance of payments, the capital account and the current account. On the capital account a country may acquire more assets abroad than other countries have acquired within its frontiers. For example, if a British chemical company has set up a plant in Germany worth £100 million and a German car company has set up a factory in Britain worth £50 million, and these are the only two items on the capital account, Britain has increased its net assets (⟨⟩ASSET) abroad by £50 million. But Britain has to pay for the assets by an outflow of currency. The capital account of the balance of payments is therefore shown as having a deficit of £50 million.

Of course, the capital account could also be in surplus in which case other countries would have increased their ownership of assets in Britain. In other words, the capital account shows whether a country owns more or less abroad than it did at the beginning of the period under consideration.

The current account measures payments for IMPORTS and EXPORTS of goods and services. If a country is buying more abroad than it is selling, it is said to be running a current account deficit. Such a deficit is similar to an excess of expenditure over income for an individual and implies that the country is incurring debt to the rest of the world. For this reason a current account deficit is normally a source of concern to the government and causes corrective measures to be taken. Aggregate demand can be reduced by DEFLATION leaving consumers and companies with less money to spend and forcing them to cut down on the foreign-produced goods they buy; the exchange rate can be lowered by DEVALUATION making exports cheaper to foreigners who then buy them in great quantity; or direct restrictions can be placed on imports by means of QUOTAS and other artificial restrictions on trade.

If the current account is in surplus the balance of payments is sometimes said to be active; if it is in deficit it is described as passive.

A clear distinction is to be drawn between the current account balance and the BALANCE OF TRADE. The balance of trade refers to transactions in tangible goods. The current account incorporates the balance of trade, but includes other transactions, such as the purchase and sale of services like insurance, tourism and transport, and receipts of income from assets owned abroad. These further transactions are known as invisible trade or invisibles. It is quite possible for a country to have a deficit on the balance of trade, but to be earning so much from invisibles that its current account is in surplus. Indeed, the United Kingdom is usually in this position. The invisible balance is positive and larger than the trade deficit.

Two further concepts relating to the balance of payments may be noted:

(a) Liquidity basis. Although a country may be acquiring assets abroad and claims on foreigners by selling more to other countries than it is receiving from them, its holdings of liquid assets may be declining (▷LIQUIDITY). For example, its reserves of foreign currencies may be spent on foreign investment in factories and mines. If there were a sudden and accidental increase in its international obligations, it might find itself in difficulties because the factories and mines could only be sold after delays and perhaps at less than their true value.

The liquidity basis of the balance of payments tries to measure the change in a country's liquid position. Assets which are generally acceptable as means of payment in international trade, such as currencies and marketable securities, are included in the liquid position.

24

(b) Official settlements basis. Transactions between countries are of two kinds, those between private companies and individuals and those between governments. If there is a deficit on one kind of a transaction there has to be a surplus on the other. The official settlements basis shows the balance on government transactions.

Balance of trade; also known as visible balance. Payments are made between countries for a variety of transactions. But the balance of trade refers to the balance of payments on transactions in tangible goods. Such goods have to be shipped and transported from one country to another. The transaction cannot be completed by a phone call or postal message, as in the case of most INVISIBLES.

A country has a trade surplus if exports of tangible goods exceed imports of tangible goods.

Balance sheet. A list of a company's assets and liabilities to show its value to the owners. A company has no wealth of its own because it belongs to the people who set it up. But many of the assets operated by a company are owned not by these people but by banks and other creditors. A balance sheet shows how much belongs to the banks and other creditors and how much to the original investors.

Balanced budget. Governments receive revenue from taxation and carry out expenditure on goods and services. If tax revenue and expenditure are equal, a government is said to have achieved a balanced budget.

Before the acceptance of KEYNESIAN ECONOMICS after the Second World War, balanced budgets were considered essential for reasons of financial prudence. But it is now understood that government spending and taxation affect employment and output. Financial considerations can no longer be seen in isolation from their effect on aggregate demand.

Baltic Exchange. The market in the City of London where shipping contracts are traded.

Bancor. The name suggested by Lord Keynes for an international unit of currency at the BRETTON WOODS Conference in 1944. It was intended to add to the world's reserves of foreign currency. The name and the proposal were rejected at the conference, but SPECIAL DRAWING RIGHTS, first issued by the International Monetary Fund in 1970, have fulfilled the same role.

Bank, Clearing. ⇨CLEARING BANKS.

Bank, Commercial. ⇨COMMERCIAL BANKS.

Bank deposits. Money put into an account at a bank by an individual, a company or some other institution. The money may be placed in either a current account where it can be withdrawn on demand or a deposit account where withdrawals can only be made after an agreed period of notice.

Bank for International Settlements (BIS).   An institution which serves as a forum for European CENTRAL BANKS. It was established in 1930 to enable European countries to coordinate policy towards the German reparations problem. However, this function soon became unimportant and its main role today is to arrange short-term loans between the central banks of Belgium, France, Italy, the Netherlands, Sweden, Switzerland, the United Kingdom and West Germany. These short-term loans can be used to combat speculation against their currencies. The BIS has acted as if it were a bank to the central banks.

Bank, Industrial.   ▷INDUSTRIAL BANKS.

Bank lending.   Banks advance money to companies and individuals to permit them to make larger purchases than they could pay for out of current income. These advances are known as bank lending. They are an asset of the banks because the borrowers are obliged to repay the loans at some future date.

Bank, Merchant.   ▷MERCHANT BANKS.

Bank of England.   The central bank of the United Kingdom. It is known colloquially in the City of London as the 'Bank'.

The Bank of England was established in 1694 by Act of Parliament. It was, however, a privately owned company whose object was to lend money to the government. It remained in private hands until 1946 when it was nationalized. By then it was realized that the Bank was immensely powerful because of its influence on monetary policy and it was felt that official control over its operations, conducted by means of Treasury directives, was necessary.

The Bank has four main functions. The first is to serve as banker to the British government. If the government has a deficit on its finances the Bank of England has to ensure that other agents in the economy, either the banking system or the private sector, lend enough money to cover the deficit. The two main ways of meeting a deficit are by sales of GILT-EDGED SECURITIES to the general public or by an increase in the government's liabilities with the banking system. The second way is commonly known as 'printing money'. Direct loans to the government by the Bank are known as ways and means advances.

The second function is to act as LENDER OF LAST RESORT to the banks and other financial institutions. Because of an unsettled economic outlook people sometimes decide to withdraw money from their bank accounts. If banks have been lending heavily they may not have enough LIQUIDITY to meet the demand for withdrawals. In such circumstances the banks may have no option but to ask the Bank of England for assistance. Bank of England help should always restore confidence because its notes and coin are liabilities of the government and it is illegal not to accept them as means of payment. In practice, the lender-of-last-resort function is less exciting than this account might suggest. The main form of assistance given by the Bank is day-to-day help to the DISCOUNT HOUSES. It removes temporary shortages of credit due to the uneven flow of government expenditure and tax revenue or to other erratic financial movements.

The third function is to operate the government's monetary policy. Monetary policy is the manipulation of interest rates and money supply to influence decisions to spend and, therefore, such variables as employment, output and the balance of payments.

The main weapons of monetary policy are open market operations or changes in MINIMUM LENDING RATE. Open market operations are conducted by the purchase or sale of certain financial assets from City institutions. A characteristic operation is the sale of TREASURY BILLS to the discount houses. This withdraws funds from the houses and tightens conditions in financial markets.

Another important part of monetary policy, less frequently mentioned, involves funding operations. These are changes in the time structure of the NATIONAL DEBT. For example, if the Bank of England succeeds in selling a large quantity of gilt-edged securities in place of Treasury bills, the average period to redemption is increased. Funding debt in this way reduces demand in the economy because it withdraws liquidity from the banking system.

Finally, the Bank of England keeps the United Kingdom's reserves of gold and foreign currency. When the United Kingdom has a balance of payments deficit it runs down the reserves to pay for the excess of imports over exports. When, on the other hand, there is a balance of payments surplus it increases the reserves. These operations are performed through the EXCHANGE EQUALIZATION ACCOUNT.

The two main parts of the Bank are the issue department, which is responsible for issuing notes and coin, and the banking department, which carries out the Bank's policy towards the discount houses and the banking system generally. This division into two departments dates from the Bank Charter Act of 1844.

Bank rate. The rate of interest charged until 1971 by the BANK OF ENGLAND on loans made to financial institutions, particularly the

27

discount houses, in the City. This rate is now known as MINIMUM LENDING RATE. There is no real difference in meaning between bank rate and minimum lending rate and the change in name was intended only to differentiate the style of monetary policy before 1971 from the style associated with COMPETITION AND CREDIT CONTROL.

Bank rate was an important barometer of financial conditions in London. Other interest rates tended to follow it up or down and this gave the Bank of England considerable power to influence the price and availability of credit.

'Bank', The. ⬦BANK OF ENGLAND.

Banking. The business of borrowing and lending money. A bank attracts deposits of money by offering a rate of interest, certain financial services and security. The companies and individuals from whom it borrows in this way are known as its depositors.

If it can be confident that the depositors will not want to withdraw their money in a rush it can lend the money to other companies and individuals in the economy. The rate of interest it charges on these loans is above the rate it pays to its depositors. The difference between the two rates is the bank's profit.

Barriers to entry. Conditions which discourage the entry of new companies into an industry. Typical examples are economies of scale, monopolistic bargaining power, and advertising. These barriers to entry mean that the costs of companies already operating in an industry are much beneath those of a company which has just begun to seek business. The new entrant may find it prohibitively expensive to maintain a foothold in the industry.

A good example is the detergents industry in the United Kingdom. Two companies, Unilever and Procter and Gamble, have dominated the industry for decades. It would be difficult for new companies to compete because both advertise their products heavily and have built up considerable customer loyalty.

Barriers to trade. Restrictions on the free movement of goods and services between countries. The main examples are tariffs, quotas and import deposit schemes. (⬦IMPORT RESTRICTIONS.)

Barter. The direct exchange of goods and services for other goods and services, avoiding the use of money. It has the disadvantage that one trader may have difficulty finding another trader whose needs match the stock of goods he has to sell. TRANSACTIONS COSTS are higher than in a money economy.

Base-period. The point of time used as the starting point for a TIME

SERIES or a time series of INDEX NUMBERS. It is, therefore, the basis for comparing with other periods. For example, if 1952 is the base-period for the retail price index and retail prices are higher in 1955, one says that retail prices are higher in 1955 than in the base-period.

Base rate. Banks lend money to a great variety of customers. Some customers are less creditworthy than others. Banks therefore charge a higher rate of interest to the unreliable customers because they are more risky. The base rate is the rate they charge to a first-class borrower with little risk attached. To other customers, personal borrowers, for example, they charge base rate plus 2 or 3 per cent.

Bear. A speculator who, in the anticipation of a fall in prices, sells stocks or shares. If he does not possess the stocks and shares to be sold, but intends to buy them when the price falls, he is said to be 'selling short'.

'Beggar-my-neighbour'. The conduct of international trade and financial relations by one country to its advantage but to the disadvantage of other countries. Tariffs are a good example of this because they damage the marketing prospects of other countries' exports, while protecting domestic industry.

The drawbacks to 'beggar-my-neighbour' policies are twofold. First, they invite retaliation by other countries and may in the end be unfavourable to those who initiate them. Second, they reduce the proportion of output which enters into international trade. The gains to all countries from international specialization are lost and living standards and employment throughout the world suffer.

The effect of short-sighted 'beggar-my-neighbour' policies on the economy in the 1930s was severe and, ever since, most advanced countries have been committed to the reduction of trade barriers and the freeing of international economic relations. (⟡IMPORT RESTRICTIONS.)

Behavioural assumption. An assumption about the way agents in an economy will act in certain situations. Behavioural assumptions play an important role in the construction of economic models.

Behavioural theory of the firm. A theory of the operation of firms which emphasizes the behaviour of employees acting in their own interests. It is to be contrasted with the conventional theory of the firm which assumes that employees attempt to maximize the profits which accrue to the firm's owners.

For example, 'rule-of-thumb' pricing is an essential part of the behavioural theory of the firm. Prices are based, according to the theory, on simple rules, such as a fixed percentage mark-up on cost price. Employees adopt these rules because they are simple and convenient to operate, not because they maximize profits.

Benefit—cost analysis. ◊COST—BENEFIT ANALYSIS.

Benelux. The CUSTOMS UNION established in 1948 between Belgium, Luxembourg and the Netherlands. It served as a forerunner to the EUROPEAN ECONOMIC COMMUNITY. The initial treaty removed some internal barriers to trade and set up a common external tariff. The aim of the union was ultimately to coordinate the economic systems of the three countries by promoting the free movement of labour and capital between them. These aims have all now been assumed by the Common Market, of which the Benelux countries were founder members in 1957.

Beveridge Report. The report, *Social Insurance and Allied Services*, prepared by Lord (then Sir William) Beveridge in 1942 for the British government. It proved to be a landmark in the evolution of the British welfare state.

The report recommended a system of social security to abolish the two great causes of need within society, sickness and poverty, and included a section on the maintenance of full employment which Beveridge later expanded and published in 1944 as *Full Employment in a Free Society*.

'Big Four'. The name given to the four largest clearing banks in England. They are Barclays, Lloyds, the Midland and the National Westminster. They were known as the 'Big Five' before the merger of the National Provincial and Westminster Banks.

Bilateral aid. . ◊AID.

Bilateralism. The tendency to make trade and financial agreements between two countries to the exclusion of others. It is to be contrasted with multilateralism, which promotes agreements between large numbers of countries. Bilateralism confines the gains for international trade to only two countries and is, therefore, disapproved of by the GENERAL AGREEMENT ON TARIFFS AND TRADE.

Bill of exchange. A trader may want to buy some goods from another trader but does not have the money immediately available. The buyer may nevertheless be able to secure the goods by giving the seller a piece of paper which promises payment at some future date, typically, in three months' time. This piece of paper is known as a bill of exchange or commercial bill.

It is still possible for the seller to obtain money at once if he can pass on the bill to a financial institution in exchange for cash. If this is done the buyer does not pay the seller in three months' time, but the financial institution instead. The risk of default and the cost of waiting have been transferred from the seller to the financial institution.

A financial institution involved in this sort of business is known as an accepting house because it 'accepts' bills. It makes its profit by charging a small discount on the bill. But banks also can perform acceptance business, in which case the bills are known as bank bills. When an ordinary trader accepts bills, they are known as trade bills.

Bills of exchange were immensely important in the development of the City of London in the second half of the nineteenth century. Bills were accepted for trade transactions between countries and therefore greatly improved the availability of credit for international commerce. These bills were and are still known as foreign bills of exchange. (◊MERCHANT BANKS.)

Bimetallism. The policy of maintaining a currency based on two precious metals. This was urged at the end of the nineteenth century when most currencies were based on either gold or silver. A combination of both, it was argued, would make the value of the currency more stable. The campaign for bimetallism was associated with the political career of William Jennings Bryan and the American presidential elections of 1896 and 1900.

Black market. Markets where goods are traded illegally, usually to avoid taxes, rationing or price controls.

Blue Book. A name given by economists to the annual publication of the British government on *National Income and Expenditure* which gives figures for the British GROSS NATIONAL PRODUCT and its components. It is so named from its blue cover.

Blue chip. An equity share of a company with a good financial reputation, where it is thought there is negligible risk of bankruptcy.

Bolton Committee. A committee set up by the government under John Bolton in 1968 to inquire into the part played in the economy by small firms which, in the report, were defined as firms employing less than 200 employees in manufacturing with similar definitions for other sectors. It found that the small firm sector in Britain contributed 19 per cent of the GNP, less than in comparable countries, but it did not recommend discrimination in favour of small firms.

Bond (1). A form of fixed-interest security, such as gilts, issued by central or local government, which is normally redeemable at some fixed date. (◇GILT-EDGED SECURITIES.)

Bond (2). Goods in bond are those in secured warehouses on which customs and excise duties have not been paid. They are generally either traded goods in transit, or goods, such as whisky, which are being allowed to mature.

Book profits. ◇INFLATION ACCOUNTING.

Book value. The value given to assets in the accounts of a company. This is often the purchase price. The book value of an asset should be distinguished from its market value, which is the amount for which it could be sold.

Bretton Woods. The international financial conference which met in July 1944 at Bretton Woods, New Hampshire, to determine the post-war international monetary system. Three plans were submitted, by the British, Canadian and American delegations, and the final agreement was influenced by the American proposals. In order that multilateral trade should be developed, the agreement proposed the CONVERTIBILITY of currencies and stable EXCHANGE RATES. To provide assistance for countries with balance of payments difficulties, the INTERNATIONAL MONETARY FUND and the International Bank for Reconstruction and Development (WORLD BANK) were set up.

Broker. ◇BROKERAGE.

Brokerage. The commission charged by a broker in a financial market. A broker buys and sells stocks and shares on behalf of his clients. In the London Stock Exchange, this is done by his asking the JOBBER for a price, without revealing whether he is a buyer or a seller. The jobber will quote two prices, for buyers and sellers, and if the appropriate price is suitable then the broker will buy. The jobber's profit is made from the difference between the buying and selling prices. The broker's profit is a certain percentage of the price of the stock that he trades, generally around $1\frac{1}{2}$ or 2 per cent, although this is higher for small deals and lower for large deals.

Budget. A budget for a household is its plan for organizing its spending based on its expected income. In the same way companies and governments that wish to plan for future expenditure must produce budgets. A company will be concerned with its profitability, the long-term relationship between income and expenditure, and its CASH-FLOW, which is the difference between its receipts and outgoings at any point in time.

A government has to organize its budget so that (a) it spends on the projects that it wants to spend on; (b) it raises its revenue in a suitable way; and (c) the net effect on AGGREGATE DEMAND of its plans for raising revenue and for spending will be satisfactory. Proposals for government revenue-raising and expenditure will be designed to satisfy the goals of fairness, efficiency and practicality. As a rough guide, the budget will increase aggregate demand if expenditure exceeds revenue, and will reduce it if revenue exceeds expenditure. This is affected to some extent by whether those on whom money is spent and those from whom money is collected would be liable to spend or save marginal increments to their income.

Compensatory or DEFICIT FINANCING takes place when expenditure exceeds revenue. This normally increases aggregate demand and can be used to reflate the economy. When this is proposed as a temporary measure it can be referred to as 'pump priming'.

The government estimates are the expected levels of expenditure that are presented to Parliament for approval. As such they represent an integral part of the budget proposals.

Budget line (1). A concept in the theory of value. In indifference curve analysis the budget line shows how much a consumer may buy of two goods with a particular income, while the indifference curves indicate his preferences between the two goods. It is the interaction between the budget line and the indifference curves, between preferences and constraints, which determines how much a consumer buys of any combination of goods. (⬦INDIFFERENCE ANALYSIS.)

Budget line (2). A now obsolete distinction made in government estimates between current expenditure, which is above the line, and capital expenditure, which is below the line. (⬦CURRENT ACCOUNT (4).)

Budgetary control. The name given to the procedure of checks carried out to ensure that actual revenue and expenditure is kept within the allowances estimated in a budget.

Building society. A British institution that provides loans for home-buyers. Building societies have expanded from localized friendly societies in the seventeenth century when potential house-buyers grouped together to share the costs of buying their houses in turn. They still retain certain characteristics from that period however; many of the names are from the towns of origin of the societies, such as the Halifax Building Society, or the Bradford and Bingley Building Society. Also, the bias in favour of making loans to those who are already investing in the societies remains, and the societies are still run on a non-profit-making basis. Deposits are made with building societies in the same way as with banks, although depositors are not given cheque books. Deposits subject to more than one month's notice are known as 'shares'. Loans, called mortgages, are given with the building acting as security, for periods up to thirty-five years. Building societies are regulated under the Building Societies Act, 1874, and the government gives both depositors and borrowers tax concessions. Probably because of this, deposits with building societies have risen quickly and are now greater than deposits with the commercial banks.

Built-in stabilizers. Government policies that automatically reflate the level of AGGREGATE DEMAND when it is low and deflate the level of aggregate demand when it is high. Examples of this are the tax system – where more tax is paid when demand is high than when it is low – and the social services – where more money is spent on, for example, unemployment benefits when demand is low than when it is high. Although these tend to stabilize the level of demand, they do not do so sufficiently to obviate the need for STABILIZATION POLICIES.

Bull. A dealer in financial markets who buys when prices are low expecting them to rise. A bullish market is a market where the prices of assets are expected to rise.

Bullion. Ingots of precious metal, normally gold. A bullion market is a financial market in which gold is traded.

Business cycle. ⟡TRADE CYCLE.

Buyer's market. A market where there is excess supply and buyers are able to force sellers to lower their prices.

C

Call option. ⟡OPTION.

'Calling'. ⟡DISCOUNT HOUSE.

Cambridge School. Cambridge University in England and, to a lesser extent, Harvard University in Cambridge, Massachusetts, USA, have been famous for the distinction and originality of their economists. Schools of thought, provoking major controversies, have developed. Three are particularly well known:

(a) The Cambridge School of Alfred Marshall (1842–1924), who became Professor of Political Economy at Cambridge University, England, in 1884. Marshall perfected the analysis of supply and demand and was the founder of modern microeconomics. He placed emphasis on marginalism (⟡MARGINAL ANALYSIS). For example, he described the profit-maximizing behaviour of firms in terms of marginal cost and marginal revenue. Marshall's successors at Cambridge, Professor A. C. Pigou and Professor D. H. Robertson, shared his interest in microeconomics, but were also known for their contributions to monetary economics.

(b) The Two Cambridges Controversy. A debate developed in the 1960s between Cambridge, England, and Cambridge, Massachusetts. It focused on the nature of capital and was important because of its relationship to the problem of income distribution and, more distantly, to the choice between different economic systems. Economists in Cambridge, Massachusetts, held that the rate of profit is determined by the MARGINAL PRODUCTIVITY OF CAPITAL, with the implication that profits are related to the efficiency of production; economists in Cambridge, England, argued, on the other hand, that there is no such thing as the marginal productivity of capital and that the measurement of profit cannot be separated from the measurement of capital, with the implication that profits might be due to exploitation or class struggle.

(c) The 'New Cambridge School' versus 'Old Cambridge School'

35

debate. In the early 1970s a group of economists in Cambridge, England, suggested that the financial deficit of the public sector and the balance of payments deficit are linked. In other words, if the government spends more than it is receiving in tax revenues, a country runs into debt with the rest of the world.

This New Cambridge School doctrine was quickly attacked by another group of economists from the same university, who became known as the Old Cambridge School. The Old School argued that the balance of payments depended on other influences, such as the competitiveness of exports, and that there is no direct link between the financial deficit of one agent in the economy and the financial surplus of another. Most economists do not take the New Cambridge School doctrine seriously, because it fails to explain why agents behave in the way required, but recognize the contribution made by the New Cambridge School in bringing FLOW OF FUNDS analysis to public attention.

Capacity utilization rate. The ratio of actual output to the output that would be produced if an enterprise were working at full capacity. It is not always clear what constitutes full capacity, since ways of increasing output – for example, by extra shift working – can often be found if there is sufficient incentive. Comparisons of capacity utilization rates should, therefore, be treated with caution.

Capital. The term 'capital', like all terms which are used with great frequency in economics, is also one of the most imprecise. There are three common usages:

(a) The wealth of a person or the value of a shareholder's interest in a company.

(b) Funds available for investment, usually in the sense of money, which can be spent without further ado to purchase machinery, buildings and so on.

(c) Physical goods which are already produced and which can be used in the production of further goods.

However, these three usages by no means exhaust the various shades of meaning which can be assumed by the word.

The capital of a company or an economy can be divided into its circulating capital and its fixed capital. Circulating capital may be regarded as goods or funds which will have been used up in the production process within a specified period of time. For example, if a year is the period under consideration, seeds and fertilizer are circulating capital because most crops are harvested annually.

Fixed capital comprises such things as machinery, buildings and land, which are fairly durable and will last for a long time.

Most of the controversies surrounding the concept of capital have arisen because it can be evaluated in several ways (for example, the Two Cambridges Controversy; ⊳CAMBRIDGE SCHOOL). There are three main methods of evaluation and they often give different answers.

The first is to consider the stream of income which will be generated by a capital asset in a number of future periods of time. It is possible to place this value on this stream of income today, known as the PRESENT VALUE. For example, if a factory is expected to yield a profit of £100 this year and next, but then to fall to pieces, its present value is probably approaching £200.

The second is to calculate the cost of replacing the capital asset to be valued. The factory in the example above might cost £150 to construct. Its replacement cost would then be beneath its present value and it would be worthwhile to set about building it.

The final method is to recall how much it cost when it was purchased. When the order for the factory was first placed the owner may have been charged £130. In this case the historical cost is beneath both the replacement cost and the present value and the owner is obviously making an attractive profit.

None of these three methods is superior to the other and the merits of each depend on the purpose for which it is required. The three are identical if the economy is in EQUILIBRIUM – that is, if it is not possible for someone to make an excessive amount of money by setting up a new plant. In the example above the economy is not in equilibrium because the owner of the factory can earn a large profit of nearly £70 from an investment of only £130.

Capital account. ⊳BALANCE OF PAYMENTS.

Capital allowances. Reductions in company taxation related to the amount of capital that is considered to have been used in a particular period. For example, if a company's capital depreciates, the DEPRECIATION is not part of profit and it would be unfair to tax profit before some adjustment had been made. In most countries capital allowances are used to stimulate investment.

Capital budgeting. A method of budgeting that allows investment projects to be evaluated separately to compare alternative uses of capital.

Capital charges. The costs a company incurs when it borrows money to increase its capital. Examples are payments of interest and DEPRECIATION.

Capital, Circulating. ⊳CAPITAL.

Capital consumption. ⟡DEPRECIATION.

Capital expenditure. The purchase of fixed capital, including the replacement of existing capital.

Capital formation. Expenditure on fixed capital, excluding the replacement of existing capital.

Capital gains. The gains obtained by the owner of an asset when it increases in value. If he sells it at a price higher than that at which he bought he is obviously better off and is said to have made capital gains.

Economists have not agreed on their theoretical status. Some argue that capital gains are part of income and should be taxed in the same way; others feel that they are not part of income because no output corresponds to them. The most important sources of capital gain are the purchase and sale of SHARES and land.

Capital goods. Physical goods, such as machinery or equipment, which are used to produce other goods.

Capital-intensive. A method of production is said to be capital-intensive if it relies on a high ratio of capital goods to labour.

Capital, Issued. ⟡ISSUED CAPITAL.

Capital, Marginal efficiency of. ⟡MARGINAL EFFICIENCY OF CAPITAL.

Capital, Marginal productivity of. ⟡MARGINAL PRODUCTIVITY OF CAPITAL.

Capital market. A market where those who wish to borrow can trade with those who wish to lend. The Stock Exchange is an example.

Capital movements. Items on the capital account of a country's BALANCE OF PAYMENTS. They arise when foreigners purchase or sell assets in other countries and can be very large, causing movements in exchange rates.

Capital, Nominal. ⟡EQUITY.

Capital–output ratio, Incremental. Additions to a country's capital stock increase its ability to produce output. The ratio between the increase in the capital stock and the increase in output is known as the incremental capital–output ratio. It is an important concept in the study of economic fluctuations because it shows how a small stimulus to demand, by calling forth more output, can later cause a much larger increase in investment.

Capital, Registered. ▷EQUITY.

Capital reserves. ▷ASSET.

Capital stock. In an economy, the accumulation of fixed and circulating capital. However, the term is commonly used to refer to an economy's fixed capital.

Capital transfer tax. ▷PERSONAL TAXATION.

Capital, Working. ▷WORKING CAPITAL.

Capitalism. An economic system which recognizes private property. Under capitalism individuals or groups of individuals own goods and land, including means of production, and dispose of these assets as they think fit. Capitalism is to be contrasted with communism, where the means of production are owned by the state.

Capitalism is typically associated with a complicated structure of credit. Owners of property lend their property to others who can use it more productively. The lenders receive interest payments or dividends, while the borrowers earn profits from the utilization of assets at their command. The possibility of receiving income for no apparent effort is sometimes considered unethical and has been singled out as the main drawback of capitalism.

Capitalism is also widely believed to be connected with the decentralization of decision-taking. In other words, decisions about output, employment and investment are taken by a large number of individuals according to their own preferences and information. In a centralized system, on the other hand, such decisions are taken by a central planning agency under political control. However, the link between capitalism and decentralization is not a necessary one. A communist society can seek to decentralize decision-taking powers also.

Capitalism has reached its furthest stage of development in the advanced industrial societies of North America, Western Europe, Japan and Australasia. These countries are mostly members of the Organization for Economic Cooperation and Development.

Capitalization (1). The issuing of shares to reflect gains in the value of a company because of the building up of reserves.

Capitalization (2). The value and structure of the capital of a company.

Capitalization (3); also known as market capitalization. The value of a company's shares on the Stock Exchange.

Cardinal utility. ▷ORDINAL UTILITY.

Cartel.   A group of producers of some good or commodity combining for mutual profit. An example of a cartel is OPEC, the ORGANIZATION OF PETROLEUM EXPORTING COUNTRIES. Cartels can cause a sector of the economy to behave as if it were under monopolistic control. They are outlawed in Britain and the United States except under certain specified circumstances.

Cash-balance effect.   The extent to which an individual's expenditure is affected by the amount of cash which he holds. The Friedmanite view of the operation of MONETARY POLICY is based on the assumption of a large cash-balance effect: people are assumed to keep a fixed proportion of the value of their assets in cash, so that a reduction in the amount of cash in the economy should bring a proportionate reduction in asset values and money income. (⊳FRIEDMANITE ECONOMICS.)

Cash-flow.   The net amount of money flowing into a firm after expenditure is taken into account. The gross cash-flow is the amount of sales minus expenditure minus provision for depreciation in the period chosen. The net cash-flow is gross cash-flow minus provision for the taxes for which the firm became liable in the period.
  Businessmen use cash-flow as an important criterion for decision-making because it indicates the change in a company's liquidity.

Central bank.   The bank which the government uses to organize the MONETARY POLICY of a nation. In Britain the central bank is the BANK OF ENGLAND. The central bank generally acts as the government's banker, issues bank notes and controls the behaviour of other financial institutions.

Central bank intervention.   ⊳INTERVENTION.

Central Statistical Office (CSO).   A British government office in Whitehall. It is part of the Cabinet Office and compiles statistical information important to government departments. In particular, it prepares the national accounts every year.

Certificate of deposit.   A marketable security issued by a bank certifying that a deposit has been made with it that is redeemable at some fixed date, generally only a short time in the future. For an individual, a certificate of deposit offers a rate of interest slightly higher than a deposit account, while giving him the ability to sell the security and obtain the money if he needs to do so.

Charge account.   ⊳TIME DEPOSIT.

Chartist.   A person who bases his opinions on the movement of prices of stocks, shares or commodities on an analysis of past trends in price rather than an analysis of the real factors that are likely to affect prices. Generally this is done with a chart showing the movement of the price over time, so that the patterns of trends and cycles can be observed and decisions about buying and selling made.

Cheap money. A deliberate government policy of maintaining low rates of interest. This policy was popular after the Depression of the 1930s when governments wished to foster expansion and growth. There was the added advantage, for the government, that it could finance its borrowing cheaply. To ensure that rates of interest are not bid up, governments following cheap money policies have to commit themselves to supplying the money that is demanded at the pre-determined rate of interest. Cheap money policies were abandoned by the British government in favour of a more flexible interest rate policy in 1951. Cheap money was most associated with the name of Hugh Dalton, the Labour Chancellor of the Exchequer from 1945–7.

Chicago School. ⇨QUANTITY THEORY OF MONEY.

c.i.f. – cost, insurance and freight. As a statistical convention, the value of imports into a country are sometimes measured c.i.f. – that is, at their cost when they enter the country, including the transport and insurance costs involved in their movements from the country of origin, while exports are measured f.o.b. (free on board), excluding transport and insurance costs.

Circular flow of income. ⇨INCOME, CIRCULAR FLOW OF.

Circulating capital. ⇨CAPITAL.

Classical economics. The school of economic thought that dominated the late eighteenth century and most of the nineteenth century, particularly in Britain. The names associated with this school of thought include Adam Smith, David Ricardo, T. R. Malthus, and John Stuart Mill, and the ideas of classical economics were developed into neo-classical economics by Alfred Marshall (⇨CAMBRIDGE SCHOOL (a)).

The essential principles of classical economics were that individuals, in the economic sphere, behaved in an essentially selfish fashion, looking after their own interests rather than those of others, but that competition from others looking after their own interests would impose a restraint on every individual. Adam Smith coined the phrase 'the invisible hand' to summarize how free competition allocated resources.

Ricardo's major contribution was to develop the labour theory of value. He claimed that since all costs other than land could be ultimately ascribed to labour, the value of a good was the cost of the labour

41

involved in producing it. Marx followed this view very closely (◇MARX-IAN ECONOMICS).

Classical monetary policy. ◇MONETARY POLICY.

Clearing banks. The banks which belong to the London Clearing House. These are the largest banks which deal directly with the public, such as Barclays, National Westminster, the Midland Bank and Lloyds, and some small banks.

Clearing House. An organization for the settlement of its members' debts with one another. The large London-based banks belong to the London Clearing House, and all cheques drawn on one bank and cashed by another are sent to the Clearing House.

Close company. This is a company effectively controlled by a small number of shareholders, generally less than five. Because these companies have been used as a device to avoid taxes, there is special legislation in Britain on the amount of their income which can be retained, and on the amount which must be distributed to the shareholders.

Closed economy. An economy that does not trade with any other economies. China has, until recently, behaved almost as a closed economy, but generally the term is a theoretical concept used to simplify the exposition of an economic MODEL.

Closed shop. A firm whose employees are obliged to be members of a union active in the firm.

Closing prices. With a market for securities or commodities where the trading period is not continuous, the closing price of a good is the price of the good when the market closes. An example of such a market is the Stock Exchange.

Cobb–Douglas production function. An important relationship in the theory of economic growth. Like all PRODUCTION FUNCTIONS it shows how a society's output responds to changes in the size of its capital stock or labour force. However, the Cobb–Douglas production function has some special properties which make it particularly suitable for inclusion in economic models.

It can be written in symbols as:

$$O = A\ L^x\ K^y$$

where O is output, L is the labour input, K the capital stock and A, x and y are constants. It can be shown that when the sum of the exponents (x and y) is equal to 1 the function exhibits constant RETURNS TO SCALE, that is a 1 per cent rise in both the capital and labour inputs causes a 1 per cent rise in output. This version of the function has been popular with economists because, as long as both factors of production are paid their MARGINAL PRODUCTS, it follows that their share in national income is unaffected by a change in the ratio of one to the other. This characteristic is noteworthy because it is consistent with the long-run constancy of the shares of wages and profits in national income despite the growing abundance of capital and increasing scarcity of labour.

Cobweb theories. Most theories of supply and demand try to show why price settles at a particular level and shows no tendency to change. But certain theories, known as cobweb theories, are instead designed to show how the interaction of supply and demand can cause a sequence of price changes. Their main application is to provide insights into volatile price movements in agricultural markets.

The explanation for price volatility is that price expectations depend on present price levels. Suppose, for example, that there is a shortage of wheat this year and that the price is high. Farmers may believe that the high price will continue next year and therefore plant much more wheat for the forthcoming harvest.

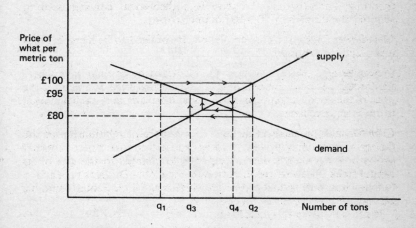

Figure 1. Cobweb theory. In year 1, the price is £100, q_1 is bought and q_2 planted.
In year 2, q_2 is bought at a price of £80 and q_3 planted.
In year 3, q_1 is bought at a price of £95 and q_4 planted.

But when next year's harvest arrives the expectations turn out to have been too optimistic. The over-planting results in an abundance of wheat which drives down the price and the farmers lose money. But this time, as the price is low, farmers do not plant enough wheat. The inevitable result a year later is another wheat shortage and a sharp rise in price.

These price movements may continue for year after year, with a high price in one and a low price in the next. When portrayed on a supply and demand diagram they suggest a cobweb (see Figure 1). Hence, the name 'cobweb theory'. In the United States the continuous upward and downward movements are also known as the 'hog cycle'.

Coefficients of production. The amount of an input in a productive process required to produce a unit of output. If they do not change they are fixed coefficients of production while if they can change then they are variable coefficients of production.

Cohen Committee. ⇨PRICES AND INCOMES POLICY.

Collusion. ⇨RESTRICTIVE PRACTICES.

Colombo Plan. An agreement signed in 1950 for the wealthier countries with interests in South and South-East Asia to provide developing countries in this area with AID and technical assistance.

Comecon. ⇨COUNCIL FOR MUTUAL ECONOMIC AID.

Command economy. ⇨PLANNED ECONOMY.

Commercial banks. The large banks which take deposits and make loans to individuals, firms and government organizations. There is no fundamental distinction between the activities of commercial and other banks although the commercial banks tend to specialize in dealings with the public at large. The major commercial banks – the 'Big Four' – and many of the others are CLEARING BANKS, although the main Scottish banks are not.

The principle attraction of the commercial banks to depositors tends to be the safety of their deposits, a large proportion of which is kept in current accounts, where the deposit is repayable on demand and where no interest is paid.

Because a large proportion of commercial banks' deposits is payable on demand, their lending, which is often to the individuals or companies keeping accounts with the branch, is generally short-term.

Commercial bill. ⇨BILL OF EXCHANGE.

Commodity shunting. If a currency is not convertible into another currency because of EXCHANGE CONTROL regulations, one way of evading the regulations is to buy commodities in the first currency and sell them in the second. The famous 'Kuwait Gap' was an example of this: when sterling was not convertible into dollars in the early 1950s, platinum was bought in London with sterling, shipped to Kuwait, and sold there for dollars.

Common Agricultural Policy (CAP).   The joint agricultural policy of the members of the EEC. Initially, when set up under the Treaty of Rome in 1957, it had three aims: the maintenance of guaranteed prices for agricultural products to provide stable and acceptable standards of living for farmers in the community, a rationalization policy to encourage the modernization of backward European farmers, and free movement of agricultural products within the Community. The guaranteed prices were maintained by intervention buying by the European Commission, and by a variable levy on imports of agricultural products. To allow for regional price differences, the guaranteed prices referred to the price at the point in the community where agricultural prices were considered to be highest, Duisberg in Germany.

Common Market.   ▷EUROPEAN ECONOMIC COMMUNITY.

Commonwealth preference.   A series of tariff exemptions and reductions once given to those goods and commodities entering the UK which had been produced in the Commonwealth or Eire or, in the case of manufactured goods, where at least 25 per cent of the VALUE ADDED was attributable to a Commonwealth country or Eire.

The concessions were negotiated in a series of bilateral agreements at the Ottawa Conference in 1932 and embodied in the Import Duties Act in the same year. Part of the Treaty of Accession between the UK and the EEC is concerned with the phasing out of these concessions or the incorporation of them in the EEC external tariffs. The tariffs were originally called the imperial preference system.

Communism.   ▷MARXIAN ECONOMICS.

Company reserves.   These can either be revenue reserves or capital reserves. Revenue reserves are profits retained in special accounts to finance future expenditure or to be distributed to shareholders as dividends. An example would be reserves that are kept for tax payments since, under the existing tax system, such payments might be made up to two years after the profit upon which the tax is assessed has been made.

Capital reserves are the result of selling new issues of shares at a premium above par or the revaluation of assets. Capital reserves are not allowed to be distributed as dividends.

Company taxation.   In Britain, company taxation is levied on profits (corporation tax) and on employees (e.g. National Insurance contributions). The complex structure of company taxation is partly due to the government's aim to tax companies fairly but in a way that will not affect the behaviour of those who are taxed. These objectives are not necessarily incompatible: for example, the government might want taxation not to affect the level of production of the corporate sector, while at the same time encouraging investment. Another reason for the complexity of company taxation is the need to ensure that the tax is actually paid, by eliminating any loopholes that make tax avoidance possible.

Since 1973, in Britain, corporation tax has been levied on distributed and undistributed profits, under what is called the imputation system. Since the profits that are distributed as dividends are also taxed as part of the income of the recipients, to avoid double taxation, they receive tax credit equal to the imputed value of the corporation tax paid on their dividends.

Against the corporation tax payable there are various schemes which allow investment to be offset against tax. Investment allowances are reductions in the corporation tax due by an amount proportional to the amount of investment. Initial allowances are tax devices where taxable profits are reduced by a proportion of the investment expenditure in the year in which the investment takes place. Companies are generally allowed to reduce taxable profits by the depreciation in assets on the grounds that such depreciation constitutes a cost. Accelerated depreciation, which is an investment incentive, arises when depreciation for tax purposes is permitted at a rate faster than that at which it takes place. Depreciation at choice is similar and arises when depreciation for tax purposes is allowed to take place at any time desired by the company. All these schemes essentially aim to encourage investment, which has been considered in Britain to be generally too low.

Companies are also liable to capital gains tax and to taxes on employment. The taxes on employment in Britain have been the employers' National Insurance contributions, and selective employment tax (now abolished), although other countries also have a payroll tax. The employers' contribution to National Insurance varies with the salary of the employee, while selective employment tax, which was used between 1965 and 1973, was a *per capita* tax that varied with industry and region, in certain circumstances becoming a subsidy, which aimed to raise revenue and move jobs into certain industries and certain regions. A payroll tax is related to the size of the company's payroll.

Tax reserve certificates enable companies to earn interest on money they are holding back in order to pay taxes at some future date. The interest on the certificates is comparable to those on other short-term government debt instruments, such as Treasury bills.

Comparative advantage. The notion of comparative advantage is basic to an understanding of the economics of trade and exchange. Although its most common application is in the theory of international trade, it is of more general significance and explains, for example, the specialization of labour within an economy.

The theory of comparative advantage tries to answer questions like 'in what branches of production will a country specialize if it engages in international trade?' It might seem that a country would specialize in all those activities where it was more efficient than its trading partners. For example, if Japan needs fewer men to make one ship or one car than Britain, it would not be worthwhile for Britain to make any ships or cars, as Japan could make both more easily.

But the theory of comparative advantage shows that this is not so. In Japan the relative efficiency of shipbuilding and car production may be such that the price of ten cars is the same as the price of one ship, while in Britain the price of five cars is the same as the price of one ship. It is therefore worthwhile for Japan to specialize in making cars because if it sends ten cars to Britain it obtains two ships in return, whereas if it makes ships itself it has to give up twenty cars to produce two ships. The comparative advantage of one country is in the production of cars and the other in the production of ships. *Both gain if they specialize according to this comparative advantage. This is true even if only one man is needed in Japan to make a ship or ten cars, whereas a hundred men are needed in Britain to make a ship or five cars.*

The theory of comparative advantage demonstrates that free trade is beneficial to all countries in the world economy. If a country imposes a tariff on an import it buys fewer of these imports from abroad. In consequence, either its consumption of the good in question declines or resources have to be transferred from other industries to increase domestic production. But these resource transfers disturb the other industries and force them to cut back production. Consumption of other goods must decline and gains from international specialization are lost.

However, international trade flows respond not only to differences in production possibilities, but also to differences in prices and costs. If a country's exports are overpriced because its exchange rate is too high it may not fully realize the potential gains from specialization. The gains can only be maximized if comparative costs are in accordance with comparative advantage.

Economists define comparative advantage in terms of opportunity cost. The opportunity cost of a good is the loss of production elsewhere which occurs because resources are devoted to making it rather than something else. For example, in Japan the opportunity cost of making a ship is ten cars. A country is said to have a comparative advantage in that line of production where the opportunity cost of specializing in it instead of another line of production is least. Japan has a comparative advantage in cars because the opportunity cost of ten cars is a ship, whereas in Britain the opportunity cost of ten cars is higher at two ships.

Comparative cost. ▷COMPARATIVE ADVANTAGE.

Comparative dynamics. ▷DYNAMICS.

Comparative static equilibrium analysis. A technique of economic analysis which simplifies problems by making certain artificial assumptions, but which improves understanding and eases exposition.

Economists are often concerned with questions of the kind 'if something happens, what will happen to something else?' In exploring such questions there is usually a complicated sequence of events to unravel because a large number of variables tends to change at the same time.

Not all of the consequences of an event are of interest and it is customary to focus on one or two variables. When these have reached a particular value and show no tendency to change they are said to have reached equilibrium. At this point the analysis is brought to a halt. It is clear what happens to these variables when there is a change somewhere in the economic system.

The equilibrium value of a variable in such an analysis is said to depend on the value of parameters. For example, in supply and demand analysis, the equilibrium price depends on the levels of demand and supply, which in turn depend on consumer preferences and costs of production. If one of the parameters changes – because of, say, an improvement in technology which lowers costs – the equilibrium price also has to change. It is possible to imagine numerous equilibrium prices associated with different values of the parameters.

Comparative static equilibrium analysis compares positions of equilibrium. This exercise can be extremely useful because it shows what will *eventually* happen after some changes in the economic system. But it has two drawbacks. It does not examine thoroughly the processes in the period intervening between two equilibria; and it does not say how long the period of time between two equilibria will be. These topics are dealt with by DISEQUILIBRIUM analysis and economic dynamics (▷DYNAMICS).

Compensation principle. A test to measure the welfare loss or gain caused by an economic change or policy. If a change affects one section of the community adversely while at the same time improving the situation of another group, the compensation principle can be used to decide whether the change has resulted in an increase in the total social welfare.

For example, if a factory is built near a residential area the owners of the factory benefit from it, while residents, who have to tolerate increased noise, extra traffic, and the damage to the environment, suffer. The compensation principle states that if the owners can compensate the residents while still remaining better off themselves, having the factory is preferable to not having it.

However, this is only true when compensation is actually paid. If compensation is not paid, use of the principle can produce contradictory conclusions. Although the details are complicated and technical, the upshot of the debate about the principle is that economists now accept that the only way to compare different situations is to make explicit value judgements about the benefits to different groups of people.

Compensatory finance. ▷BUDGET; DEFICIT FINANCING.

Competition and credit control. A new style of monetary management in the United Kingdom introduced in September 1971, following the publication of a consultative document entitled *Competition and Credit Control* by the Bank of England.

It had two main intentions: to promote competition in the financial system and to improve the Bank of England's control over the major monetary aggregates. In the late 1960s monetary restraint had been achieved by imposing 'ceilings' on lending for the main financial institutions, particularly the banks. This had resulted in a lessening of competition because efficient banks who wanted to capture an increased share of business were unable to do so because of the ceiling constraints. Under the new system, therefore, no ceilings on bank lending were contemplated. Instead, restraint, if necessary, was to be enforced by withdrawing liquidity from the banks by calls for SPECIAL DEPOSITS. The Bank of England's tactics in the gilt-edged market were also to be changed. Until 1971 the Bank had tried to keep the gilt-edged market steady in value by stabilizing interest rates. But this involved substantial increases in the money supply if the government's borrowing requirement was excessive. It was hoped that, after September 1971, the Bank would give priority to money supply objectives and allow interest rates to rise to the level required by the state of financial markets.

In the event only some of the changes envisaged by the consultative document were put into practice. In 1972 and 1973 the Bank of England pursued its traditional policy of supporting the gilt-edged market despite unprecedented rates of money supply growth. However,

49

Competition and Credit Control remains an important landmark in British post-war monetary policy.

One of the new control mechanisms associated with competition and credit control involved the use of reserve ratios. Banks are not allowed to increase their liabilities to an unlimited extent, but must ensure that their reserve assets do not fall beneath a particular ratio to liabilities. As the Bank of England can influence the rate of growth of reserve assets, the enforcement of a particular reserve ratio also enables it to control the growth of the banking system's liabilities and, thereby, the money supply. Reserve assets consist of balances at the Bank of England, holdings of Treasury and local authority bills, MONEY AT CALL with the discount houses, commercial bills, gilt-edged securities with a life of up to a year and tax reserve certificates (⟡COMPANY TAXATION).

Complement. ⟡COMPLEMENTARY DEMAND.

Complementary demand. When an increase in the demand for one good causes an increase in the demand for another, the two goods are said to be in complementary demand. Left and right shoes, cars and tyres, and roast beef and Yorkshire pudding are examples. Such pairs of goods are said to be complements or complementary goods.

Complementary goods. ⟡COMPLEMENTARY DEMAND.

Composite demand. The total demand for a product with different uses. For example, a cow can produce milk, beef and leather, and the composite demand for cattle is the combined demand for all these purposes.

Compound interest. Interest payments can be either simple or compound. A payment of 10 per cent per annum simple interest on a loan of £100 for five years involves the payment of £10 for each year, so that after five years a repayment of £150 is made. Compound interest works on a different basis. After the first year the borrower owes the lender £100 plus £10. The 10 per cent interest charge for the second year is therefore calculated on £110, not £100. This makes the interest charge for the second year £11 and for the third year £12.10. After five years over £160 would be paid back.

Compound interest is much the most common system used in business and commerce.

Concentration. The extent to which an industry is dominated by its largest members. The most extreme example of concentration is a monopoly where one company controls all of an industry's output.

Concentration is normally considered to be undesirable because the fewer the number of companies in an industry the greater the influence each one has on the price. Economic theory shows that socially beneficial behaviour results when individual companies are unable to control prices and have to accept the price level established by competition among numerous rivals.

The degree of concentration is measured by the concentration ratio. It can be expressed either as the percentage of industry sales accounted for by the largest two, three or four companies or as the smallest number of firms producing a particular percentage of industry sales.

Concentration ratio. ⊳CONCENTRATION.

Confederation of British Industry (CBI). The organization which represents management and employers in British industry. It was formed in 1965 after a merger between the British Employers Federation, which concentrated on industrial relations, the Federation of British Industry, which promoted British industry abroad and negotiated with governments, and the National Association of British Manufacturers.

The CBI carries out the tasks of all these organizations and represents industry in formal systems of consultation with government and trade unions such as the NATIONAL ECONOMIC DEVELOPMENT COUNCIL. It is not linked to any political party.

Conglomerate. A company form which developed in the 1960s. Unlike most companies a conglomerate does not specialize in one activity, but has operations in several industries. Its typical structure is a HOLDING COMPANY with subsidiaries only loosely controlled by the main board of directors.

Conglomerates have serious disadvantages compared to the traditional specialized company because they are unable to build up know-how or expertise in particular areas. Their management resources are often severely stretched.

Consolidated fund. An account which shows the expenditure of central government in Great Britain. It does not include expenditure by local government or the nationalized industries, although the rate support grant, a payment made by the central government to the local authorities, is included. Figures for the consolidated fund are published every month in the *London Gazette*, but do not normally receive much publicity.

Consols. The name given to certain UNDATED SECURITIES issued by the British government. It is an abbreviation for 'consolidated stock', so called because it replaced a number of other stocks which constituted part of the NATIONAL DEBT.

Conspicuous consumption. Most forms of consumption are desired because they yield satisfaction in themselves. However, certain forms yield satisfaction because other people see and admire the act of consumption. A good example is the ownership of a Rolls-Royce. Although it is comfortable to drive in and mechanically reliable, the main pleasure is the thought that most people do not own Rolls-Royces and are envious of those who do. These forms of consumption are known as conspicuous consumption.

Consumer durables. ⟡DURABLE GOODS.

Consumer expenditure. ⟡CONSUMPTION.

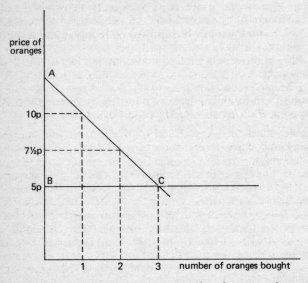

Figure 2. Triangle ABC measures consumer surplus when price of oranges is 5p.

Consumer surplus. A consumer buys a batch of goods because the benefit he expects to receive is valued more highly than the costs he has to pay. This gain is known as consumer surplus. It is most easily understood with the help of a demand curve. (⟡DEMAND (2).)

In Figure 2, when the price is 5p per orange the consumer buys three oranges. If the price were 10p he would buy only one and if it were 7½p two. A price of 5p, therefore, gives him a special gain on both the first and second oranges he buys. This special gain is consumer surplus and is measured in Figure 2 by the area ABC. Clearly, if the price goes up, the consumer loses consumer surplus and if the price goes down he gains.

Consumers' sovereignty. A condition in which the supply of goods in the shops depends on what consumers want, rather than what the supplier finds it convenient to put on sale. It has been claimed that consumers' sovereignty is no longer found in advanced industrial societies because tastes are influenced by advertising.

Consumption. A term used in two distinct but related senses in economics. The first is the enjoyment of goods and services. If a product has given someone satisfaction it is said to have formed part of his consumption. The second usage is as a category in national accounts (◊GROSS NATIONAL PRODUCT). An economy's consumption is that part of its production which is used up in a year and is not added to its capital stock.

The difference between income and consumption is called saving. But it is possible for consumption to exceed income in which case there is said to have been dissaving.

Consumer expenditure is consumption by private individuals and constitutes most of Britain's total national expenditure.

Consumption function. A relationship which shows how consumption in an economy depends on income. It plays an important role in macroeconomics.

Economists have long been impressed by the stability of consumption, particularly in comparison with the instability of investment. When national income goes down by a large amount, investment almost invariably falls more than consumption. Lord Keynes emphasized this contrast in his famous book, *The General Theory of Employment, Interest and Money*, published in 1936. Consumption, he suggested, depends on income, whereas investment and other components of demand depend on interest rates and business optimism and are responsible for changes in income.

However, the precise nature of the relationship between consumption and income has been much debated since Keynes's work. Most evidence shows that consumption does not change much as a proportion of national income over long periods of time, but that at any moment in time rich people save more than the poor and therefore have a lower AVERAGE PROPENSITY TO CONSUME.

Contango; also called a carry-over or continuation. A transaction which involves settling a debt on the Stock Exchange after the end of the ACCOUNT (2). Some interest payment is usually made.

Continuous variable. A mathematical term for a variable which can take any value between two numbers which are its extreme values. For example, in a macroeconomic model, consumption may be said to be a continuous variable which can never exceed income. If income amounts to £100, consumption could take any value – including a number expressed to several decimal places – up to £100. It might be, say, £80.68. But if consumption could only take two or three values beneath £100, such as £70, £80 and £90, it would not be a continuous variable. A continuous variable is easy to manipulate mathematically.

Contract curve. A tool in WELFARE ECONOMICS and general equilibrium analysis (⟡COMPARATIVE STATIC EQUILIBRIUM ANALYSIS). It shows a number of points where, after trading between two parties has taken place, it is impossible to make one better off without making the other worse off.

Conversion. The issue of STOCK (2), either fixed interest or equity, to replace some other stock. A good example is a decision by the government to offer holders of gilt-edged securities another gilt-edged security as their present holdings become due for redemption. (⟡DEBT MANAGE-MENT (2).)

Convertibility. Governments often impose restrictions on the use of their currencies in international trade and finance. They forbid holders of the currency to convert it into dollars, gold or any foreign currency whatever. The currency is then said to have lost convertibility.

Since the Second World War, convertibility has tended to have a fairly restricted meaning. A currency is said to be convertible if it can be freely exchanged into dollars. But this is not the only use of the term. In 1971 the dollar itself became inconvertible. This meant that the United States Treasury refused to give gold in exchange for dollars in future. Until 1971 the US Treasury had done so at a price of $35 an ounce.

Corporation tax. ⟡COMPANY TAXATION.

Correlation. A measure of the association between two or more economic variables. If two variables move in the same direction at the same time they are said to be strongly and positively correlated; if they move in opposite directions at the same time they are said to be strongly and negatively correlated; if they move at different times they are said to be weakly correlated.

Correlation is measured by either the coefficient of correlation or the coefficient of determination. The coefficient of correlation is the square root of the coefficient of determination. The coefficient of correlation varies from +1 to −1. The nearer its value to either +1 or −1, the stronger the correlation. In most economics books the coefficient of determination, which varies from 0 to 1, is more commonly used and is denoted by r^2.

Correlation can be between two variables when it is known as simple correlation; or between one variable and two or more variables when it is known as multiple correlation. It is calculated by fairly complicated statistical techniques.

Cost—benefit analysis; also known as benefit—cost analysis. A method of determining the value to society of economic change. It is particularly useful for evaluating the advantage, or disadvantage, to society from a large project, such as the building of a dam or road. It is therefore sometimes referred to as project evaluation. It is widely used by governments and international agencies.

Cost—benefit analysis can be used to compare the results of two competing projects or to decide whether or not a project should be undertaken at all.

Cost—benefit analysis is similar to the calculation of profit by a private businessman, except that the profit under consideration accrues to society. All of the costs and all of the benefits involved in a project are added up and then the costs are subtracted from the benefits. If benefits exceed costs and there is no other project which shows a bigger advantageous difference between benefits and costs, the project should be carried out.

There are two main difficulties with cost—benefit analysis. First, the benefits and costs have to be measured by a yardstick which is generally believed to represent the wishes of the community. But this is elusive because what is regarded as a benefit by one person may be a cost to someone else. The only way to resolve this problem is to attach weights to everyone's welfare. For example, it may be decided that an extra £100 to a poor man adds more to his welfare than an extra £100 to a rich man. If a project causes an increase in the poor man's income of £100 and a reduction in the rich man's of the same amount, society as a whole is better off and the project should be encouraged.

This kind of procedure is widely regarded as undesirable because it involves making judgements about people with which they may disagree. It is also immensely difficult in practice to decide how to weight one person's welfare against another's because so many factors have to be taken into account.

The second difficulty is the measurement of benefits which accrue over a number of periods of time. It is clear that benefits in later periods are valued less highly now than benefits in nearby periods. It is therefore agreed that future benefits have to be discounted at some rate of interest. But what rate of interest should apply? Some economists believe that it should be equal to the rate of interest charged to private companies on their loans; others that it should be equal to the SOCIAL RATE OF TIME PREFERENCE.

Cost–benefit analysis can never give final answers to questions about the desirability of projects. Much in practice depends on political judgements about how much one section of the community should benefit.

Cost curves. ▷SUPPLY.

Cost, Marginal. ▷MARGINAL COST.

Cost-of-living index. ▷RETAIL PRICE INDEX.

Cost, Opportunity. ▷OPPORTUNITY COST.

Cost, Overhead. ▷FIXED COSTS.

Cost-push inflation. ▷INFLATION.

Cost, Replacement. ▷REPLACEMENT COST.

Cost, Social. ▷SOCIAL COST.

Costs, Fixed. ▷FIXED COSTS.

Costs, Historic. ▷REPLACEMENT COST.

Costs, Prime. ▷PRIME COSTS.

Costs, Supplementary. ▷FIXED COSTS.

Council for Mutual Economic Aid. Generally referred to as Comecon, this body was set up in 1949 and is the supranational agency through which the Eastern European countries, Bulgaria, Czechoslovakia, East Germany, Hungary, Poland, Romania, and the USSR together with Mongolia and Cuba attempt to plan their economies on the basis of self-sufficiency, making the maximization of trade with one another a common policy. In practice it is frequently claimed that Comecon is merely the façade behind which the USSR exerts control over the economic life of the other members, a claim which is supported, to some extent, by the attempts of the smaller countries, notably Romania, to frustrate and ignore Comecon policies and plans.

Countervailing power. The concept associated with J. K. Galbraith (1908–   ) that a stable economy can be maintained by a balancing of political power between opposed interest groups, such as consumers against employers and trade unions, or employers against trade unions.

Cover; also called dividend cover. The ratio of profits to DIVIDENDS for a company.

Crawling peg. ⟡FLOATING EXCHANGE RATES.

Credit. It is sometimes possible to obtain goods without paying for them immediately. Instead a promise is made to the seller to pay him at some future date. The goods are then said to have been purchased on credit.

Credit is given, in other words, when the buyer has incurred a LIABILITY to the seller.

Credit account. An arrangement whereby the person with the account can buy goods and pay for them later. Credit accounts are generally given either by shops or by credit organizations, who issue credit cards which entitle the users to make purchases on account with firms subscribing to the organization.

Credit control. ⟡COMPETITION AND CREDIT CONTROL.

Credit restrictions. ⟡CREDIT SQUEEZE.

Credit squeeze. A method of DEFLATION which restricts demand by making CREDIT less easily obtainable. Expenditure financed by credit is reduced and fewer goods are purchased. A credit squeeze is also referred to simply as a squeeze.

The two main forms of credit squeeze are controls on hire-purchase and restrictions on bank lending or credit restrictions. Hire-purchase controls are enforced by increasing the minimum deposit payable or by reducing the maximum period over which repayments can be made.

Restrictions on bank lending can be either the direct imposition of a 'ceiling' on lending (for example, lending is not allowed to exceed a particular percentage of the level of lending at a particular date) or the operation of monetary policy to discourage the banks from increasing their advances. A strict monetary policy of this kind is known as tight money or 'dear money' because it raises interest rates.

Cross elasticity of demand. The proportional change in the quantity of one good demanded per unit proportional change in price of another good. When the cross elasticity of demand is positive, as with butter and margarine (the demand for butter will increase when the price of margarine rises), butter is said to be a SUBSTITUTE for margarine. When the cross elasticity of demand is negative, as with cars and petrol (since the demand for cars will increase when the price of petrol falls), cars and petrol are said to be complementary goods (⟡COMPLEMENTARY DEMAND).

Cross-section analysis. Analysing statistical data obtained from a single moment in time. Statistical analysis is generally either time-series analysis or cross-section analysis. For example, to investigate the relationship between savings and incomes one might either compare savings and income for some group or for the whole economy as their income changes over time, which would be time-series analysis, or else one might compare the savings and income of those earning different incomes at a single moment in time, which would be cross-section analysis.

Cross subsidy. A system where one uneconomic product of an enterprise is subsidized by the profits from another product. For example, the postal service in the UK has often been cross-subsidized from the profits of the telephone service.

Crowther Committee. A committee set up in 1968, under the chairmanship of Lord Crowther, to investigate the provision of credit to consumers. The report was published in 1971 and concluded that the growth and level of consumer credit gave no cause for alarm, and recommended that credit of all types be treated under similar legislation with the replacement of existing credit legislation by a single act on the subject. Many of its recommendations were included in the Fair Trading Act of 1973.

Cumulative preference shares. ▷PREFERENCE SHARES.

Currency. The form of MONEY used in an economy.

Currency appreciation and depreciation. Currency appreciation is the increase in the value of a currency relative to other currencies. Currency depreciation is the fall in value of one currency relative to other currencies.

Current account (1). A bank account where deposits are repayable on demand (in the USA called a demand account), generally paying no interest.

Current account (2). That part of the BALANCE OF PAYMENTS that does not include CAPITAL MOVEMENTS.

Current account (3). In the national accounts, the current account of a sector shows the difference between its income and its expenditure on consumption or on goods that are used up on production. (▷GROSS NATIONAL PRODUCT.)

Current account (4). Government expenditure is divided between capital account and current account expenditure. By and large, current account expenditure is expenditure which does not increase the value of the CAPITAL STOCK owned by the government.

Current assets. ▷ASSET.

Current expenditure. Economists and accountants distinguish between current expenditure and CAPITAL EXPENDITURE. Current expenditure is typically on items which are to be used up fairly quickly for consumption or in a production process. Such items also tend to be purchased recurrently. Raw materials and fuel are good examples. The differentiation between current and capital expenditure is a matter of convention; there is no clear-cut dividing line.

Customs drawback. ▷NON-TARIFF TRADE DISTORTIONS.

Customs union. An agreement between two or more countries to abolish tariffs or quotas on trade amongst themselves and to equalize their tariffs and quotas with other countries. The EEC is the best-known example of this. A free trade area is a customs union where tariffs and quotas with outside countries have not been equalized.
   The advantage of a customs union, trade creation, is the result of members being able to obtain from one another goods at a lower cost than if the goods were made domestically. The disadvantage of a customs union, trade diversion, is that some goods are bought from other members that cost the country more than goods that would otherwise be bought from outside the customs union.

Cyclical. A cyclical economic variable is one which rises and falls by large amounts when economic activity fluctuates. It differs considerably from its TREND level at various stages of the trade cycle. For example, investment is a highly cyclical variable because it changes by large amounts from year to year and normally by much more than other components of demand such as consumption and government spending.

Cyclical unemployment. Unemployment caused by a cyclical downswing in demand. It is usually less of a concern than STRUCTURAL UNEMPLOYMENT because it is thought to be temporary and can be eradicated when demand recovers.

D

Dated securities. SECURITIES which have a specified date of redemption. The government is one of the main issuers of such securities, in which case they are known as gilt-edged securities or government stock. Long-dated securities have a distant redemption date, normally more than five years away; short-dated securities are to be redeemed sooner.

'Dear money'. ⟡CREDIT SQUEEZE.

Debenture. A fixed-interest security issued by companies in return for a loan. Debentures can be traded on the Stock Exchange like equity or gilts.

Fixed-interest securities are also sometimes known as loan stock or loan capital. These terms are roughly synonymous with debenture, although collateral is offered on loan stock in case of default whereas no collateral is offered for a debenture.

Debt. An obligation to pay money to another individual or institution now or at some future date.

Debt management (1). Any operation or set of operations intended to alter the composition or structure of debt.

Debt management (2). Operations by the central bank of a country, usually with the approval of the government, to alter the composition or maturity structure of the NATIONAL DEBT. For example, a decision to issue long-dated gilts as a short-dated gilt-edged stock approaches redemption is an exercise in debt management because it increases the average age of the national debt. (⟡CONVERSION.)

Debt ratio. ⟡GEARING.

Debt-servicing. When a company is in debt to another company it usually has to pay interest for the privilege of using money it does not own. Such interest payments are known as debt-servicing and the practice of paying interest is known as servicing debt.

Decentralized decision-taking. In certain economies the important decisions about the allocation of resources and the distribution of income are taken by numerous individuals responding to market signals at a local level. They are able to do as they wish with the property at their command. They do not receive instructions from the central government or from a central planning agency and they are not constrained by official restrictions. This system is known as decentralized decision-taking.

It is to be contrasted with a PLANNED ECONOMY where major decisions are taken at the centre and individuals throughout the system are obliged to accept and follow instructions they receive from a planning agency.

Decentralized decision-taking is associated with political democracy and a capitalist economy recognizing private property. Communist societies have tried to introduce aspects of decentralized decision-taking into their system, but have found it difficult to reconcile with the absence of private property rights in the means of production.

Decreasing returns. ⊳RETURNS TO SCALE.

Deferred rebate. A restrictive practice which encourages a customer to keep on buying from the same company because the company promises to give him a rebate if he does so.

Deferred shares. A share issued by a company which has a fixed or highly stable dividend pay-out to its equity shareholders. Any profits outstanding after these dividend payments have been made accrue to the holders of deferred shares. They are a risky investment and are now little known.

Deficiency payments. A method of subsidizing farmers in the United Kingdom since 1947, but now being phased out because of membership of the EEC. Farmers are told of a guaranteed price for their products, but they have to sell them on the free market. The difference between the two prices is then paid to them as a subsidy or deficiency payment.

Deficit (1). A condition in which expenditure exceeds revenue.

Deficit (2). A condition in which liabilities exceed assets.

Deficit financing. When a government deliberately allows expenditure to exceed revenue it is said to have embarked on a programme of deficit financing. This is normally intended as part of a planned expansion of demand to stimulate output and employment. Budget deficits add to the economy's spending power by putting more money into the economy than is taken out by taxation, but for the same reason they are sometimes regarded as a cause of inflation. A planned expansion of this sort is sometimes called 'pump-priming'.

Deflation. A policy of reducing aggregate demand. Deflation is usually adopted when aggregate demand is believed to exceed aggregate supply in an economy, a situation which is associated with rising prices, a balance of payments deficit and too full utilization of resources. It is carried out by a combination of monetary and fiscal methods – for example, by raising interest rates, reducing public spending and increasing taxation.

Demand (1). The total amount of spending power which companies and individuals want to commit to buying goods and services in an economy over a specified period. Demand is used in this sense in the sentence: 'The government tried to increase demand by reducing taxes.'

Demand (2). The desire for and ability to buy a particular good or service. Demand is used in this sense in the sentence: 'The demand for tobacco increased because the habit of smoking pipes spread.'

It is this sense of the word which is referred to in the theory of demand and in such phrases as the demand curve and the demand function. The theory of demand is one-half of the theory of value, the other half being the theory of SUPPLY. The theory of value constitutes the core of economics and most other branches of the subject may be regarded as applications of its findings. It tries to explain price in terms of utility on one hand and scarcity on the other.

The modern theory of value developed in the late nineteenth century when it superseded older theories which had failed to solve the 'diamond and water' paradox. It had been noticed that diamonds were extremely valuable, whereas water was usually cheap and occasionally even free. But water was essential for life while diamonds were a luxury.

The modern theory of value gave two insights into this problem. First, it said that diamonds were scarce and would therefore command a higher price than a commodity like water which is abundant. It is not correct, the theory suggested, to concentrate solely on the essential nature of a commodity because supply considerations are also important.

Second, the theory argued that a distinction should be made between total utility and marginal utility. When a consumer is considering whether or not to buy more or less of a particular commodity he is concerned with the extra benefit he expects from one more unit, or its marginal utility, and not with the total benefit he receives from all the units he has, or its total utility.

The notion of marginal utility is central to the theory of demand. It is usually true that the more someone has of something the less is the extra benefit he obtains from a further unit. This psychological generalization is the basis for the law of diminishing marginal utility, that marginal utility decreases as the quantity bought increases. The law can be represented on a diagram with utility on one axis and quantity bought on the other (Figure 3).

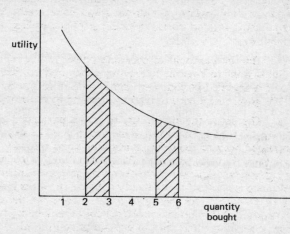

Figure 3. The law of diminishing marginal utility. When a consumer has five units and buys one more his marginal utility, measured by the shaded area, is less than when he has two and buys one more.

Obviously a consumer will buy another unit of a good if its marginal utility is greater than its price and he will reduce his purchase if its marginal utility is less than its price. He can only be satisfied if marginal utility is equal to price. In that case he can gain no advantage from changing his purchasing plans. (⬦CONSUMER SURPLUS.)

It follows that the curve of marginal utility in Figure 3 could also be looked at as a curve relating price to quantity demanded. The higher the price, the less the consumer wants to buy. This curve is known as a demand curve (Figure 4).

The demand curve is to be distinguished from the demand function. The demand function shows how quantity demanded depends on a number of variables, such as price, income and tastes, and not solely on the one variable of price.

Rationing involves the frustration of demand by artificial restrictions, usually imposed by a government. These restrictions say that only a particular quantity of a good can be purchased. The demand may be so strong that the price consumers are willing to pay for this particular quantity is much above the cost of production. Although suppliers would like to put more of the good on sale they are unable to do so and both consumers and suppliers are not as well off as they might be.

Demand curve. ▷DEMAND (2).

Demand function. ▷DEMAND (2).

Demand inflation. ▷INFLATION.

Department of Economic Affairs (DEA). A government department set up in 1964 by the new Labour administration. It was intended to work out policies for improving Britain's prospects of economic growth. In 1965 it published a five-year national plan based on an expansion of the national output at 4 per cent a year. In practice, the national plan was frustrated by a succession of balance of payments crises which forced the government to hold back the economy and prevented the attainment of the growth targets. The Department of Economic Affairs was wound up in 1969.

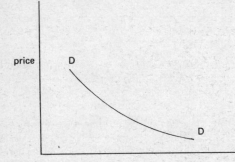

Figure 4. DD is a demand curve.

Dependent variable. An economic variable determined by some other variable or group of variables. For example, consumption depends on income and is, therefore, a dependent variable.

Deposit account. A bank account which yields a rate of interest, but which is not as liquid as a current account because it is only possible to withdraw money after a period of notice. In the United Kingdom the usual period of notice is one week. (▷CURRENT ACCOUNT (1).)

Depreciation. Most capital goods do not have indefinite lives, but fall to pieces because of wear and tear and become uneconomical to use. Companies have to subtract the loss this involves from their gross profits to produce a realistic estimate of their true income. By setting aside money for depreciation companies are also able to buy a new capital good when an old one eventually becomes unusable.

Capital consumption is a synonym for depreciation.

Depreciation measures the reduction in the value of a company's or country's capital stock which would occur if there were no investment at all. If investment is taking place depreciation must be deducted to arrive at an estimate of the increase in the capital stock. After this adjustment the increase is known as net investment.

Depreciation at choice. ◊COMPANY TAXATION.

Depressed areas. ◊REGIONAL POLICY.

Depression. A period when economic activity is at a low level. It is associated with heavy unemployment and reduced output. Depression is a stronger term than recession which is usually regarded as a short period of slow growth of output

The most serious world-wide depression occurred between the two wars. It began in 1929 after a dramatic collapse in share prices on Wall Street in New York and in some countries continued throughout the 1930s. In Britain in 1933 there were nearly three million people registered as unemployed.

Derived demand. The demand for a factor of production depends on the demand for output. For example, the demand for textile operatives depends on the demand for clothes. The demand for a factor of production is therefore said to be a derived demand.

Devaluation. A reduction in the value of a currency in terms of other currencies. If a currency is devalued it cannot be exchanged for as many units of foreign currencies as before. For example, when the pound was devalued in 1967 it could only buy $2.40 whereas it could previously have bought $2.80.

Devaluation occurs because the supply of a currency exceeds the demand and price has to be adjusted downwards. It is a standard method of curing a balance of payments deficit because it makes exports cheaper to foreign countries, who therefore buy more, and imports more expensive to domestic consumers, who buy less.

Developing country. A country which is poor in comparison with the industrialized countries of North America and Western Europe. Although the benchmark is a matter of choice, many economists regard countries with an annual income per head of under $1000 as falling within the category. The Third World is the term used to describe developing countries as a group.

In addition to having low living standards, developing countries are usually dependent on exports of raw materials to the advanced Western economies for much of their national income. The industrial sector is small because most people are employed on the land in technologically backward agriculture. Developing countries often have large inequalities in the distribution of income and wealth and tend to be politically unstable.

Some improvement in conditions in developing countries has occurred in recent years, partly because of attempts to industrialize and partly because of the 'green revolution'. The green revolution is a dramatic increase in agricultural productivity in certain countries because of the adoption of better farming methods, particularly the planting of more productive seeds.

A developing country is also sometimes known as an underdeveloped country. (⟡ECONOMIC GROWTH.)

Development areas.   ⟡REGIONAL POLICY.

Differentials.   Differences in wages and earnings between workers in different jobs or in different grades in the same job. They are also sometimes called relativities. They are a major source of industrial disputes because one group of workers tries to maintain its position compared to another even if underlying economic circumstances justify a change.

Differentiation, Product.   ⟡PRODUCT DIFFERENTIATION.

Diminishing marginal utility.   ⟡DEMAND (2).

Diminishing returns, Law of.   When a company increases the number of inputs it uses in a production process it expects there to be some increase in output. But the extra output to be achieved from a given quantity of input is not fixed and depends on the company's scale of operations.

If there are two inputs, and the quantity of one input is fixed, an increasing application of the other leads after a time to a smaller increase in output. For example, a company may have two inputs, a factory and men. The size of the factory cannot be changed and, if higher production is needed, the only method is to hire more men. When the company is making 100 units another man may cause 5 more units to be produced; when it is making 150 units he may contribute 4 more units to output; and when it is making 200 units only 3 more units. In other words, as output increases the marginal productivity of labour declines. This tendency is known as the law of diminishing returns. (⟡MARGINAL PRODUCTIVITY OF CAPITAL.)

The law of variable proportions is slightly different. It is sometimes the case that marginal product rises over a certain range of output before beginning to decline. This is the tendency described by the law of variable proportions, not the tendency for marginal product to decline continuously.

Direct costs. ▷VARIABLE COSTS.

Direct investment. The buying of machinery, plant and buildings by a company, in contrast to the purchase of financial assets.

Direct taxation. ▷PERSONAL TAXATION.

Discount house. A financial institution in the City of London. A discount house borrows money from banks and uses it to purchase a variety of financial assets, most of them riskless and highly liquid. When a bank is itself short of money it is able to withdraw a certain amount from the discount houses. This operation is known as 'calling' because a bank is 'calling back' the money it has lent.

The discount houses are also extremely important for the conduct of monetary policy. When they are short of money, for example, because of heavy calling, they can borrow from the Bank of England. The rate of interest the Bank charges for the loans has a significant effect on the credit position of the houses and eventually on that of the financial system as a whole.

The market in which discount houses borrow and lend with other financial institutions is known as the discount market. Today most of the deals are made by telephone.

Discount market. ▷DISCOUNT HOUSE.

Discounted cash flow (DCF). A technique for appraising INVESTMENT projects by which the costs and the receipts for the project are quantified, and the times when they are likely to occur are estimated. For example, a receipt of £110 at the end of the first year of the project will be worth £100 at the beginning of the project if the annual interest rate is 10 per cent, since the £100 would have been worth £110 after a year, had it been invested. Similarly a cost of £121 at the end of the second year would be discounted to £100 at the beginning of the project applying the same interest rate. When all the discounted costs have been subtracted from the discounted receipts, the net present value (NPV) of the project is obtained. This is the sum of money which, if invested at the prevailing interest rate, would bring in as good a return as the project. If the calculations take into account all costs and risks, then all projects showing a positive NPV should be undertaken. Another way of using DCF is to calculate the interest rate at which the NPV is zero. This gives the INTERNAL RATE OF RETURN

(IRR) and if this is above the discount rate chosen, then the project should be undertaken.

Discretionary income. The income accruing to a company or individual after deducting interest payments owed on loans.

Discriminating monopoly. A monopoly which charges different prices in different markets. The object of this policy is to take advantage of differences in the elasticity of demand.

Diseconomy. An increase in the average cost of production associated with an enlarged scale of operations. For example, in a company employing 10000 people, it is more difficult for the management to keep control over labour relations than in a company employing 1000 people. There may be more strikes and dissatisfaction with working conditions which raise production costs.

Disequilibrium. A situation in which economic forces have not worked themselves out fully and some change is about to occur. It is to be contrasted with EQUILIBRIUM, where all companies and individuals involved in a particular situation are as satisfied as they can be and no change is likely.

Disequilibrium dynamics. ⟡DYNAMICS.

Disguised unemployment. In most economies, but particularly in developing countries, many people are employed in jobs with low productivity. Indeed, their output is at times so small that they might just as well be unemployed. Workers in this situation are said to constitute disguised unemployment.

Disposable income. The income that an individual or company is free to spend as he or it wishes. Personal disposable income is roughly equivalent to gross income minus tax and social security payments.

Dissaving. ⟡CONSUMPTION.

Distribution, Theory of. The branch of economic theory which explains how income is distributed between different factors of production and between different individuals. (⟡INCOME DISTRIBUTION.)

Diversification. A business strategy of increasing the number and variety of interests in which a company is involved. It is used in two main contexts – to describe a decision by an investment company to buy assets rather different from those which it has traditionally held; and to describe a decision by a manufacturing company to move into an industry different from that in which its main operations are concentrated.

Dividend.   The payment made by a company to its shareholders.

Dividend cover.   ⇨COVER.

Division of labour.   In primitive societies where trade and commerce are almost non-existent most people have to do a great variety of tasks. They do not specialize in one activity. This is inefficient because they are unable to build up experience or develop their skills.

As societies progress, however, it is customary for some people to specialize in certain occupations. They produce more of a good or service than they need for themselves and sell the surplus to other people who specialize in different occupations. This system of social organization is known as the division of labour. It is only possible when trade and commerce are extensive and the degree of specialization depends on the size of the market. It results in substantial increases in productivity because the more someone does something, the better he becomes at it.

Dollar.   The currency of the United States of America. Because of the size of the US economy, which accounts for about half of the output of all the developed countries, the USA has a dominant influence on world trade.

As a result the dollar is used both for accounting purposes and as the means of payment in a large number of international transactions. In the immediate aftermath of the Second World War, when the economies of the European countries were still suffering from the effects of hostilities, they were forced to run large balance of payments deficits with the relatively healthy US economy, paying out more dollars for their imports than were received for their exports.

The consequence was a dollar shortage or 'dollar gap'. It was remedied by suspending the CONVERTIBILITY of certain European currencies, notably sterling, by Marshall Plan aid from the USA, and by the gradual recovery of European output.

In the 1960s the opposite problem occurred. International trading conditions were less favourable to the USA because the prices of its primary product exports were depressed, other developed economies had made a strong recovery from the war, and the USA itself became involved in a long and costly overseas war in Vietnam. The resulting balance of payments deficit caused the 'dollar glut' and in 1971 the convertibility of the dollar into gold was suspended.

During the period of the dollar gap, EXCHANGE CONTROL regulations were instituted in the UK which forbade portfolio investment in the USA. However, investments already made were allowed to continue and these investments constituted the dollar pool. The amount by which the price of the dollar purchased from this pool exceeds the price of the dollar at the official exchange rate is known as the dollar premium. It is intended to discourage overseas investment by British citizens.

Dollar area. The area, including the USA and certain countries in South America, where sterling accounts were freely convertible into dollars during the period of dollar shortage after the Second World War. The term was abandoned in official usage in 1958.

Dollar gap. ⟡DOLLAR.

Dollar glut. ⟡DOLLAR.

Dollar pool. ⟡DOLLAR.

Dollar premium. ⟡DOLLAR.

Domestic credit expansion (DCE). A measure of the growth of credit in an economy. It is sometimes preferred to the main alternative measure, the increase in the economy's money supply. The drawback to the use of money supply figures is that a bank can grant credit to a customer who intends to buy goods from another country. If he does so, nothing is added to domestic bank deposits and, therefore, to the money supply, even though the decision to grant credit has affected the community's spending power. Domestic credit expansion is equal to the increase in the money supply *and* the economy's balance of payments deficit.

It is also equal to the public sector borrowing requirement plus the increase in bank lending to the private sector *minus* sales of government debt to the non-bank public.

Domestic credit expansion became prominent in 1968 because the INTERNATIONAL MONETARY FUND required the British government to control this variable as a condition for receiving certain loans.

Double option. ⟡OPTION.

Double taxation. A citizen or company belonging to one country may be in another country, earning income or receiving profits. This income may be liable to tax in both countries, a situation known as double taxation. Double taxation agreements are arrangements between countries whereby income is taxed only once.

Dow Jones index. The main index of share prices on Wall Street, the USA's leading stock exchange which is located in New York.

Dual economy. An economy – usually that of a developing country –

with a modern technologically advanced sector employing a small fraction of the labour force and a poor backward sector with a much lower level of productivity. As the backward sector is typically subsistence farming with little trading for cash, the two sectors can develop at different rates with only limited contact between them.

Dumping. The export of goods at prices below the cost of production. Dumping is often condemned by the governments of the importing countries because, although they receive goods at a lower price than they would otherwise pay, this temporary advantage may be offset by the long-term harm done to domestic producers. Dumping is contrary to GATT laws and countries are allowed to impose tariffs to prevent it. In many cases, however, complaints against dumping are the result of producers' campaigns against foreign competition to preserve domestic monopoly or OLIGOPOLY.

Duopoly. A market where there are only two producers or sellers.

Duopsony. A market where there are only two buyers.

Durable goods. These are goods that are not wholly consumed at, or shortly after, the time of purchase. Capital goods fall into this category as do certain consumer goods called consumer durables. These range from clothes, which are 'used up' relatively quickly, to vehicles or television sets which may continued to provide service for a considerable length of time.

Dynamics. The analysis of economic change over time. Dynamics usually refers to the theoretical aspects of economic change; the term is rarely used to describe a process which has actually taken place.

For example, economists may want to discuss the effects of an increase in demand on price. In the first period, when supply has not had a chance to adjust fully, the price may rise much above the cost of production. Only in the second and third periods, as competition strengthens, does price come down to production costs again. A discussion of these changes in price through time is said to be a discussion in economic dynamics.

Comparative dynamics is a form of analysis which compares two processes of change through time. For example, one process of economic growth might be caused by an increase in population, another by an increase in savings. A comparison of the two would be an exercise in comparative dynamics.

Change from one period to the next occurs for two main reasons: a change in the value of one or more PARAMETERS; or a sense of dissatisfaction with the present outcome. When the individuals concerned

71

are dissatisfied with the present outcome they are said to be in DIS-EQUILIBRIUM and the process of change is analysed by means of disequilibrium dynamics.

These branches of economic theory are complicated and difficult, and they do not usually form part of an introductory course in economics.

E

Earnings (1). The total payment received by an employee. Earnings are to be contrasted with wage rates, which usually specify minimum entitlements, because they are affected by bonus and overtime payments. Earnings are often 50 per cent higher than envisaged in agreements on wage rates because of these additional items.

Earnings (2). That part of a company's profit which is available for distribution to shareholders. Much of a company's earnings may, however, not be paid out in dividend because the directors consider it to be in the shareholders' interest if it is retained in the business for investment or to maintain adequate liquidity.

Ease, To. When prices fall on commodity and financial markets they are said to ease. An easing of prices is a small downward movement, not a large one.

Econometrics. The study of past economic relationships by statistical techniques. The object of econometrics is to discover the strength and reliability of these relationships. If a strong and reliable relationship is found, particularly when it is plausible on theoretical grounds, it can be used for forecasting and policy-making purposes. For example, if statisticians have shown that in previous years there has been a clear link between the money supply and money national income, they will feel encouraged to say that control of the money supply should influence the growth of money national income in future.

The main methods of econometrics are simple and multiple regression. (⟡REGRESSION ANALYSIS.)

Economic development. A general phrase to describe the progress of an economy. It can be roughly equated with ECONOMIC GROWTH, but it is less precise. It refers to the adoption of new and more advanced production methods, the change in the structure of the economy from agriculture to industry, and the improvement in living standards. Unlike economic growth it is not measured by a figure, but is more vague and qualitative.

Economic dynamics. ⟩DYNAMICS.

Economic efficiency. The success with which resources are used is the main task of economics, the maximization of UTILITY. Two concepts of efficiency can be distinguished, allocative efficiency and productive efficiency.

Allocative efficiency refers to the distribution of resources between industries. When the welfare of the community cannot be increased by shifting resources from one industry to another, allocative efficiency has been achieved. There is a more restrictive notion of allocative efficiency which makes use of the idea of Pareto optimality. A distribution of resources between industries and employments, or a system of resource allocation, is said to be Pareto optimal when it is not possible, by transferring resources from one industry to another, to make one person better off without making another worse off.

This is different from the loose idea of allocative efficiency which turns on 'the welfare of the community'. An observing economist might say that the welfare of the community has been increased by a resource-shift which makes one group much better off while making another only slightly worse off. This might be so, but the resource-shift would *not* be Pareto optimal because one group is worse off.

In most economies resource allocation is determined by the price mechanism. Labour and capital flow to industries which are profitable and leave industries which are making losses. Industries are profitable only if there is strong demand for the product and price is above average cost. Resource-shifts should continue until profit rates are the same in all industries. When it is no longer worthwhile to transfer resources, prices should be equal to MARGINAL COSTS in all branches of production.

Productive efficiency refers to the productivity of a given set of inputs in one industry. For example, it may be possible, given the existing technology, to obtain 20 cars a year from one man. A factory which is only obtaining 10 cars a year per man has a lower level of productive efficiency than a factory which has reached maximum output at 20 cars a year.

In most popular discussions 'efficiency' means productive efficiency. Economists on the whole have little to say about this form of efficiency because it is regarded as a problem for engineers and managers. They are more concerned with questions of allocative efficiency.

Economic growth. The process whereby a nation's output increases through time. It is sometimes considered more narrowly as the process whereby output per head in a country increases.

The subject of economic growth was in the forefront of economists' minds for most of the 1950s and 1960s, but it has now been replaced by concern for inflation, unemployment and some of the problems which have followed the rapid expansion of the world economy since the Second World War. The main object of studying economic growth was to discover its causes. On the whole the results of this study have been rather dissatisfying and few economists would be certain of the reasons for high or low growth.

But they do agree that an increase in the quantity and quality of inputs raises the level of output. An increase in the capital stock and the advance of technology are, therefore, widely regarded as the principal causes of economic growth, although education is also sometimes mentioned, and no one has worked out a reliable method of distinguishing between the contribution of technology and the contribution of investment.

It has been argued, notably by the American economist, Professor Rostow, that the increase in output per head which has created modern industrial society occurred in a sequence of stages of economic growth. The most important stage was the take-off, associated with extremely rapid rates of growth, an increase in the ratio of output devoted to investment, the adoption of new and more advanced methods, and the transfer of workers from agriculture to industry. The take-off took place in Britain in the late eighteenth century and in Germany in the late nineteenth century and it has reached a number of DEVELOPING COUNTRIES in recent years. For example, Brazil in the 1960s and early 1970s is often said to have experienced economic take-off. After take-off most economies have lower rates of economic growth, but continue to expand.

One of the most serious questions in the theory of economic growth was posed by Sir Roy Harrod, the British economist, in the late 1930s. He distinguished between the warranted rate of growth and the natural rate of growth. The warranted rate of growth is an economy's CAPITAL–OUTPUT RATIO divided by its savings ratio (the proportion of total income saved). The capital–output ratio depends on technology and the savings ratio on the community's preferences between present and future consumption.

The natural rate of growth is determined by the growth of the labour force and the increase in productivity caused by the advance of technology. It depends on quite different factors from the warranted rate of growth. The warranted growth rate could therefore be higher or lower than the natural growth rate. This might create difficulties because if, for example, the warranted growth rate were above the natural, an economy's capital stock would be rising more rapidly than the labour force and many of the new machines would be standing idle.

Much of growth theory is an attempt to explain why the warranted and natural rates should eventually be come equal and why difficulties of this kind have never proved insoluble for long.

Economic imperialism. The domination of an economy, usually that of a DEVELOPING COUNTRY, by foreign companies or governments.

Economic rent. A factor of production is induced into employment by the promise of payment. The level of payment required to induce it is known as its 'supply price'. But the payment it actually receives may be higher than this. The difference between the supply price and the actual payment is known as economic rent.

The best examples of economic rent are in the entertainment industry. Many popular performers would be happy to appear in a show or to make a record for much less than they in fact receive. It is possible to lower their incomes or to tax them heavily and thereby eliminate their economic rent while still providing them with enough incentive to work.

Super-normal profit is a similar concept, but it applies to companies. A company is earning super-normal profit if its rate of profit is higher than that necessary to induce it to remain in production in the LONG-RUN. (⟡NORMAL PROFIT.)

Economies of scale. Reductions in the average cost of production as the level of output increases. Economies of scale are extremely common in modern industry and enable prices to fall as a new technology is exploited and companies expand. Internal economies of scale are cost reductions confined to one company; external economies of scale are cost reductions which occur because of the expansion of an industry.

Elasticity. When a company lowers the price of its product, it expects the quantity demanded to increase. More consumers should be willing to buy the product. But the response to the reduction in price may vary. It might be that a 10 per cent reduction in price is followed by a 15 per cent increase in quantity demand, by a 10 per cent increase or by a 5 per cent increase.

The responsiveness of quantity demanded to price is obviously a very important consideration in business and economics. The switch in demand which accompanies price changes affects other products and alters the distribution of spending and the allocation of resources in an economy. The term adopted by economists for this responsiveness of quantity demanded to price is elasticity. If elasticity is high the economy is responsive to price changes and they cause a large number of con-sequential adjustments. If it is low the economy is insensitive to price changes and they have little effect on its behaviour.

There are two main concepts of elasticity, the elasticity of demand

and the elasticity of supply. The elasticity of demand (or price-elasticity of demand) is defined as:

$$\frac{\text{the percentage change in the quantity demanded}}{\text{the percentage change in price.}}$$

When the price under consideration is the same as that of the product being demanded the elasticity is known as the own-price elasticity of demand. When the price is that of another product, it is known as the CROSS ELASTICITY OF DEMAND.

The elasticity of supply is:

$$\frac{\text{the percentage change in quantity supplied}}{\text{the percentage change in price.}}$$

If the elasticity of supply for a product is high, its suppliers increase output by a larger percentage than an increase in price; if it is equal to 1 they increase output by the same percentage; and if it is low, they increase output by less than the increase in price. The same distinction between high, unity and low applies to the elasticity of demand.

Elasticity of substitution. A manufacturer can often produce the same level of output with different combinations of inputs. The particular combination chosen depends primarily on the comparative cost of the inputs. If the comparative cost changes, he may decide to alter the mix between them. He reduces the quantity of one input used and increases the quantity of another.

The elasticity of substitution is a term used when there are only two inputs. It measures the increase needed in the quantity of one input if less is used of another and the level of output is to remain unchanged.

The term is also sometimes found in MACROECONOMICS. It shows how the ratio between capital and labour in an economy responds to a change in the ratio between the rate of profit and the rate of wages.

Eligible paper. A security that can be converted into cash by being sold to the Bank of England or accepted by the Bank as security for a loan to a DISCOUNT HOUSE. Treasury bills, short-dated government stock and accepted bills of exchange are eligible paper.

Endogenous variable. In an economic MODEL, an endogenous variable is a variable which is generated within the model. An exogenous variable is a variable which is not generated within the model.

Engel's law. The theory that the proportion of income spent on food declines as income increases.

Entrepôt. Trade which passes through a third country on its way between the initial producer and the final consumer.

Entrepreneur. When property is privately owned it is possible to venture into new and risky lines of business in an attempt to obtain profits. Individuals who perform this risk-bearing function are known as entrepreneurs. They are often said to operate in a free enterprise or market economy because they are free to take advantage of opportunities created by market forces or the laws of supply and demand.

Equilibrium. An economic system is in equilibrium when the amounts of each good that buyers wish to buy are equal to the amounts of each good which sellers wish to sell. The prices associated with this balance are known as the equilibrium prices. The quantities of each good bought and sold in equilibrium are known as the equilibrium quantities.

In partial equilibrium analysis only the equilibrium of a particular market is under consideration. The equilibrium price and quantity in this market is not unique since a change in other markets could affect it. For example, if the market for cars is not in equilibrium, any partial equilibrium in the market for tyres is likely to be disturbed since an increase in car sales causes an increase in the demand for tyres.

In general equilibrium analysis the equilibrium of all markets in an economy is under consideration. The connections between markets are recognized. Under certain assumptions it can be shown that the equilibrium set of prices and quantities is unique. The general theory of equilibrium analysis was pioneered by Leon Walras (1834–1910), Professor of Economics at Lausanne University. The Lausanne school is therefore associated with this branch of economics.

Equilibrium price. ▷EQUILIBRIUM.

Equilibrium quantity. ▷EQUILIBRIUM.

Equity. Companies normally have obligations to a wide range of people, to banks and individuals who have lent them money at fixed interest, to suppliers of raw materials who extend trade credit and to the government if they have to pay taxes. But when all these obligations have been met there are usually assets remaining. These assets belong to the shareholders and are known as the equity of the company.

Equity can, therefore, be considered as the shares issued by the company. Most of these tend to be ORDINARY SHARES which yield a dividend and entitle their owners to vote at the annual general meeting where the board of directors is chosen. But there are other kinds of share, such as 'A' shares which only yield dividends and do not give an entitlement to vote.

When a company is set up, its constitution usually refers to registered or nominal or authorized capital. This is the number of shares it may issue if it wishes to do so. But, at the outset, it may issue only a fraction of this number, known as the issued capital.

For example, a company may have a registered capital of one million shares of £1 each. But its issued capital may amount to 500000 shares of £1 each. The purpose of this system is to issue more shares in future so that the proceeds can be used for expansion or to buy out another company.

Estimates.   ⟁BUDGET.

Euro-currency.   International trade and finance are conducted with a number of currencies. For example, an exporter in West Germany may receive payment for his goods in dollars or sterling even though the domestic currency he uses is the mark. He may deposit these foreign currencies at his bank rather than exchange them into marks. When, at some future date, he wants to buy machinery or raw materials from the United States or the United Kingdom, he can withdraw the dollars and sterling from his deposit with minimal inconvenience.

A currency which is deposited in banks in a foreign country on a large scale is known as a Euro-currency. This name has developed because the most sizeable foreign currency deposits are found in European countries, particularly the United Kingdom, West Germany and Switzerland, although it is quite common for companies to have dollar deposits in banks in South America or Asia.

The main Euro-currency is the Euro-dollar. Euro-dollars are dollar deposits held by companies and individuals outside the United States. Banks which have received such deposits can, of course, on-lend them to other companies and individuals. A huge market, centred on London, has emerged since the late 1950s based on credit transactions of this kind. The growth of the Euro-dollar market was encouraged by the Interest Equalization Act passed by the US Congress in 1963. It was intended to check capital outflows from the United States, but its main result was to force American companies to borrow dollars abroad and it therefore shifted banking business in dollars to the other side of the Atlantic.

Lending in dollars is usually in the form of an ordinary bank advance, but it is sometimes performed by means of Euro-bonds. A Euro-bond is a long-term loan (usually for more than five years) to a government or large international company. Several banks participate in the loan to reduce the risk of default to each one. The sums raised by Euro-bonds in recent years have been enormous and may be measured in billions of dollars.

Euro-dollar. ⊳EURO-CURRENCY.

European Coal and Steel Community (ECSC). ⊳EUROPEAN ECONO-MIC COMMUNITY.

European Commission. ⊳EUROPEAN ECONOMIC COMMUNITY.

European Common Market. ⊳EUROPEAN ECONOMIC COMMUNITY.

European Economic Community (EEC); also called the European Common Market. The Treaty of Rome was signed between 'the Six', France, West Germany, Italy and the three BENELUX members, Belgium, Luxembourg and the Netherlands, in 1957. Under the Treaty, the countries agreed to establish a FREE TRADE area, then to harmonize their external tariffs and at the same time to eliminate barriers to the free movement of labour and capital. The Treaty also provided for the development of common policies towards agriculture, transport and external trade, and eventual co-ordination of economic policies within the community.

In 1971 negotiations took place between the UK, Ireland, Denmark and Norway and 'the Six' on terms for their joining the Community. The terms were accepted by referenda in Ireland and Denmark who joined the community in January 1973, but rejected in a referendum in Norway. In the UK, which also became a member in January 1973, the terms were accepted by Parliament, but subsequently, after the Conservative government was replaced by a Labour government that was less in favour of entry, a renegotiation of the entrance terms took place and revised terms were submitted to a referendum in which the country voted to accept them.

The executive body of the EEC is the European Commission. The Commission has two commissioners appointed by each of the larger countries and one from each of the smaller countries and staff recruited from the member countries on a quota basis.

The Treaty of Rome laid down a time-table for the abolition of internal tariffs and the erection of a common external tariff, but the programme was accelerated so that the common external tariff came into force in 1968, two years early. The COMMON AGRICULTURAL POLICY, which replaced the individual agricultural policies of the member countries, operates by guaranteeing free movement of goods within the Community and setting intervention prices. When the price of the good is below the intervention price the Commission will buy to increase the price and when the price is higher than the intervention price the Commission sells. Imported products have levies charged on them to raise their prices to the EEC levels.

A forerunner of the EEC was the European Coal and Steel Community (ECSC), which was established in a treaty signed by the Six in 1952. The treaty made provisions for a reduction of tariff barriers in iron and steel products.

The European Social Fund promotes policies concerned with the amelioration of industrial relations and the retraining of the unemployed, particularly where redundancies have been due to the creation of the Community.

The European Regional Fund provides assistance to the poorer regions in the Community, particularly in Italy, Ireland and the UK.

European Free Trade Association (EFTA). The seventeen countries in the Organization for European Economic Cooperation (OEEC) other than the six founder members of the EEC negotiated with the Six in 1958 to form a free trade area. When the negotiations broke down, the European Free Trade Association was formed by Sweden, Norway, Denmark, Austria, Switzerland, Portugal and the UK in 1959. Finland joined in 1961 and Iceland in 1970. The members of the Association agreed to phase out tariffs on goods from the other members; tariffs on goods certified as at least 50 per cent manufactured within an EFTA country were virtually eliminated in the original members by December 1966. The UK and Denmark withdrew from EFTA in 1973 when they joined the EEC.

European Fund. ⊳EUROPEAN MONETARY AGREEMENT.

European Monetary Agreement (EMA). The European Payments Union (EPU) was the organization founded by the OEEC countries in the immediate post-war period to clear balances between members. It extended credit to members with balance of payments deficits. The European Monetary Agreement, which was signed in 1955, replaced the EPU in 1958. The European Fund was set up and assumed the banking role of the EPU. Settlements had to be made in convertible currencies or gold.

European Monetary Union. A scheme intended to unify the monetary systems of the members of the European Economic Community. It was originated by M. Pierre Werner, the then Finance Minister of Luxembourg, in a set of proposals put forward in 1970. The proposals were accepted by all the members of the Community and the aim was to achieve monetary union by 1980. Fluctuations in value between the currencies of member countries were to be eliminated and, eventually, a new European currency would be introduced to replace them.

In practice, it has proved impossible to achieve harmonization of monetary policy and no one now believes that monetary union will be attained by 1980. At first fluctuations between the currencies concerned were held within a narrow band known as the 'SNAKE'. But the United Kingdom was only briefly within the 'snake' and, since its inception, France, Italy, Ireland and Denmark have all been outside it for a period.

European Recovery Programme. ⇨MARSHALL AID.

European Regional Fund. ⇨EUROPEAN ECONOMIC COMMUNITY.

European Social Fund. ⇨EUROPEAN ECONOMIC COMMUNITY.

European unit of account. The unit used for accounting purposes by the European Economic Community. One unit was originally equal to 0.88671 grams of fine gold or one dollar. But the devaluation of the dollar in 1971 has meant that the unit of account is now worth rather more than one dollar.

Ex ante. An adjective used to describe the propensity to carry out some economic action before it takes place. For example, if someone wants to spend £800 in the near future his *ex ante* expenditure is said to be £800. In the end he may only spend £750 because he finds the goods he intended to buy were more expensive than anticipated. Looked at after the event or *ex post*, his expenditure is lower than his expenditure *ex ante*.

Ex post. ⇨EX ANTE.

Excess capacity. If a company is not using its plant and labour force fully, its output is beneath the highest attainable level and it is said to have excess capacity.

Excess demand (1). In microeconomics, excess demand is the excess of quantity demanded over quantity supplied at a particular price level. It can be eliminated by a rise in price to the EQUILIBRIUM level.

Excess demand (2). In macroeconomics, excess demand is a condition in which aggregate demand is higher than aggregate supply. People want to buy more goods at their present price level than are available.

Exchange control. In most international transactions companies and individuals have to exchange their domestic currency for foreign currency. If the domestic currency is priced too high or too low and they believe that some adjustment is likely in the near future they can speculate in foreign currency. For example, if someone in Britain thinks that the pound is soon to be devalued he can buy foreign currency, wait for the DEVALUATION to take place and then exchange his foreign currency for more pounds than he had in the first place.

Governments try to prevent behaviour of this kind, even if, by doing so, they inhibit normal commercial practices. They impose exchange control which specifies conditions under which residents cannot exchange domestic currency into foreign currency. The main forms of exchange control are restrictions on the amount of money which can be invested in foreign financial markets and on the amount of money which travellers can take out of a country for their own use. Exchange control reduces the CONVERTIBILITY of the currency concerned.

Exchange Equalization Account. An account operated by the Bank of England for buying and selling gold and foreign currencies. It is used to stabilize sterling's exchange rate and transactions are made in both the spot and forward markets.

Exchange rate. The price at which one currency can be exchanged for another. For example, if someone can buy $2 for £1 the exchange rate is said to be '$2 to £1'. If the exchange rate varies for different types of transaction there is said to be a system of multiple or two-tier exchange rates.

Exclusive dealing. ⇨RESTRICTIVE PRACTICES.

Ex-dividend. The buyer of a stock or share which is ex-dividend is not entitled to the next instalment of dividends or interest. When a share becomes ex-dividend its price usually goes down.

Exogenous variable. ⇨ENDOGENOUS VARIABLE.

Expectations. Beliefs about future events. In any economic decision influenced by future events, expectations are obviously important. An example is found in wage negotiations where the expectation of future price increases influences the demand which a trade union makes for higher pay.

Export Credits Guarantee Department (ECGD). A United Kingdom government department which insures exports against certain risks. The main risk is that a British company sends exports to a foreign customer before the customer has paid for them and may incur a loss if the customer does not, in fact, have the money.

Export incentives. Special assistance given to companies to encourage them to export goods. Tax rebates on foreign sales are one of the most important forms.

Export-led growth. A phase of economic expansion at unusually high rates associated with larger percentage increases in exports than in national output. The doctrine of export-led growth has been advanced by Professor Kaldor of Cambridge University. He has claimed that manufacturing industry shows higher rates of PRODUCTIVITY growth than national output as a whole. But much of manufacturing output is exported. If demand for exports can be stimulated – for example, by lowering the exchange rate – manufacturing industry should be able to expand quicker and the growth rate of the whole economy should benefit. This doctrine influenced policy in the United Kingdom in the mid-1970s when the government restricted domestic demand and lowered the exchange rate while arguing that other economies should boost demand to pull the world economy out of recession.

Exports. Goods and services produced domestically and sold abroad in exchange for foreign currencies. The foreign currency earned by exports can be used to purchase imports. (◊BALANCE OF PAYMENTS.)

External deficit. A balance of payments current account deficit.

External economies. ◊ECONOMIES OF SCALE.

Externalities. These occur when a decision to consume or produce by one person or firm affects the welfare of others. A classic example is the case of a firm that discharges effluent into a river in the course of production.

An essential aspect of externalities is that their effects are not taken into account by market prices. However, a large variety of arrangements for compensation can be made. If A wants to build a wall between his and B's house, and B does not want the wall, it is possible that a bribe can be made from B to A so that A will not build the wall. The question of compensation will depend on the laws and institutions under which the externality occurs. Government can also correct externalities by a system of taxing consumption or production with socially undesirable external effects and granting subsidies when the external effects contribute to social welfare.

Externalities are important in COST–BENEFIT ANALYSIS, where their effects are quantified and compared with the other effects of projects. (◊ COMPENSATION PRINCIPLE.)

F

Face value. The nominal price at which a security is redeemed, a share issued or a coin denominated. The face value and the market value of a security do not generally coincide.

Factor incomes. ▷INCOME DISTRIBUTION.

Factor of production. Anything which contributes to the production of goods is known as an input or a factor of production. The standard examples are capital, labour and land.

Factor payments. The returns paid to factors of production. For example, wages are the factor payments to labour.

Factor price equalization theorem. When countries engage in international trade, prices for particular goods should become the same throughout the world. If the price of a good is higher in one country than in another it is worthwhile for a trader in the cheap country to buy there and export at a higher price to the more expensive country. This should raise prices in the cheap country and lower them in the expensive country.

If production methods are identical in all countries, equalization of product prices should also lead to an equalization in factor prices. In other words, a unit of capital or labour in one country will be paid the same as in every other country. This result, which depends on a number of assumptions and is quite complicated to prove, is known as the factor price equalization theorem. Its importance is that it shows that, as long as there is free trade, there is no need for capital or labour to migrate for them to achieve the highest possible return.

Two Scandinavian economists, Eli Heckscher and Bertil Ohlin, were the first to study in this area. They concluded that a country will specialize in producing goods which require large amounts of the factor which is abundant in it. This principle is known as the Heckscher–Ohlin theorem.

Factoring. If A owes money to B and is unlikely to pay in the immediate future, then B can sell the debt to C for an amount below its face value, thus insuring himself and borrowing money at the same time. Factoring has developed very slowly in the UK in comparison with the USA where it is an accepted method of raising money on debts.

Fair trade policy. ⟡RECIPROCITY.

'Fancy accounting'. A euphemism for misleading accounting procedures which place too high a value on a company's assets.

Farm price review. Under the traditional method of subsidizing British agriculture, which was to be phased out as a result of joining the EEC but which became an issue in the renegotiation of terms in 1975, the prices that farms were to receive for their produce during the next year were announced in advance at the farm price review. The difference between the guaranteed price and the market price was the amount of the subsidy given (provided that the market price was below the guaranteed price).

Federal reserve system. The system of central banking in the United States, which consists of twelve regional CENTRAL BANKS with twenty-four branches. The reserve banks are owned by the 6000 member banks who receive a fixed dividend. The surpluses after the dividends are paid are kept by the US Treasury.

The regional banks perform the functions of central banks, providing clearing facilities and acting as LENDERS OF LAST RESORT. They come under the control of the Federal Reserve Board, which is appointed by the President and confirmed by the Senate. The Board is responsible for carrying out monetary policy in the USA.

Fiduciary issue. Money issued by the government that is not backed by gold or silver. When the fiducary issue was first introduced (in 1844), the amount of such money was limited by law, but now such restrictions have been waived.

Final products. Products that are consumed rather than being used as inputs to produce other goods.

Finance house. A financial institution providing hire-purchase finance and other loans. The major finance houses are the seventeen members of the Finance Houses Association. Although there is no clear-cut distinction between the business of finance houses and banks, finance houses tend to make loans on a more risky basis at higher interest rates.

Finance houses are among the non-bank financial intermediaries singled out for control under the document *Competition and Credit Control*. The others include investment trusts, building societies, insurance companies and pension funds. ($\diamond$COMPETITION AND CREDIT CONTROL.)

Financial intermediaries. Institutions such as building societies and hire-purchase companies which trade in money, borrowing from those who wish to lend and lending to those who wish to borrow. Banks and non-bank financial intermediaries are distinguished from each other, as the liabilities of the latter are not considered to be part of the MONEY SUPPLY.

Financial Times **Actuaries Share Indices.** $\diamond$FINANCIAL TIMES STOCK INDICES.

Financial Times **Stock Indices.** The *Financial Times* newspaper publishes indices of various stock prices. These take two forms, the *Financial Times* Stock Indices and the *Financial Times* Actuaries Share Indices. The latter are more detailed and calculated in a more accurate fashion, while the former are calculated by taking a goemetric mean of the values of the shares involved. The *Financial Times* Industrial Ordinary Shares Index is the best known of all the indices and is based on the geometric average of the prices of thirty BLUE CHIP shares. ($\diamond$AVERAGE.)

Financial year. The financial year for which government accounts are produced starts at the beginning of April. As a result most private concerns time their arrangements to coincide with this financial year.

Firm, Theory of the. The branch of economic theory that explains the behaviour of companies, particularly the quantities of each good that are produced and the prices at which the goods are sold.

The traditional theory, which assumes profit maximization, competition and a given market structure, is in many ways unrealistic, but provides a good basis for understanding real-world business behaviour, with limited liability for the shareholders. More modern theories have emphasized the divorce between ownership and control in joint-stock companies, suggesting that managers are as much concerned with objectives like the growth of the firm or the growth of their own departments as with the maximization of profits.

Firm, To. A price is said to firm on the Stock Exchange when it ceases to fall, or rises slightly.

Fiscal drag. The tendency for tax payments to rise at a faster rate than money national income as money national income increases. The reason for fiscal drag, which is found in almost all countries, is that the tax system is progressive. This means that tax rates are higher on large than on small incomes. As incomes rise, an increasing proportion is absorbed by tax payments unless the government decides to take off-setting action by lowering tax rates. Fiscal drag is particularly powerful during periods of rapid inflation.

Fiscal policy. The government's attempts to influence spending in an economy by changes in taxation and public expenditure are known as its fiscal policy. Fiscal policy is to be contrasted with MONETARY POLICY which tries to influence spending by changes in the money supply and interest rates. A reliance on fiscal policy to control fluctuations in output and employment was common in the advanced industrial economies in the 1950s and 1960s, but increasing emphasis is now being placed on monetary policy.

Fisher equation. ▷QUANTITY THEORY OF MONEY.

Fixed capital. Most companies have buildings and equipment as part of their productive capacity. But much of this capital cannot be increased quickly if demand for their products rises. In the short-run, therefore, part of a company's productive capacity is fixed capital. Fixed capital is to be contrasted with circulating capital, such as raw materials and semi-finished goods, which can be purchased in larger or smaller amounts at short notice.

Fixed costs; also called overheads or overhead costs or supplementary costs. Costs are divided into fixed and variable costs. The latter are the costs which vary in the short-run when output is varied, while the former do not.

Fixed exchange rates. EXCHANGE RATES which are maintained or pegged at a particular level, or within certain bands. They have the advantage of reducing trading risks through exchange rate changes, but have the disadvantage that when there are structural reasons for exchange rates changing, these changes are at first prevented and then when they finally take place are larger and more disruptive than they need to be.

Fixed interest. A rate of interest that is fixed in advance.

Floatation. Raising capital from the public at large rather than through a private deal with a FINANCIAL INTERMEDIARY.

Floating debt. Any short-term debt that is continually renewed. For example, government keeps a large part of its floating debt in the form of TREASURY BILLS.

Floating exchange rates. EXCHANGE RATES which are either allowed to move freely in response to market forces or which are maintained at levels which shift gradually in response to economic conditions. The latter system is called the crawling peg.

Flow of funds. In any economy, payments are being made between groups of people. Companies make payments to individuals in the form of wages and dividends and individuals make payments to companies when they buy goods and services. These financial transactions are known as the flow of funds.

Whenever there is a buyer there is a seller, and whenever someone incurs a liability someone else obtains an asset. It follows that the flow of funds cancels out. An economy can be thought of as consisting of four sectors – the personal sector, the company sector, the government sector and the overseas sector. One sector, by receiving more financial assets than it pays out, can have a financial surplus; or, by paying out more than it receives, it can have a financial deficit. But the sum of the financial surpluses and deficits of all four sectors must cancel out to zero.

This truism has important implications. If it is possible to say that one sector is certain to have a financial deficit, it must be the case that the other sectors considered together have a surplus. For example, if the government spends more than it receives in taxes, which creates a deficit, the overseas, personal and company sectors must have a surplus. The New Cambridge School (⟡CAMBRIDGE SCHOOL (c)) of the mid-1970s argued that the company and personal sectors never have a large surplus, implying that the government's deficit must be matched by a balance of payments deficit.

f.o.b. – free on board. Traded goods can either be valued f.o.b. or c.i.f., that is, after the inclusion of commission, insurance and freight charges incurred in transit. F.o.b. prices are lower than c.i.f. prices. The importance of the distinction is that trade figures are sometimes given in f.o.b. terms and sometimes in c.i.f. terms and the choice of measure affects the size of the deficit or surplus.

Food and Agricultural Organization (FAO). An organization set up in 1945 under the auspices of the United Nations to improve the production and distribution of food.

Forced saving. Saving which is caused by the consumer being unable to consume for some institutional reason or because of the absence of goods. Compulsory pensions contributions are an example of forced savings.

Foreign exchange. The currency of some other country. Foreign exchange can be held either directly as cash, or indirectly as securities denominated in and exchangeable for the foreign currency. The primary need for foreign exchange is to finance purchases from abroad, but there is a large speculative market as well, since movements in exchange rates are often relatively large and sudden. There are both SPOT and FORWARD MARKETS in foreign exchange and traders attempt to make profits by ARBITRAGE between different markets.

Foreign investment. Investment by individuals or institutions from one country in another country. This can either be direct investment, where capital goods or similar assets are purchased, or PORTFOLIO investment where financial assets are purchased.

Foreign trade multiplier. ⟡MULTIPLIER.

Forward cover. Avoiding the risk of future fluctuations in some price by buying for future needs at the present price in the FORWARD MARKETS. This is most likely in overseas trade where the importer may commit himself to paying in foreign exchange at some point in the future. To avoid possible losses through changes in the exchange rates he may buy the foreign exchange that he will need on the forward market.

Forward exchange market. ⟡FORWARD MARKET.

Forward market. A market where a contract can be made for the delivery of goods or financial assets at some stated point in the future. One such market is the forward exchange market where foreign exchange is traded forward.

Free goods. · Goods where the supply is effectively infinite or the cost of production negligible, such as air, water and some kinds of information.

Free market. A market where buyers and sellers are allowed to make the deals that they wish to without interference from governments or other institutions.

Free trade. International trade that is not hampered by tariff or non-tariff barriers imposed by governments. It is promoted by international organizations such as GATT and OECD on the grounds that restrictions reduce trade which can be beneficial to both parties involved. Free trade was largely accepted internationally until the inter-war Depression. In the period after the Second World War there has been a movement back towards free trade.

Frequency distribution. The relationship between the size of some variable and the number of occurrences of that particular size. For example, the frequency distribution of income would show how many individuals or households had incomes within each income group (see Figure 5).

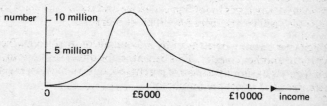

Figure 5. Frequency distribution.

Frictional unemployment. Unemployment that takes place while workers are moving from one job to another. Unless the labour force stays in the same jobs there will generally tend to be some frictional unemployment.

Friedmanite economics. The emphasis on money supply as a method of controlling the economy and the support of the free-enterprise system associated with Professor Milton Friedman of the University of Chicago.

Friedman has argued that, over long periods of time, the money supply holds a fairly stable relationship to money national income. The prime reason, he suggests, is that people hold money to finance transactions. If the supply of money is held back they are unable to finance a much larger level of transactions and the value of transactions is held back too.

Friedman has also put forward the theory that governments are unable to control the rate of unemployment, except in the short-run. In the long-run, he believes, either the rate of unemployment is determined by such factors as labour market mobility and the quality of job information or, if governments try to keep unemployment beneath this 'natural' rate, the system degenerates into HYPERINFLATION. Friedmanite economics is the most important intellectual challenge to Keynesian economics and fierce controversies have raged between the contending systems of thought.

Fringe banks. Banks outside the normal banking system involving themselves in high risk, high interest lending. They tended to grow in the early 1970s but many met with financial problems in 1974–5.

Full-cost pricing. A system of pricing where the profit margin is a fixed proportion of the average total costs of production.

Full employment. A condition in which a low proportion of the total labour force does not have permanent employment. Full employment has been an objective of government policy since the end of the Second World War.

The precise definition is still a matter of controversy. Some economists believe that, in any economy where people are changing jobs, there is certain to be FRICTIONAL UNEMPLOYMENT. Full employment has been reached, they suggest, when this is the only remaining form of joblessness. It has also been argued that many of those included in official unemployment statistics are actually unemployable, because they are mentally or physically unsuited to work, and that they should be deducted from the unemployment total to discover the number who are actively in the labour market looking for jobs.

Full-line forcing. ⟡RESTRICTIVE PRACTICES.

Fundamental disequilibrium. An excess supply or excess demand that is perpetuated for some institutional reason. In some interpretations of the Keynesian system, the economy can be in fundamental disequilibrium because of the inability of prices to adjust to a changed economic situation.

Funding. The replacement by central bank action of short-term public debt by long-term public debt. Funded debt in the United Kingdom consists primarily of gilt-edged securities quoted on the London Stock Exchange. Funding has an important bearing on monetary policy because long-term debt is less liquid than short-term. A change in the ratio between the two types of debt therefore influences behaviour because people find that their assets are held in a more or less liquid form. If people's assets are less liquid, they tend to be more cautious and to cut down their consumption.

Futures. Contracts made in a FORWARD MARKET to sell certain specified goods in the future.

G

Galloping inflation. A condition of rapidly rising prices. It may be thought of as synonymous with HYPERINFLATION which has been defined as a rise in prices faster than 50 per cent a month.

Games, Theory of. In much of economic analysis it is assumed that a decision by one economic agent has so little effect on other agents that the interaction between them can be ignored. However, it often happens that there are only two or three rivals in an industry or market and that each rival bases his own decisions on what he expects the response of the others to be. The theory of games is the branch of economic theory which examines the implications of this interdependence between economic agents. It consists largely of analyses of alternative strategies in hypothetical situations involving considerable risk or uncertainty. It can become highly mathematical and complicated.

Gearing; also known as leverage. Companies can finance investment in two ways – with funds borrowed from outsiders, such as banks and financial institutions, or with funds generated internally from profits. Most external finance tends to be fixed interest. In other words, companies have to pay an annual interest charge to the lenders. This kind of finance can be risky because profits in a bad year may drop beneath the interest charges. Gearing is the ratio between fixed-interest debt and shareholders' funds in a company. If a company is highly geared it is normally considered to be a bad risk and banks may be reluctant to extend it more credit.

General Agreement on Tariffs and Trade (GATT). An international organization founded in 1947, the members of which are pledged to promote free trade between countries. Multilateral bargaining for the reduction of tariffs and the abolition of other import restrictions has taken place on six occasions to date.

General equilibrium analysis. ▷EQUILIBRIUM.

Genoa Conference. Two financial conferences at Brussels in 1920 and

Genoa in 1922 discussed international debt settlements and reparations. It was agreed that each country should have a CENTRAL BANK to control domestic financial movements.

Giffen goods. When the price of a good falls there are two effects on the consumer. The first is that his real income has risen because he can buy more of all goods than he could before. The second is that the lower price makes the good more attractive compared to other goods. The second effect, known as the SUBSTITUTION EFFECT, is bound to make him buy more of the cheaper good. But the first effect is not. It may be that, at the higher income level, the consumer's preferences have changed and that he would like to alter the structure of his purchasing decisions. He may want to buy less of the cheaper good, despite the reduction in price. A good like this, where a negative INCOME EFFECT outweighs the positive substitution effect, is known as a Giffen good. Its characteristic is that a fall in price causes a reduction in the quantity demanded, not an increase.

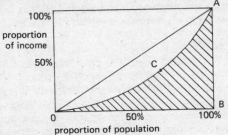

Figure 6. Gini coefficient.

Gift tax. ◊PERSONAL TAXATION.

Gilt-edged securities. Fixed-interest government securities traded on the London Stock Exchange. They are called gilt-edged because they are liabilities of the Treasury and are, therefore, almost completely free of risk. They are also known simply as gilts. (◊CONVERSION.)

Gilts. ◊GILT-EDGED SECURITIES.

Gini coefficient. This is a coefficient of inequality of distribution of some variable. It is formed by graphing the proportion of a variable such as income held by the x per cent of the population with least income. When this is done for all values of x, a curve such as OCA in Figure 6 is produced. The Gini coefficient is the ratio of the area under the curve OCA (the shaded area) to that of the triangle OAB.

The line O A represents the proportion of income that different proportions of the population would have if income was distributed equally throughout the population.

Gold. ⇨TWO-TIER GOLD MARKET.

Gold and foreign exchange reserves. Most countries have a stock of gold and foreign currencies which are used to settle foreign debts. The size of the reserves that is considered necessary depends on the balance of payments deficits that are considered likely in the future and the possibilities of financing such deficits.

Gold exchange standard. A variant of the GOLD STANDARD in which the central bank does not exchange gold into the domestic currency unless an international transaction is to be carried out. A gold exchange standard was in operation between the end of the First World War and 1971 because most countries held gold in their reserves and used this gold to meet balance of payments deficits. But the suspension of the dollar's convertibility into gold in 1971 has left the metal's position in the international monetary system in doubt.

Gold points. ⇨GOLD STANDARD.

Gold standard. A country is on the gold standard if its CENTRAL BANK will exchange gold for its currency on demand. The domestic money supply is, therefore, linked to the central bank's gold reserves because enough gold has to be held to honour this obligation.

The gold standard has never worked in a pure form, but in theory it helps economies to maintain equilibrium on their international transactions. If a country is running a balance of payments deficit the reduction in the gold reserve obliges the central bank to raise interest rates and reduce the money supply. Demand in the economy should, therefore, be restricted, resulting in fewer imports and more exports. The balance of payments deficit is removed automatically.

The United Kingdom was on the gold standard until the First World War and from 1925 to 1931.

Central banks were never able to promise to redeem the domestic currency into gold at a single price, but charged one price to buyers of gold and a lower one to sellers. These two prices were known as gold points or specie points. They defined the very narrow range within which currencies could fluctuate.

Government securities; also called government stocks. Government fixed-interest debt.

Government stocks. ⇨GOVERNMENT SECURITIES.

Green revolution. ⬦DEVELOPING COUNTRY.

Gresham's law. The law that states that 'bad money drives out good'. It was formulated in Elizabethan times by Sir Thomas Gresham, one of Queen Elizabeth's economic advisers, to explain how, if there were two forms of currency with the same face value but containing different amounts of gold, the currency containing more gold would be melted down into more coins of the type containing less gold.

Grey areas. ⬦REGIONAL POLICY.

Gross domestic product (GDP). ⬦GROSS NATIONAL PRODUCT.

Gross domestic product deflator. The price deflator used to value GDP at constant prices. This is so that the effects of price changes on the value of GDP can be removed and an estimate of the change in the number of goods produced can be made. The index used is a Paasche index, which means that the weights given to the individual prices are the proportions of the goods currently purchased when the deflator is applied. (⬦INDEX NUMBERS.)

Gross investment. ⬦INVESTMENT.

Gross national product (GNP). Government departments prepare estimates of the volume and value of output in nearly all countries. The most important measure of a country's output is known as gross national product.

The gross domestic product (GDP) is the sum of all the output produced domestically. It is equal to domestic expenditure plus exports minus imports. Gross national product is equal to gross domestic product plus income received from abroad minus payments made abroad.

Estimates of gross domestic product can be made on an expenditure basis (how much money has been spent), on an output basis (how many goods have been sold) and on an income basis (how much income has been earned). In principle all three should be equal.

There is a number of minor, but complicating, statistical adjustments which have to be made to some of the estimates to obtain a true picture. For example, adding up expenditure at market prices is misleading because it includes indirect taxes which plainly do not correspond to output. It is necessary to subtract indirect taxes and add subsidies to arrive at an estimate for output at factor cost. National income, sometimes known as the national dividend, is equal to gross national product at factor cost.

Net national product or net domestic product is gross national product or gross domestic product minus the DEPRECIATION of the country's capital stock.

Group of Ten. ⟡INTERNATIONAL MONETARY FUND.

Growth. ⟡ECONOMIC GROWTH.

Growth theory. ⟡ECONOMIC GROWTH.

H

Hard currency. A currency that is generally acceptable internationally for trading purposes, normally because its exchange rate is not expected to fall.

Harden, To. A currency hardens when demand for it at the existing price is high so that in the absence of government transactions its price will tend to rise.

Harmonization. Systems are harmonized when differing systems in different countries are replaced by systems which are the same in each country. The EEC promotes harmonization in many fields, from standards and safety regulations to agricultural and tax policies.

Harmonization, where the result is two similar systems run separately, is different from integration, where the result is a single system run centrally. For example, it is intended that the EEC countries have integrated anti-monopoly policies and regional policies where, in both cases, the policies would be administered from the European Commission rather than by the national governments.

Heckscher–Ohlin principle. ⟡FACTOR PRICE EQUALIZATION THEOREM.

Hedge. To reduce the risk in a contract by making purchases in FORWARD MARKETS.

Hicksian economics. In the 1930s a number of new theoretical tools were developed in economics, particularly indifference curves, isoquants and associated concepts such as the elasticity of substitution. They were an advance on the previous tools which had relied heavily on demand and supply analysis. Sir John Hicks (1904–), the famous British economist who was joint winner of the Nobel Prize for economics in 1974, pioneered these new ideas in his book on *Value and Capital* in 1939 and they have formed the core of Hicksian economics. *Value and Capital* was also important as a synthesis of existing work on general equilibrium theory. (⟡INDIFFERENCE ANALYSIS; EQUILIBRIUM.)

Historic cost. ⇨ REPLACEMENT COST.

Hoarding (1). Buying goods and not consuming them.

Hoarding (2). Accumulating money and not spending it. This has a deflationary effect on demand since the income is generated but then not matched by expenditure, so that part of output will not be bought.

Holding company. A company for the purpose of holding shares in other companies. Theoretically it is possible to control a large company with a small investment if there are sufficient layers of holding companies, since one man can control the first holding company with 51 per cent of its shares, and the first company can control the second company in the same way. This kind of behaviour is known as pyramiding.

Horizontal integration; also called lateral integration. A merger between two firms in the same line of business, to take advantage of the economies through sharing certain facilities, or to attempt to increase MONOPOLY power.

Hot money. Foreign funds invested in short-term securities in a country to take advantage of exchange rate movements or attractive rates of interest. As it is only invested in short-term securities this money is extremely volatile.

Human capital. Skills and abilities that people have as a result of investment in education and training.

Hyperinflation. A condition of rapidly rising prices. The distinction between inflation, galloping inflation and hyperinflation is a matter of degree, but hyperinflation has been defined as a rise in prices in excess of 50 per cent a month. The fall in the value of money becomes so rapid that the economy may begin to regress to a barter economy. The most serious hyperinflations in the past have been due to excessive government spending financed by the printing of money, typically in the aftermath of war. Examples are Germany between August 1922 and November 1923, when prices rose at an average rate of 322 per cent a month, and Hungary between 1945 and July 1946, when the average rate was 19800 per cent a month.

I

Imperfect competition. A technical term used to describe a degree of competition which is less effective in bringing prices down to costs than PERFECT COMPETITION. The reasons for this include lack of knowledge, discrimination between buyers and collusion between sellers. Imperfect competition is to be distinguished from OLIGOPOLY, because it is associated with a fairly large number of competitors, whereas oligopoly is characterized by a small number.

Imperfect market. A market in which the assumptions of PERFECT COMPETITION are not satisfied and which, therefore, has less beneficial effects on welfare. Artificial restrictions on sale, particularly where these arise because of agreements between sellers, and lack of product divisibility are examples of factors which disturb the smooth functioning of markets. A feature of imperfect markets is for non-price competition to be more important than price competition. A good example is the agreement between major international airlines to have the same fares on certain routes. The result is that they compete by advertising heavily or improving the service. In consequence, prices are above MARGINAL COST and resources are not allocated as efficiently as in perfect markets.

Imperial preference. ◇COMMONWEALTH PREFERENCE.

Import deposits. A scheme intended to correct a balance of payments deficit without the need for deflation of the domestic economy. It operates by obliging importers to deposit funds in commercial banks (or, sometimes, the central bank) equal in value to some percentage of their import bills. This discourages imports because the money is tied up and is not earning interest.

Although similar in effect to import duties, import deposit schemes are usually more acceptable to international opinion, partly because they reduce the MONEY SUPPLY in the economy imposing them. They are, therefore, popular with governments which, although expecting an eventual improvement in the payments position, are reluctant to take more drastic steps, such as changing the value of the currency or cutting spending power in the domestic economy.

Roy Jenkins, as Chancellor of the Exchequer, introduced an import deposits scheme in 1968, because the recovery of the British balance of payments after the 1967 devaluation of the pound was slower than had been hoped. The Italians have also adopted import deposit schemes.

Import duties. ▷IMPORT RESTRICTIONS.

Import Duties Act 1932. ▷COMMONWEALTH PREFERENCE.

Import restrictions; also known as import controls. Attempts to reduce the value of imports, usually carried out with the backing of the government of the country concerned. They take a wide variety of forms, but they have one feature in common. They try to cut back imports while leaving the EXCHANGE RATE unchanged. Several international organizations, notably the General Agreement on Tariffs and Trade, have since the Second World War actively discouraged the extensive use of import restrictions because of the unfavourable effect on the growth of world trade. A preference has gradually developed, especially among the advanced countries, for using the exchange rate for correcting imbalances between exports and imports.

The most important type of import restriction is the IMPORT TARIFF. When a good is imported, the importer has to pay a sum of money to the government related to the nature or price of the good he is buying from abroad. This import duty is over and above the price which has to be paid to the exporter. Because the cost to the importer altogether is above the cost he would have to incur without the tariff, he buys fewer imports.

The second most common type of import restriction is the QUOTA. This sets an overall limit to the quantity of a good which may be imported from abroad. Although more certain in impact than the tariff, it has several disadvantages.

In the last ten years governments in advanced countries have refrained from using import restrictions on a permanent basis, using them mainly as a bargaining counter in international negotiations on trade and international monetary affairs. However, in the 1930s, there were frequent 'tariff wars' of a 'BEGGAR-MY-NEIGHBOUR' character. In the nineteenth century, Friedrich List advocated import restrictions because they insulated domestic industries from foreign competition and, therefore, he argued, made it easier for them to grow. The industrial development of Japan is, to some extent, an example of the application of this INFANT INDUSTRY principle.

Import substitutes. Import substitutes are rivals to imported products. They are made within the economy. Promotion of import substitutes lessens dependence on foreign suppliers and has, therefore, become a common policy in developing economies trying to assert their freedom from commercial links with advanced economies.

Import tariff; also known as import duty. When a country buys a good from abroad its government may decide to levy a tax from the importer before giving him permission to sell it. This tax is called an import tariff.

A tariff can be levied as a fixed sum (for example, it might be 10p per gallon of petrol regardless of the price) or as a percentage rate (say 10 per cent of the price). In this case the two tariffs would yield the same sum to the government only if the price were £1 per gallon.

Tariffs have two main purposes. The first is to raise revenue for the government. In this respect it is similar to taxation, but the burden falls partly on foreign producers rather than entirely on domestic taxpayers.

The second is that they protect domestic industry. If Britain can produce petrol at £1 per gallon whereas the Middle East can produce it for 60p per gallon, it would plainly pay no one in Britain to produce petrol because he could not compete with the Middle Eastern producers. But if the British government were to charge a 100 per cent tariff on imported petrol, then the price of Middle East petrol would rise to £1.20 and the British industry would be competitive. Tariffs have been defended on these grounds because they promote output and keep up employment.

However, tariffs do have undesirable effects. If Middle East oil is so cheap, it might be better for Britain to make more machines and export them in exchange for imported petrol. The effect of protecting the British oil industry is to cause resources to be diverted to extracting petrol so that fewer are available for making machines.

In other words, tariffs may distort resource allocation ($\Diamond$ECONOMIC EFFICIENCY). Consequently governments since the Second World War have tried to eliminate tariffs as far as possible, mainly through negotiations under the General Agreement on Tariffs and Trade (GATT).

There is a branch of economic theory known as the theory of effective protection which is based on the idea that taxing imports of inputs has different effects from taxing imports of FINAL PRODUCTS because manufacturers may be using inputs produced abroad. This theory tries to determine the best tariff structure after account has been taken of these side-effects on domestic industry. ($\Diamond$INTERMEDIATE PRODUCTS.)

Imports. Goods and services purchased from abroad. They form the debit items on the balance of payments and, over a period of years, must be matched by equivalent sales of goods and services to other countries. The phrase 'capital imports' is also sometimes used. This means an inflow of funds into a country, which is, therefore, incurring liabilities to other countries.

'In the Bank'.   A phrase used to describe the activities of a DISCOUNT HOUSE which has been forced to borrow from the Bank of England. Normally discount houses would like to borrow money from the clearing banks, because they charge a lower rate of interest. To be 'in the bank' is, therefore, a sign of slight financial difficulty. However, in some parts of the financial year, notably around the TAX GATHERING SEASON, it is a daily occurrence.

Income.   The concept of income is one of the most basic, but also most complicated, in economics. The popular usage is that income per period is the sum of receipts by an individual, or firm, or an economy in that period. The receipts are of three main kinds – wages and salaries (income from work), profits (income from capital) and rents (income from land).

However, economists have never been happy with this definition. For example, someone may be paid monthly and in the first fortnight of the month he is receiving nothing. But it cannot be said that his income is nothing. In practice he will probably not be making too bad a mistake to suppose that this income in the fortnight is exactly half of his monthly income. On the other hand, if he had substantial savings, and he were receiving income over a long period of time, it would not be right to say, after he had been given half of his interest payments on his assets, that he had already received half his income. The reason is that he probably discounts the income he will be obtaining in future years at a particular rate of time preference. As the saying goes, 'a bird in the hand is worth two in the bush'. Future income, although relevant to how much someone wants to spend now, is valued less highly than present income. (◊INTEREST, THEORY OF.)

Because of this problem, another definition has been chosen in preference to the simple 'receipts in a period' concept. The central idea is that income is the maximum amount an individual can spend without making himself worse off. In other words, income is the consumption that an individual can have in a period which will leave him at the end of the period with the same stock of goods, and expectations of future goods, as he had at the beginning.

There are two main difficulties arising from this definition. The first is that net income must be distinguished from gross income. Often individuals or companies are receiving income from an asset which is gradually losing value. For example, a company may have bought a machine which will last five years and is worth less after four years than after one. This loss in value – or depreciation – must be deducted from the firm's profits to reach an idea of its true income.

A similar adjustment has to be made to national income. Although a society could consume all it produced in a year, it could only do so by not replacing some of its capital equipment which had grown old and fallen to pieces. A term for depreciation is, therefore, deducted from output to determine net national income.

The second difficulty is that the value of capital is changing through time. For example, someone may own shares which in 1968 were worth £100, but which, in 1975, are worth £150. Is this £50 income or is it a capital gain which only exists on paper and should not affect behaviour?

Despite these problems, income is an immensely important notion for economists. It is the most significant determinant of consumption and plays a central role in the theory of the CONSUMPTION FUNCTION in MACROECONOMICS. It also is crucial in discussions about the distribution of income between factors of production and different social classes.

Income, Circular flow of. All income is spent in some form or other – apart from a usually small amount which individuals lay aside to increase their money balances. But all receipts by businesses and corporations are eventually passed on to other individuals as income. This continuous flow is known as the circular flow of income.

Income determination, Theory of. The theory of income determination is concerned with the level of national income. It must be distinguished from the theory of income distribution which is concerned with the amount of income received by different individuals and FACTORS OF PRODUCTION.

The main purpose of the theory of income determination is to explain why national income settles at a particular level; why, in other words, it is at £20000m instead of £18000m, for example. As such it is important for determining the level of employment, because higher incomes and output are associated with higher employment.

The modern theory of income determination developed in the 1940s and 1950s on the foundations laid by Keynes in *The General Theory of Employment, Interest and Money* which was published in 1936. The central notion is that national income is determined by AGGREGATE DEMAND, or, more crudely, by the amount people are spending. There are several components of aggregate demand, but they fall into two main categories.

The first are endogenous. What this means is that their level depends on how much people in the economy are receiving in income. For example, consumption is endogenous because, generally speaking, the amount that individuals have to spend depends on how much they are receiving from their employment or from the ownership of capital. Such endogenous components of demand clearly are not going to determine the level of national income. On the contrary, the relationship is the other way round. They are determined by the level of national income.

The second category is exogenous. These are unrelated to the present level of national income. Investment, for example, is not constrained by the level of current receipts, because it is typically financed by borrowing from banks or savings institutions. It tends to be determined by such things as profits and the rate of interest. Similarly, exports depend on the exchange rate and the level of demand in foreign countries.

It is the exogenous components of demand which matter in deciding whether or not national income will go up or down or settle at a particular level. Movements in exogenous demand cause fluctuations in national income; fluctuations in national income cause movements in endogenous demand.

Keynes introduced a further refinement. He said that, on the basis of observable experience, endogenous components of demand responded to national income in a stable way. When national income rose by 10 per cent, imports rose by 10 per cent also. Or, if they did not rise by 10 per cent, they rose by 8 per cent or 6 per cent. The important point was not the figure itself, but the fact that relationship between the two figures remained the same.

These two ideas – that exogenous demand caused fluctuations in national income and that the response of endogenous demand to these fluctuations did not vary through time or in different circumstances – were extremely valuable. They permitted the development of forecasting techniques which have subsequently been helpful to governments when they want to find out how much demand – and, therefore, how much unemployment – there will be in a particular year.

The MULTIPLIER theory of income determination hinges on the two ideas. It states, in its simplest form, that national income is equal to the reciprocal of 1 minus the MARGINAL PROPENSITY TO CONSUME multiplied by the level of investment. The vital point to understand here is that the marginal propensity to consume is something known from past experience. It can be assumed that it will not change in the future because it is a stable aspect of an endogenous component of demand. A forecaster can, therefore, determine what national income will be if he can find out what investment will be. Equally, a government can alter national income by stimulating or deterring investment. It has been the realization that this is possible which has led to the elimination of mass unemployment in most advanced countries since 1945.

Income distribution. In economics, income distribution refers to the distribution of income between individuals, social classes or FACTORS OF PRODUCTION. Unless where specifically stated, it does not refer to the distribution of income between regions or between the public and private sectors.

Incomes are of two main kinds – factor incomes and transfer incomes. Factor incomes or factor payments are received for the performance of an activity for which there is an economic demand. They are received by the owners of factors of production as a reward for their employment. Transfer incomes, on the other hand, are not paid for productive services. They tend to arise, instead, from charity or government-backed arrangements to provide income support to those who are unable to work to obtain a livelihood. Pensions are a good example.

There are numerous theories of income distribution and the area remains one of the most debated and contentious in economics. The main theory is that the price of factors of production is determined in the factor markets by demand and supply. According to this theory, if the demand for, say, rented accommodation rises, and there is no increase in the quantity supplied, rents will also rise. An important extension of this approach is the marginal productivity theory of income distribution. (⬦MARGINAL PRODUCTIVITY OF CAPITAL.)

The principal alternative theory is the Marxian theory of distribution. This places less emphasis on demand and supply in the factor markets and more on the balance of power between social classes. (⬦MARXIAN ECONOMICS.)

There are three sorts of income: wages and salaries (income from employment), profits (income from capital), and rents (income from land). The theory of income distribution is concerned with two types of question: 'What determines the distribution between wages and salaries, profits and rents?' and 'What determines the distribution between one individual and another, and between one group of individuals and another?' It is not concerned with other questions, such as, 'What determines the distribution of wealth between individuals?' or 'What determines the rate of interest?' However, these two further questions are closely related and much of the complexity and uncertainty in the theory of income distribution arises from a failure to distinguish the issue at stake.

Income effect. With given tastes, there are two reasons why an individual might want to buy more of a good: a reduction in its price or an increase in his income. There is, however, a complication. If someone has an income of £100 and he is spending it all on, say, 100 loaves of bread, a reduction in the price of bread from £1 to 50p is equivalent to doubling of his income. A change in price has an income effect.

If the person's income had been doubled to £200, with prices remaining unchanged, he might not have spent all of the extra income on loaves. At the higher income level he might have begun to buy fish – say 150 loaves and 50 fish.

The same possibility arises when income has been doubled because of a price change. In this case more loaves will probably be bought, partly because loaves are now cheaper compared with other things (the SUBSTITUTION EFFECT), partly because the person is now better off. It is this second reason for a change in consumption which is known as the income effect.

It is important to understand that the income effect arises because of a change in prices. Other 'income effects' are sometimes found in economic discussions, but the strict meaning is 'that part of the change in the consumption of a good caused by the change in real income arising from a change of price'.

Income elasticity of demand. The income elasticity of demand is a concept used to describe how people alter their consumption habits as they become better off. It is defined as

$$\frac{\text{the percentage change in quantity demanded}}{\text{the percentage change in income.}}$$

For example, suppose that, when incomes rise by 10 per cent, the demand for telephones rises by 20 per cent. Then the income elasticity of demand for telephones is 20/10 or 2. Most luxury goods have a high income elasticity of demand, while most necessities have a low income elasticity of demand.

Income tax. ♢PERSONAL TAXATION.

Income velocity of circulation. When people receive incomes, they spend them and they become the incomes of other people. But other people will also be spending their incomes as they are received. In this way, money circulates continuously through the economy. The income velocity of circulation is the rate at which this money is circulating. It plays an important part in the QUANTITY THEORY OF MONEY.

Incomes policy. ♢PRICES AND INCOMES POLICY.

Increasing returns. The tendency for MARGINAL PRODUCT to rise as output increases. Increasing returns are, therefore, the opposite of DIMINISHING RETURNS. They must be distinguished from ECONO-

MIES OF SCALE – or the tendency for average product to rise or average costs to fall as output increases. However, many economic discussions use the phrase 'increasing returns' in this second sense and, in many cases, it makes little difference.

Incremental capital–output ratio (ICOR). ⇨ CAPITAL–OUTPUT RATIO, INCREMENTAL.

Independent variable. An important notion, central to the economist's use of models and to the direction of causation in them. When something happens its cause is said to be a change in a variable. From the economic point of view, independent variables tend to be those determined by social or political factors, such as population in models of economic growth or government economic policy. They cause changes in DEPENDENT VARIABLES through economic relationships.

Index numbers. Indicators of change in the value of economic variables. Their importance is that they are able to point out the direction of change (upwards, downwards, or the same) when several variables are involved.

A good example is provided by the price of shares on the Stock Exchange. Suppose that the price of a 5 shilling ORDINARY SHARE in ABC Co. Ltd has risen from 100p to 150p. Then it is obvious that the value of the share has gone up. But, suppose that someone is also holding shares in XYZ Co. Ltd, and that the value of these shares has fallen from 100p to 60p. Is the investor better or worse off? Clearly, it depends on the relative importance – or weighting – of the two shares in his PORTFOLIO. If he held 100 ABC shares and 50 XYZ shares he would be better off; if he held 50 ABC shares and 100 XYZ shares he would be worse off.

There are several economic problems where it is necessary to weight variables to discover the direction of change. Index numbers, of which there are many kinds, are different ways of carrying out the weighting.

One of the most important issues to which index numbers are addressed is the rise in prices. A price index is used to show if prices have risen, stayed the same or fallen. The two main price indices are the Laspeyres index and the Paasche index. In both the weights are quantities of goods. If one is trying to find out how the price of goods as a whole has gone up, one clearly needs to decide on the relative importance of the different goods under consideration. The other point to remember is that one is comparing prices at an earlier date with prices at a later date, to see how much prices have risen in the meantime. This poses a problem. Should one use a weighting determined by the relative importance of the different goods at the earlier or at the later date?

There is no clear-cut answer to this question. Consequently, both kinds of weighting systems have been calculated. The Laspeyres index is based on the relative importance of the different goods at the earlier date; the Paasche index is based on their relative importance at the later date.

To give an example, suppose we want to find out if the cost of motoring has increased. The two main items in motoring expenditure are the price of cars and the price of petrol. Suppose that, in the first period, the price of a car was £1000 and accounted for 50 per cent of all motoring expenditure, while the price of petrol was 30p a gallon and it accounted for the remaining 50 per cent. In the second period, though, the price of a car was still £1000, but it accounted for 40 per cent of expenditure, and the price of petrol had risen by 66 per cent to 50p a gallon so that it accounted for 60 per cent of expenditure. If a Laspeyres index is calculated the rise in prices emerges as 33 per cent. If a Paasche index is calculated, however, it comes out as 39.6 per cent. The reason for this is that the Paasche index attaches more weight in the example chosen to the item which has risen most in price. This might not always be so. Usually, in fact, because consumers buy less of those things which rise most in price, the Laspeyres index will be higher than the Paasche index.

Indexing. The adjusting of the terms of long-term contracts to take account of inflation. The purpose of indexing is to prevent one or other party to certain kinds of contract from taking advantage of continually rising prices.

For example, suppose that someone borrows money in 1970. In 1971 and 1972 the rate of inflation is 10 per cent – or the value of money has fallen by about 20 per cent. Consequently, the real value of the debt has fallen and the borrower is better off, purely because of the inflationary environment in which he is working. Indexing would raise the money value of the debt by the rise in prices. If the borrowing amounted to £1000 in 1970, £1200 would have to be repaid in 1972.

Indicative planning. ⊳PLANNED ECONOMY.

Indifference analysis. A technique for analysing the demand for goods. It is an alternative to the traditional demand curve analysis, and is considered to have several advantages. However, it is more complicated. The simplest way of discussing indifference analysis is by means of diagrams.

The first idea is the indifference curve (see Figure 7). Suppose that you have 10 apples. Then you are clearly better off than if you have 8 apples. But suppose that you have 10 apples and 3 oranges, or 7 apples and 4 oranges. Probably you feel as well off with either of these two combinations as you do with 10 apples. You are indifferent between the three alternatives. An indifference curve plots these points of indifference – with these three alternatives all on the same line.

An indifference map is built up from a number of indifference curves. If you are on a higher indifference curve you are obtaining a higher level of satisfaction. It is extremely useful to be able to make statements about differing degrees of satisfaction when two goods are involved. It

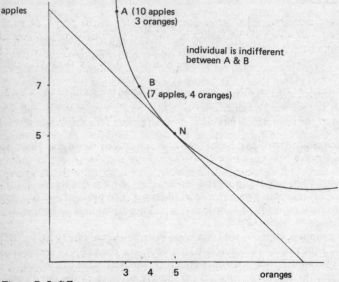

Figure 7. Indifference curve.

is easy enough to see that someone is better off when he has 20 apples and 10 oranges rather than 10 apples and 5 oranges. But what about when he had 12 apples and 13 oranges instead? An indifference map enables one to say if he prefers this combination to 20 apples and 10 oranges.

The next tool is the budget line. If you have a certain amount of money you can spend all of it on apples or all of it on oranges. But you will probably want to spend some of it on both. You can buy various combinations – for example, 7 apples and 1 orange or 9 oranges and 1 apple. Obviously, the more you spend on apples the less you spend on oranges and the fewer you buy.

As you are trying to maximize your satisfaction you will want to reach the highest indifference curve possible within your budget line. In the example chosen this is clearly at N where you buy 5 apples and 5 oranges (see Figure 7).

Indifference analysis has some advantages over demand curve analysis. The main one is that it is possible to isolate the INCOME EFFECT and the SUBSTITUTION EFFECT of a price change. With demand curve analysis this cannot be done because the effect of a reduction in price on the real value of someone's income cannot be represented.

Indirect taxation. The government has two main ways of raising revenue – through direct taxation, which is primarily on incomes and is immediately noticed by the person paying the tax, and by indirect taxation, usually on spending and not noticed by the taxpayer, except through higher prices.

In the United Kingdom most indirect taxes are paid to the Customs and Excise, while direct taxes are paid to the Inland Revenue. The main direct tax is income tax and the main indirect tax is value added tax (or VAT).

Because indirect taxes are less obvious to the tax payer there is a considerable temptation to the political authorities to prefer them to direct taxes. This is despite that fact that the taxpayer still has to pay in the end and preferring one to another does not reduce his burden. However, the United Kingdom has a tradition of fairly heavy direct taxation and lower indirect taxation, unlike countries such as France and Italy.

The disadvantage of direct taxes is that they are disincentives to effort. If you have to pay the government a particular percentage of what you are earning, you are evidently going to be more reluctant to earn an increased income than if you were paying no tax at all. But indirect taxes have their drawbacks, too. The most important is that they tend to be REGRESSIVE – that is, the poorer people pay them more than the rich. This is particularly true in the United Kingdom where excise duties on petrol and luxuries cut into the spending power of the less well off. This is because the so-called 'luxuries', such as drink and tobacco, are heavily taxed for social and health reasons, although spending on them is a high proportion of low-income group spending.

A turnover tax is identical to the present system of value added tax. The operation of the tax is quite complicated. At each stage of the production process value is added to the article being made. The object of VAT is to tax the producers at each point in the process. 'Value added' is determined by subtracting the cost of inputs from the value of output.

VAT was introduced in the UK in 1973. It replaced purchase tax –

a tax on several items of expenditure such as consumer durables and certain luxury goods. It was selective and did not apply to the whole range of goods. Because it was selective only 70000 stores had to liaise with the Customs and Excise to make it effective. By contrast, VAT covers all goods and all retail outlets have to keep records. This is the principal objection to VAT.

Indivisibilities. The concept of indivisibility is a difficult one in economic theory. The assumption of divisibility is needed to prove a number of theorems, although its significance is technical and not vital to an understanding of what they mean.

The law of demand says that, as price goes up, the consumer will buy less of a good. If the price is 10 pence, he will want one apple; if it is 5 pence, he will want two; but what happens when the price is 7½ pence?

The assumption of divisibility is that the consumer could buy one and a half apples, and that he would not have to pay anything extra to the greengrocer for cutting one. In practice, of course, this would not happen and he would buy either one or two.

But if he bought one, the law of demand would be violated. As the price fell, the consumer would not buy more. Because of this, a formal statement of the law of demand would include the assumption of no indivisibilities.

Induced investment. INVESTMENT has two causes. The first is an increase in income and, hence, output, which forces firms to use their capacity more fully. Because capacity may become stretched, they may decide to acquire some more capital – in other words, to invest. This type of investment is known as induced investment. The second type includes, for example, higher profits and a lower rate of interest. These are not related to output movements and are known as AUTONOMOUS INVESTMENT.

Industrial banks. Industrial banks provide finance to industry. Their distinctive feature is that the finance is usually of a medium- or long-term nature, with a repayment period of more than two years. They are much more strongly represented in some European countries and Japan than in the United Kingdom or the United States of America. The reason for this is that, in the UK and the USA, companies have traditionally used the Stock Exchange for long-term finance.

Industrial banks take more risks than most kinds of banking operation. But, as creditors, they can become extremely powerful and obtain a stranglehold over industry. When a firm finds itself in financial difficulties it may have to appoint someone from an industrial bank to its board of directors, because it owes the bank money.

Industrial production. The output of the industrial sector of an economy. In the UK this includes the output of the electricity and gas industries, mining and quarrying and construction. The output of manufacturing industry – which consists of finished goods for the home market and abroad, and of semi-finished goods solely for export – is a more restricted notion.

Industrial production should be distinguished from GROSS NATIONAL PRODUCT, which includes the output of service industries, agriculture and the government.

Infant industry argument. There a number of arguments in favour of PROTECTION. But one of the most persuasive is that imports should be limited because they stifle the growth of a domestic industry. The infant industry argument is that if the domestic industry is protected from the competition of imports by tariffs or quotas it will, in due course, become sufficiently efficient to dispense with protection. The argument relies heavily on ECONOMIES OF SCALE – which lower costs as production is stepped up.

Inferior good. One which consumers buy less as their income goes up, assuming that its price compared to the price of other things does not change.

Inflation. Rising prices within an economy. It is the main economic problem of modern times and no solution has yet been found to it which does not involve equally or more painful alternatives.

In recent years inflation has gradually accelerated. In the United Kingdom retail prices rose by 3.6 per cent a year on average between 1965 and 1967; by 5.5 per cent a year between 1968 and 1970; and by 8.2 per cent a year between 1971 and 1973. In other countries the acceleration has been even more pronounced. In Japan, for example, retail prices have been rising at over 20 per cent a year for most of the 1970s.

Inflation must be distinguished from REFLATION, which means an addition to AGGREGATE DEMAND. Economists do not talk of an 'inflation of demand' when the government raises its expenditure or lowers taxes.

There are main schools of thought on inflation – those who believe in cost-push inflation; and those who believe in demand-pull inflation. (Or, more simply, those who believe in cost rather than demand inflation.)

The cost-push theorists consider that inflation is caused by the monopoly pressure of the unions on wages and, hence, on costs. The large firm of modern times is thought to be so powerful that it does not lose business if it raises its prices after cost increases.

113

The demand-pull theorists, on the other hand, consider that excess demand in the economy – or 'too much money chasing too few goods' – is responsible. People want to spend more money on output than the value of output at the old prices. If they do spend the money prices go up, profits rise and then, after a LAG, wages rise too. Most economists probably recognize merits in both views of inflation. In practice there are both cost-push and demand-pull elements in the inflationary process.

For example, it is clear that the power of trade unions is easier to curb if unemployment is high than if it is low. It is also clear that, if the government is operating a strict MONETARY POLICY, it will be more difficult for firms to obtain overdrafts. They will, therefore, be more cautious in giving way to union demands for higher pay.

In the modern world inflation has become international and it has become difficult for a small country, intent on maintaining price stability, to insulate itself from the international trend. This has led to the phenomenon of imported inflation. Three main mechanisms are responsible. The first is the direct one of an increase in the price of imported goods.

The second and third are more interesting. The second consists in the disruption of domestic monetary policy because of a payments surplus. If a country is selling more abroad than it is buying, its money supply increases and this fuels a higher rate of inflation.

Finally, if world demand is strong, this probably has a favourable effect on exports. But as exports increase the demand for labour in export industries also goes up – obliging employers to offer higher wages. This then spreads to other industries which have to raise prices because their costs are higher.

Inflation accounting. Inflation brings with it a number of difficulties in the identification of profits. For example, suppose a company buys a machine in 1970 for £1000 which is expected to last for five years. If the company wanted to renew the machine in 1975 the wise course might appear to be to make a provision of £200 a year for DEPRECIATION.

This £200 a year should be deducted from gross profits to yield a figure for net profit. But suppose that inflation is running at 5 per cent a year. This would raise the price of the products the firm was selling and make the profits record look very healthy. These profits would be known as book profits.

But it would also mean that the company would have to pay about £1250 in 1975 to buy another machine and would only have £1000 to do it with. It would have been better to have operated a system of inflation accounting in which the net profit figure for each year would reflect depreciation *and* the effect of inflation on the cost of replacing the machine.

Inflation accounting is, therefore, a method, or set of methods, for presenting accounts in REAL TERMS.

Inflationary gap. ◊AGGREGATE DEMAND AND SUPPLY.

Infrastructure. A country's infrastructure is its system of roads, rail and other transport links, and its accumulation of social overhead capital. Social overhead capital includes such things as street lighting, parks and schools, which in most countries are provided by public authorities.

Innovation. The economic application of a scientific or technical idea which raises the output obtainable from a given quantity of inputs or puts a new product on the market superior to previous alternatives. It must be distinguished from invention, which is the discovery of the scientific or technical idea. Many inventions do not lead to innovation because they are not economically worthwhile. (◊SCHUMPETERIAN THEORY OF THE TRADE CYCLE.)

Input. Anything which contributes to the production of a good or service. The two main kinds are raw materials, or physical inputs, and workmen and management, or labour inputs.

Input–output analysis. A complicated technique which has proved a helpful supplement to economic planning. One industry buys output from another industry, and then sells output to another industry. The sales of the output of one industry are, therefore, the input of another.

It is possible to build up an input-output matrix, or a picture of all these linkages between all the industries in an economy. This is helpful because planners can identify industries where a supply bottleneck would hold up a particular growth rate. For example, it might not be feasible to increase the output of shoes because the output of shoe-making machinery cannot be stepped up sufficiently. Since leather might be freely available, the shoe-making machinery industry would be a bottleneck. (◊PLANNED ECONOMY.)

Input–output matrix. ◊INPUT–OUTPUT ANALYSIS.

Insider dealing. The purchase or sale of shares by insiders, or people with knowledge of future developments denied to the general public. This enables them to make unfair gains. Because of this, insider dealing is illegal in the United Kingdom.

Insolvency. When a firm has spent so much money (or agreed to spend so much money) that it cannot expect to recoup the money from sales of its product, it will be unable to repay its debts. It is said to be in a state of insolvency.

Institutional investor. Because individuals are usually not well informed about the best place to put their savings they often lend it to an institution with investment expertise. The institutional investors – such as life assurance companies, banks and building societies – then lend money to companies or buy shares. They are very important to financial markets because they are in control of large funds.

Integration. ▷HARMONIZATION; VERTICAL INTEGRATION.

Interbank market. Banks occasionally need to obtain money at short notice for short periods to keep their books balanced. The sums involved may be large and it may be easier to find them from other banks than from the public. When the money is lent at the end of a session to be repaid the following morning it is called overnight money. The market where these transactions takes place is known as the interbank market.

Interest equalization tax. ▷EURO-CURRENCY.

Interest, Theory of. When someone borrows money from, for example, a bank, he will probably have to pay back a slightly larger sum in the future. The difference between the amount he had borrowed and the amount he has to pay back is interest. The rate of interest per cent is usually expressed at an annual rate and is the amount someone has to pay at the end of the first year of the loan for each £100 of that loan.

There a number of theories to explain the origin of interest. The main one is that most people prefer to consume something now to consuming it in the future. To put it another way, a typical individual probably prefers to consume £100 today rather than £100 in a year's time, but he may be indifferent between consuming £100 today and £110 in a year's time. If he was offered a loan of £100 and had to pay back £105 in a year's time it would obviously be worth his while to take the loan. He would be happy to pay back £110 but in fact has only to pay back £105. The £10 the individual would be willing to pay per £100 is a measure of his rate of time preference. Because his rate of time preference is greater than the rate of interest, he borrows now to increase his present consumption.

Some writers in the Middle Ages protested against the payment of interest. Their argument was that a lender who made money merely from waiting was receiving a reward from no effort. He was extracting usury from the borrower. It should be clear from the example that this is rather misleading. By borrowing money someone is able to buy more things now, which he values highly, than he otherwise could manage. Indeed, in this case, because the rate of interest is beneath the rate of time preference, a sort of profit of £5 is made by *the borrower*.

Interlocking directorates. Occasionally a director of one company is also a director of another. When this happens on an extensive scale there are said to be interlocking directorates. They are usually considered to be undesirable because they enable firms to exchange information and, therefore, reduce competition.

Intermediate areas. ⇨REGIONAL POLICY.

Intermediate products. A product which is traded between producers. For example, timber, when sold to a builder, is an intermediate product, because it is sold from one producer, a timber merchant, to another, the builder. A house, however, is a final product because it is sold to the person who eventually consumes it.

The notion of intermediate products is important for a complicated new development in economic theory known as the theory of effective protection. The basic idea is that it is impossible to estimate the effectiveness of a tariff from the way it is levied on imported final products. For example, suppose a 10 per cent tariff is charged on imported textiles and a 50 per cent tariff on imported cotton. Then the effective rate of protection is not 10 per cent because the foreign supplier does not have to pay the 50 per cent on cotton which the domestic textile producers face.

Internal balance. If an economy is fully employed and enjoys price stability, it is said to have internal balance. More formally, this probably involves the equality of SAVING and INVESTMENT. It is to be contrasted with external balance, which is a condition in which the value of exports equals the value of imports.

Internal economies. When companies expand they are often able to lower their average costs. These cost reductions may be confined to a particular firm or they may be obtainable by all firms in an industry. When they are confined to a particular firm they are known as internal economies.

Internal rate of return (IRR). A method of INVESTMENT APPRAISAL. It is the rate of interest you would pay on a loan for a profitable investment project which would leave you no better off at the end than at the beginning. For example, suppose you borrow £100 and make £10 profit in both the first and second year. If the rate of interest were 5 per cent you would be better off in each of the two years and £10 better off altogether. But if the rate of interest were 10 per cent you would be paying all of your profits to the lender and you would be no better off. This 10 per cent is the internal rate of return on the proje ct

International Bank for Reconstruction and Development (IBRD).. ⇨WORLD BANK.

International commodity agreements. The price of most PRIMARY COMMODITIES traded in world markets is highly volatile. This has an unfavourable effect on the incomes of countries specializing in the production of these commodities, particularly the poorer countries because the incomes tend to fluctuate so much that it is difficult to plan for economic growth. Consequently a number of agreements between producing countries has been arranged, aimed at keeping supply and demand in balance. Their most usual form is for each member country to agree to restrict its output to a particular fraction of total output. The most successful example in recent years has been OPEC – the Organization of Petroleum Exporting Countries – which, in 1973 and 1974, was successful in quadrupling the price of oil.

International company. ⇨MULTINATIONAL CORPORATION.

International investment. ⇨FOREIGN INVESTMENT.

International liquidity. When countries buy and sell goods from one another they have to use some means of payment in the same way as when individuals buy and sell goods they use money. The money used in international payments is known as international liquidity.

Countries hold stocks of international liquidity in their reserves of foreign currency and gold. The most important form of international liquidity is the DOLLAR which is acceptable as payments for imports from almost any country. For example, if an Indian wants to buy a Japanese machine tool, the Japanese manufacturer may not want rupees, but he may be happy to accept dollars. As long as India has some dollars the Indian can exchange his rupees for dollars and then use the dollars to pay the Japanese businessman. Obviously trade between countries can only work smoothly if there are adequate amounts of international liquidity.

International Monetary Fund (IMF). The International Monetary Fund performs the same function for countries that banks perform for individuals. It provides them with money to tide them over if they run into debt.

If a country is buying more abroad than it is selling, it will lose its reserves of internationally acceptable currency. If the reserves run out completely it will no longer be able to import goods. In this situation it may go to the IMF and ask for a loan. Each member of the IMF has a quota which specifies the size of the loan allowed. The IMF may grant the loan only on condition that the country stops buying more than it is selling.

The IMF was established in 1944 at the BRETTON WOODS Conference to come into operation in 1947, and the system of international monetary relations associated with it was known as the Bretton Woods system. With the return to FLOATING EXCHANGE RATES, the IMF has become less useful because countries let their currencies lose value rather than borrow to cover payments deficits.

Complicated negotiations between members of the IMF are often linked to negotiations between the Group of Ten (the leading industrial economies including the United Kingdom and the United States). The finance ministers of these countries meet in Basle every month to ensure that international economic relations are amicable and their economic policies are not in conflict.

International Settlements, Bank for. ⬦BANK FOR INTERNATIONAL SETTLEMENTS.

Intervention. Intervention, or central bank intervention, describes the action of a CENTRAL BANK in supporting or (occasionally) depressing the value of currency. For example, suppose that many traders and banks are selling sterling. Then, as few people will want to take on the currency, its value would decline against, say, the dollar in a free market. But suppose the Bank of England intervenes to buy sterling by selling its dollars. This should prevent the pound losing its value if the intervention is sufficiently large.

Invention. ⬦INNOVATION.

Inventories (USA). Inventories is the American term for stocks of raw materials or finished goods.

Inventory analysis. ⬦STOCK CONTROL.

Inventory investment (USA). Inventory investment is the American term for stockbuilding. When firms increase the amount of raw materials they have for future production, or their STOCKS (1) of finished goods for future sales, they are investing money for expected profits. This can, therefore, reasonably be called inventory investment.

Inventory investment cycle. ⬦TRADE CYCLE.

Investment. (a) In everyday language, the purchase of any asset, such as ordinary shares on the Stock Exchange, intended to yield a profit or benefit to the investor in the future.

(b) In strict economic terms, the acquisition of capital goods, such as

119

machinery and houses, which will give satisfaction to the investor in the future, probably in the form of profits.

It is important to distinguish between gross and net investment. If a company is spending £100 000 a year on machinery and equipment it might be tempting to say that it has invested £100 000 and that the value of its CAPITAL STOCK had gone up by the same amount. But this may not be true because the company may stop using some of its old equipment, or possibly, the old equipment may be falling to pieces. It may, therefore, be taking £50 000 worth of equipment out of service. Its net investment is the increase in the capital stock – or £100 000 minus this £50 000. Its gross investment is the total amount it is spending on machinery and equipment – or the full £100 000.

In national accounts, gross investment is divided into investment on types of capital which will last many years (gross fixed capital formation) and investment on stocks and work in progress (stockbuilding). It is gross fixed capital formation which is relevant for seeing how much extra capital the economy has available for increasing production.

Investment allowances. ▷COMPANY TAXATION.

Investment appraisal. When a company invests in a project it wants to make sure that, when it has paid interest on any borrowing and all other costs, it will be earning a profit. There a number of techniques available for assessing this and together they are known as investment appraisal.

One of the simplest techniques is the pay-back method. A businessman may have £100 to invest on a project and he discovers that it would yield an annual profit of £33. It would pay back his investment in three years, whereas another project would pay back in four and is, therefore, rejected.

The difficulty with this method is that profits in the fourth year might be very high – say £70 – and this should affect the business-man's decision. A better technique, known as DISCOUNTED CASH FLOW (DCF), should, therefore, be adopted for projects where the flow of profits varies through time. It works on the principle that £100 today is worth more than £100 tomorrow and the £100 tomorrow is worth more than £100 the day after tomorrow. In other words, it places a discount against future earnings. (▷INTEREST, THEORY OF.)

Investment function. A concept in MACROECONOMICS which shows how investment in the whole economy changes as national income changes. (▷INDUCED INVESTMENT.)

Investment incentives. Forms of government assistance to firms to encourage them to invest. They are often aimed at promoting investment in depressed regions such as the development areas in this country.

The two main types of investment incentive are grants to firms wishing to invest – the government providing, say, 25 or 30 per cent of the cost of equipment – or favourable tax treatment to firms who have invested heavily. A common kind of favourable tax treatment is to allow the firm to deduct DEPRECIATION from profits at an early stage of the investment. ($\Diamond$COMPANY TAXATION; REGIONAL POLICY.)

Investment trust. An investment trust puts money in a wide variety of ASSETS. Its object is to reduce risk because, with a large number of assets owned, the danger that one or two will lose value matters less. People who wish to reduce their risks, therefore, lend money to an investment trust and the investment trust then uses its skill and knowledge to increase the value of the lender's money by investing in, for example, stocks and shares on their behalf.

Invisible balance. $\Diamond$BALANCE OF PAYMENTS.

Invisible trade. $\Diamond$INVISIBLES; VISIBLE TRADE.

Invisibles. Payments between countries are of two kinds – those for goods and those for services. Because payments for services are not accompanied by movements of any tangible object they are known as invisibles. They include payments for tourism, shipping, receipts of interest and dividends from capital owned abroad, and the remittances of foreign workers to their home countries.

Irredeemable securities. $\Diamond$UNDATED SECURITIES.

Iso-cost lines. In the theory of production it is useful to have a geometric technique for analysing the effect of a change in the price of an input on the quantity of the input used. An iso-cost line serves this purpose by showing positions on a diagram where total costs are constant although the mix between two inputs is varying.

Iso-product curves. $\Diamond$ISOQUANTS.

Isoquants. Isoquants are important geometric tools for economists working on the theory of production. They show what combinations of inputs are sufficient to produce a given output.

Suppose a businessman wants to produce 100 nails. He can do this with 2 machines and 10 men or with 3 machines and 7 men or with 4 machines and 6 men. As in Figure 8 it is possible to draw an isoquant showing these possibilities.

The value of isoquants is that the response of the businessman to a change in the price of machines compared to the price of labour can be represented on a diagram. Clearly, if prices of machines fall, he uses more machines and less labour. Isoquants are also known as iso-product curves.

Issued capital. When a company is set up legally it is entitled to borrow a certain amount of money by the issue of shares. But it may not take out its full entitlement. That part of its full entitlement which is issued is known as its issued capital.

Issuing houses. When a company wants to borrow money from the public it may not understand how to present information on its credit-

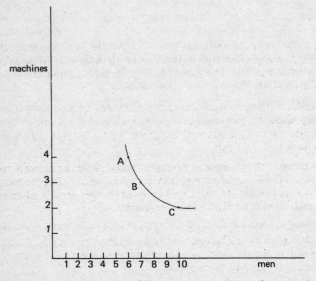

Figure 8. The line through A, B and C is an isoquant. 100 nails are made with 4 machines and 6 men at A; 3 machines and 7 men at B; and 2 machines and 10 men at C.

worthiness or how to set about obtaining the funds from the STOCK EXCHANGE. It will, therefore, go to a financial institution, probably a MERCHANT BANK, which will carry out the issue of shares on its behalf. If the public does not want to lend all the money to the company, the financial institution may have to provide the remainder. Financial institutions performing this role are known as issuing houses.

J

Jobber. A trader on a STOCK EXCHANGE. He owns shares and, if a stockbroker approaches him with an order to buy or sell shares from a member of the public, the jobber will be able to complete the order. (⬦BROKERAGE.)

Joint costs. When two or more products are being made together, they may all require inputs of the same kind and it may be impossible to separate the contribution of the inputs to each output. This is said to be a case of joint costs.

Joint demand. When someone buys certain articles, he is likely to buy others of a similar and related kind. For example, if someone buys books, he will probably want to buy bookshelves shortly afterwards. Books and bookcases are in joint demand.

Joint products. When certain articles are produced, other articles are often made as an inevitable part of the production process. For example, sheep farming yields both wool and mutton. Wool and mutton are described, therefore, as joint products.

Juglar. ⬦SCHUMPETERIAN THEORY OF THE TRADE CYCLE.

K

Kaldorian theory of distribution. An unorthodox attempt to explain the rate of PROFIT and the share of profits in national income by the propensity to save of different classes, the share of investment in national output and the rate of growth. The details are complicated, but its importance is in arguing that income distribution is not determined by marginal productivity or by conflict between classes. Nicholas Kaldor (1908–   ), the notable economist from Cambridge, England, has claimed that it is the true Keynesian theory of income distribution. (◊MARGINAL PRODUCTIVITY OF CAPITAL; KEYNESIAN ECONOMICS.)

Kennedy Round. An important round of trade negotiations between countries held between 1964 and 1967. It resulted in large reductions in tariffs. Unlike previous trade rounds, these reductions were often across the board rather than item by item.

Key currency. ◊RESERVE CURRENCY.

Keynesian economics. A branch of economic thought which, when developed in the 1930s and 1940s, was revolutionary. Its main characteristic is that it deals with the behaviour of the economy as a whole, not with the behaviour of individuals and firms. Its objective is to discover what determines the level of NATIONAL INCOME and, therefore, of employment. It was fathered by Lord Keynes, the famous Cambridge economist who lived between 1883 and 1946.

The central contribution was Keynes' book, *The General Theory of Employment, Interest and Money*, which was published in 1936. Its argument was that fluctuations in the level of national income are determined by changes in the level of INVESTMENT. Investment is carried out to make profits and depends on expected profitability and the rate of interest. If the rate of interest is too high it may not be worthwhile to borrow money to finance investment.

Keynes argued that, in the 1930s, investment had not been sustained at an adequate level. There were two reasons for this. First, the innovations and geographical discoveries of the nineteenth century had come to an end and the opportunity for profitable investment had declined as a result. Second, although this development might not have mattered if the rate of interest had fallen very low or become negative, in fact the rate of interest could never fall below a certain point. If someone saves money and receives a negative rate of interest he will have less money at the end than at the beginning.

Consequently, investment had fallen to extremely low levels. National income had dropped and, because aggregate demand was weak, unemployment was unacceptably high. Keynes claimed that it was impossible for MONETARY POLICY, which operates on the money supply and the rate of interest, to correct this situation because it could never force the rate of interest low enough. The only answer was for the government to boost demand by increasing its expenditure or by lowering taxation. Moreover, it was vital, in the interests of stability, that the government sector be expanded so as to counteract any tendency for weak investment opportunities to cause excessive unemployment.

It is this theory which has been behind the increased role of the state in economic life since 1945 and has contributed to the eradication of mass unemployment.

One of the consequences of Keynesian economics, which is MACRO-ECONOMIC in character, has been an increasing reliance on FISCAL POLICY to stabilize aggregate demand and maintain a high level of employment. This has been criticized by a group of economists, who have been called MONETARISTS, who believe that an active monetary policy involving control over the money supply is also essential.

Keynesian monetary policy. ▷MONETARY POLICY.

Kitchin. ▷SCHUMPETERIAN THEORY OF THE TRADE CYCLE.

Kondratieff. ▷SCHUMPETERIAN THEORY OF THE TRADE CYCLE.

L

Labour-intensive. A technical concept in economics which is often used carelessly in popular discussions. A process that uses a high proportion of labour input to capital input is labour-intensive. This idea is often confused with inefficiency, but there is no necessary connection between a labour-intensive and an inefficient method of production.

Labour, Marginal productivity of. ⋄MARGINAL PRODUCTIVITY OF CAPITAL.

Labour market. The MARKET in which workers find jobs and employers find labour. It occasionally takes an institutionalized form, as with the Employment Offices in the United Kingdom where lists of job vacancies are drawn up for the unemployed. But it is usually informal and depends on the exchange of information between employers and workers about where jobs are being offered and what rates of pay are to be expected.

An important aspect of a free labour market is labour turnover or the phenomenon of men leaving one employment to find employment elsewhere. If a firm finds that it is losing a high proportion of its labour force and that new recruits are often unsuitable, it may be forced to put up wages to keep labour turnover down.

Labour-saving technical progress. ⋄TECHNICAL PROGRESS.

Labour, Specialization of. ⋄DIVISION OF LABOUR.

Labour theory of value. ⋄MARXIAN ECONOMICS.

Labour turnover. ⋄LABOUR MARKET.

Lag. There is sometimes an interval of time between one economic event and another, although one has probably been caused by the other. This interval is known as a lag. For example, a rise in income now may cause a rise in consumption in six months' time – or after a six months' lag.

Laissez-faire. An important economic philosophy dating from the early nineteenth century. *Laissez-faire* is the belief that governments should abstain from active participation in business or commerce. The role of the government should be to enforce law and order and to provide for national defence, while economic affairs should be left to the private sector.

This belief is accompanied by a conviction of the virtues of FREE TRADE and the price mechanism. It is hostile to the use of subsidies to encourage industry or to selective and discriminatory economic measures of any kind. *Laissez-faire* has not been widely adopted and its influence on policy has gradually been undermined by KEYNE-SIAN ECONOMICS.

Land. Land is the primary input into production. It is one of three factors of production – land, labour and capital – and is distinguished from the others in that its supply cannot be increased.

Laspeyres index. ⟡INDEX NUMBERS.

Lateral integration. ⟡HORIZONTAL INTEGRATION.

Lausanne school. ⟡EQUILIBRIUM.

Law of diminishing returns. ⟡DIMINISHING RETURNS, LAW OF.

Least-squares regression. A statistical technique to determine how one variable changes when another variable changes. For example, one may want to know if consumption increases with an increase in income and also by how much it will increase for a given income increase. The technique is based on the examination of past data, which will give a wide range of income and consumption figures. If income went up 2 per cent in 1970 and consumption went up 1.8 per cent, it might seem that if income went up by 4 per cent in 1972, consumption should go up by 3.6 per cent. But it may have gone up by 5 per cent. Least-squares regression is the simplest technique of deriving a good relationship (the 'best fit') suitable for predictive future behaviour from apparently conflicting past experience of this kind.

Leftward-shifting. ⟡RIGHTWARD-SHIFTING.

Lender of last resort. When a firm borrows money it sometimes happens that the money is badly spent and cannot be repaid. This may put the lender in a difficult position and he may have to go bankrupt. The lender may, in turn, have borrowed some money from a third firm and his bankruptcy may embarrass this third firm. In order to prevent the process becoming cumulative, most financial systems have a lender of last resort – usually the CENTRAL BANK – which can lend money with government backing. No one can refuse to accept money from the central bank because the government can legally force people to take it in exchange for goods.

Less developed country (LDC). ⟡DEVELOPING COUNTRY.

Leverage. ⟡GEARING.

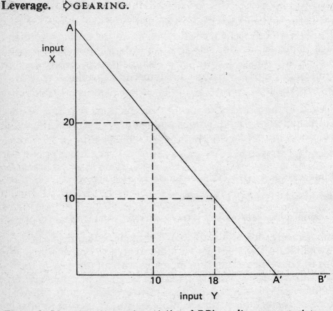

Figure 9. Linear programming. AA' and BB' are linear constraints.
At every point on AA' 100 units of output can be produced, although with varying combinations of inputs. For example, if there were no other constraints, constraint AA' would allow 100 units to be produced with either 20 of input X and 10 of input Y or with 10 of input X and 20 of input Y.

Liability. When a firm or an individual borrows money (or other assets) from another firm or individual, it is taking on a liability. This means that the borrower is obliged to pay back the money at some date in the future or, in other words, is liable for the sum involved.

Limited liability. When a firm takes on a liability by borrowing money and uses the money unwisely, it may be unable to pay it back. Although the owners of the firm then become responsible for paying back the loan, they may not as private individuals have sufficient resources. The risk of this situation might have deterred them from setting up the firm in the first place and, thereby, have discouraged enterprise. Consequently, most countries permit companies to be formed as distinct legal entities and, although the owners may lose all of their investment in the company, their liability is limited to this investment. For example, two people invest £100 in a company and the company makes a loss of £250 they will only lose £100, not £125. Limited liability takes a variety of legal forms and does not protect businessmen from losses caused by their own negligence.

Linear programming.   A technique used by businessmen to maximize output subject to linear constraints. A constraint is a restriction on output from, say, a lack of inputs. It is a linear constraint if it can be drawn as a straight line on a diagram of production possibilities (see Figure 9).

Linear relationship.   When the response of a DEPENDENT VARIABLE to an INDEPENDENT VARIABLE is the same whatever the value of the independent variable, the relationship between them is said to be linear. For example, consider two situations. The first is where a level of national income of £100 million rises to £110 million while consumption rises from £80 million to £88 million. In the second situation, national income is £200 million, which rises to £220 million. If now consumption rises from £160 million to £176 million, the relationship between income and consumption, or the CONSUMPTION FUNCTION, can be seen to be linear. At two very different levels of national income, a 10 per cent rise in income is accompanied by a 10 per cent rise in consumption. A linear relationship can be drawn as a straight line on a diagram.

Liquid.   ◊LIQUIDITY.

Liquidity.   When people wish to obtain things from other people they have to offer something in return. Certain ASSETS – such as money – are acceptable to the great majority of other people. If you hold your assets in a form which can be exchanged quickly and easily for different assets with a large number of other people you are said to be liquid. To have liquidity is to have a high proportion of your total assets in money or assets such as riskless government securities which can be readily exchanged for money. Short-dated government securities and building society deposits are sometimes referred to as near money.

Companies like to remain fairly liquid because it enables them to meet unforseen contingencies and to pay for their inputs as the need arises. Most of their working capital – or the capital needed for the day-to-day running of the business – is, therefore, in liquid form. Companies also keep capital reserves. These are accumulations of profit which have not been paid out to shareholders, but which have either been re-invested in plant and buildings or set aside in cash and investments on financial markets. Capital reserves are unlikely to be highly liquid, although they are a good indication of how much a company is worth.

Liquidity basis. ⊳BALANCE OF PAYMENTS.

Liquidity preference. When companies or individuals are afraid to take risks or feel that the return from investment is too low, they may decide to keep a large part of their assets in the form of money. They are said to have strong liquidity preference.

Liquidity ratio. A bank has to be able to provide cash to its depositors if the depositors wish to have their money back in this form. But a bank makes a profit by lending out to companies. The bank, therefore, has to make a decision about the proportion of its assets which will be held in liquid form (cash, money with other financial institutions and certain short-term government securities) and which will be held in illiquid form. A high liquidity ratio is a safeguard against risk, but a high porportion of illiquid assets is likely to be more profitable.

Liquidity trap. When the government expands the money supply the usual result is a reduction in the rate of interest which stimulates investment. The rise in investment then causes an increase in aggregate demand and leads to greater economic activity.

The fall in interest rates occurs because people use their extra money to buy financial assets, such as fixed interest securities. This raises their price and lowers their yield. Consequently, if the government or a company now wants to raise money by issuing more securities, it does not need to offer such a high rate of interest as before.

However, circumstances could arise in which interest rates have fallen so low that, when people find they have more money in the bank, they are happy to leave it there, rather than buy financial assets. In this case an expansion in the money supply does not lower interest rates or lead to an increase in aggregate demand. There is no way in which monetary policy can boost the economy and the government is facing a liquidity trap.

Loan capital. ⊳DEBENTURES.

Loan stock. ⊳DEBENTURES.

Location theory. A branch of economic theory which explains why industry is located in particular regions. Location is governed by transport costs and depends on the balance between the cost of transporting raw materials to factories and the cost of transporting goods to the consumer.

Lombard Street. A street in London where the DISCOUNT HOUSES are situated. Lombard Street is used, therefore, as a synonym for the MONEY MARKET.

Long-dated securities. ◊ SECURITIES.

Long-run. In economics long-run means that period of production in which the quantity of all INPUTS is variable. It must be distinguished from the short-run in which only some inputs are variable and others are fixed.

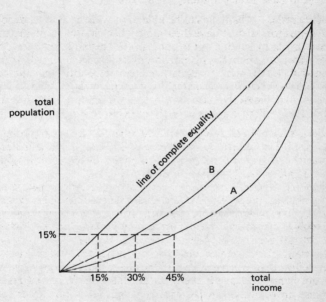

Figure 10. The Lorenz diagram. With the line of complete equality, 15 per cent of the population receive 15 per cent of income.
  With Lorenz curve B they receive 30 per cent of income.
  With Lorenz curve A they receive 45 per cent of income.
  Lorenz's curve A therefore indicates greater inequality than Lorenz curve B.

For example, when a company has a factory it is not possible to change the number of machines in a short period, although it may be feasible for the size of the labour force to be changed. CAPITAL, in this instance, is a fixed input, while labour is variable. Over a longer period, though, the management may want to alter the size of the factory. The

131

difference between the long- and short-run will, therefore, depend on the method of production and will vary from industry to industry.

Lorenz curve. A Lorenz curve is used in three areas of economics: population, industrial concentration and income distribution. It shows how unequally a variable is distributed. For example, in Figure 10, income distribution is more unequal with Lorenz curve A than with Lorenz curve B.

Loyalty rebates. ⇨RESTRICTIVE PRACTICES.

Lump-sum tax. ⇨PERSONAL TAXATION.

M

M1, M3. M1 and M3 are different definitions of the MONEY SUPPLY. M1 is the narrowly defined money supply and, in the United Kingdom, includes notes and coin and current accounts at the banks. M3 is the broadly defined money supply and includes M1 plus deposit accounts at the banks, deposits with the discount houses, accounts owned by UK residents in foreign currencies, deposits owned by the public sector, and sterling deposits held by foreigners in UK banks.

Both definitions of the money supply are indicative of the community's spending power, but M3 is larger than M1 and is sometimes regarded as a more reliable guide.

Macmillan Committee. Set up in 1929, under the chairmanship of Lord Macmillan and with J. M. Keynes as a member, to examine the sources of finance for British industry, as well as to investigate its difficulties at the beginning of the Depression. It found a 'gap' between the easy availability of finance from the Stock Exchange for large companies and similarly easy credit from banks for very small businesses. It considered that the small- and medium-size companies found it most difficult to obtain funds.

Macroeconomics. Macroeconomics is a branch of economic theory which has developed since the 1930s, mainly from the impetus given by KEYNESIAN ECONOMICS. It is concerned with the behaviour of the economy as a whole and with the major components of total spending, such as consumption, investment and public expenditure. Unlike MICROECONOMICS, it is not concerned with the behaviour of individuals and firms. It has given rise to elaborate forecasting exercises in which the future levels of national income and employment are predicted.

Malthusianism. Societies have always been concerned that too rapid a growth of population will lead to a reduction in living standards because there is only a limited quantity of natural resources available. These fears have rarely been expressed more forcefully than by Thomas

Malthus (1766–1834), an English clergyman and thinker, in his *Essay on the Principle of Population as it Affects the Future Improvement of Society* (1789). Consequently, gloomy forecasts of future disasters caused by lack of resources or rapid growth in population have been labelled Malthusian.

Managed currency. A currency whose value is affected by central bank intervention in the foreign exchange market.

Margin of forecasting error. Most forecasts of future events are based on samples of similar past events. However, these samples may not have occurred in the same conditions and, as a result, the forecasts may be slightly misleading. The margin of forecasting error shows how large the largest possible mistake in such a forecast might be.

Marginal analysis. Marginal analysis is basic to an understanding of economics and, in particular, is the main technique of MICROECONO-MICS. It tries to answer the question, 'If we changed our economic behaviour in a particular way by a particular amount, would we be better off or worse off?' For example, a businessman might ask himself 'If I changed my input of labour would this increase or lower my profits?'

The hallmark of marginal analysis, therefore, is the emphasis on small changes. It has been criticized by Keynes (◊KEYNESIAN ECONOMICS) because it is no use in any analysis of the economy as a whole, and by Schumpeter (◊SCHUMPETERIAN THEORY OF THE TRADE CYCLE) because it obstructs a full investigation of the causes and consequences of a revolutionary change in production methods.

Marginal cost. When a businessman increases his output by one unit, his total costs will in most cases also increase. This increase in total costs is known as marginal cost.

There are few more fundamental ideas on which so much confusion abounds. The first confusion is that marginal cost is the cost of the last unit produced. This is not correct, because it will in many cases be impossible to distinguish the share of costs attributable to the final unit of output and because the cost of the last unit is not always the same as the increase in total costs caused by increasing output by one unit.

The second confusion is that one can talk of the 'marginal cost of producing apples' or the 'marginal cost of producing eggs'. This is also not correct, because marginal cost varies with the scale of output. For example, it may be much more expensive to produce one more unit in a pin factory when four hundred pins are already being produced than to produce one more when only one hundred are being produced. The variation of marginal cost with the size of output is one of the most important ideas in MICROECONOMICS and, in particular, is crucial to the law of DIMINISHING RETURNS.

Marginal cost is central to the theory of WELFARE ECONOMICS. The cost of the same input is, in a majority of cases, identical in all industries. If, therefore, the same input produces more if it is allocated to industry A than if it is allocated in industry B, it would be desirable for the input to be transferred from production in industry B to production in industry A. These transfers should continue until additions of input in one industry bring no greater benefit than additions in another – or when marginal costs are equal to MARGINAL UTILITIES throughout the economy.

This argument is basic to the economist's defence of PERFECT COMPETITION and marginal cost pricing. Marginal cost pricing is the practice of setting price equal to marginal cost and has been advocated as the right pricing policy for nationalized industries because it maximizes social welfare. It is easy to explain the rationale of such a policy.

Marginal utility is a measure of the increases in social benefit from consuming one more unit of output. Marginal cost is a measure of the cost to society of producing one more unit of output. If marginal cost is less than marginal utility it is evidently worthwhile to have the extra unit of output because the extra benefit exceeds the extra cost. According to the law of demand, consumers act to equate their marginal utility to the price of the objects they buy. It follows that nationalized industries should set prices at marginal costs.

In a perfectly competitive market, businessmen behave in such a way that prices are, in EQUILIBRIUM, equal to marginal costs. As long as markets are competitive, there is, therefore, no point in the government interfering with firms' behaviour. The belief that a free enterprise economy is competitive in this sense is the principle economic justification for LAISSEZ-FAIRE.

Marginal cost pricing. ▷MARGINAL COST.

Marginal product. When a businessman hires another man or buys another machine he expects his output to increase. The increase in output which follows the hiring of another man or the purchase of another machine is known as the man's or the machine's marginal product.

When output increases, price may fall because of the law of demand. The increase in total revenue which follows an increased use of inputs is known as the marginal revenue product of these inputs. It should be distinguished from the marginal physical product, which is the increase in the number of units produced following an increase in inputs; and the marginal value product, which is the increase in total revenue that would take place after an increase in inputs if the price did not change.

Marginal productivity of capital. The marginal productivity of capital is the extra output that would be generated or lost if one extra or one less unit of capital were used, in a project or a production process, where the level of other inputs stayed the same. If a washing machine took one person to operate it, and cost one unit of capital, then the marginal productivity of capital in this case would be the extra number of clean clothes that could be produced in a unit time period by using the washing machine instead of washing them by hand.

The importance of the marginal productivity of capital is that it gives rise to a theory of the distribution of income between capital and labour. This theory says that the amount of labour used in production will be increased while the marginal productivity of labour (defined in the same way as the marginal productivity of capital) exceeds the price of labour. In the same way, the amount of capital applied will be increased while the marginal productivity of capital exceeds the price of capital.

The return to capital is the price of capital multiplied by the amount supplied. The return to labour is the price of labour (the wage rate) multiplied by the amount of labour supplied. Output is shared between the seller of capital and the labour in the proportions indicated by the ratio of the returns to capital and to labour.

Marginal productivity theory can be criticized on several points. The first is that the theory does not explain what happens if output is not sufficient to pay the technically determined returns to labour and to capital, or if there is a surplus left over after these returns have been allocated. It can be shown that, when there are INCREASING RETURNS to scale, there is insufficient output to pay the marginal products of labour and capital to each factor, while when there are DIMINISHING RETURNS to scale there will be a surplus left over after the factors are paid. It is only when there are exactly constant returns to scale that the factors can be paid their marginal products and output is exactly exhausted.

The second criticism is that the cost of capital is itself determined by the marginal products of capital and labour, since capital goods are made using capital and labour. This can cause difficult problems if capital goods are less CAPITAL INTENSIVE than consumption goods. It is because of such problems that the interest in the Austrian theory of capital has been revived recently. (◊AUSTRIAN SCHOOL.)

A similar criticism might be made concerning the supply of labour. Suppose that, when wages went up, people were unwilling to work as much as before, because the same income could be obtained for less work. In this situation, it is at least theoretically possible that there is no wage rate at which the amount of labour the economy would be willing to supply would be as great as the amount that the producers would demand.

The power of these criticisms depends on the extent to which the problematical situations are liable to occur in real life. Some simulated models suggest that the problems of the supply of capital goods may not be likely to occur, while the problem of higher incomes reducing the incentive to work also seems to be mainly theoretical.

Marginal productivity of labour. ⋄MARGINAL PRODUCTIVITY OF CAPITAL.

Marginal productivity theory of wages. When a businessman employs one more man there will be an increase in output and then an increase in his total revenue. If the wage which he has to pay the extra man is less than the increase in total revenue the businessman's profits will obviously have increased.

It follows that the businessman will keep on increasing his labour force until the increase in total revenue from employing one more man is equal to the wage he has to pay. The increase in total revenue from employing one more man is known as the marginal revenue product. It follows that the wage is equal to the labour force's marginal revenue product.

This theory of wage determination is known as the marginal productivity theory of wages. It has been much criticized by Marxist economists who believe that wages are determined by a struggle between classes for a higher share in national output and is conditioned by their relative bargaining strengths. (⋄MARXIAN ECONOMICS.)

Marginal propensity to consume (MPC). When NATIONAL INCOME increases consumers will want to enjoy a higher standard of living and raise their expenditure on CONSUMPTION goods. The marginal propensity to consume is the relationship between the increase in national income and the increase in consumption. The strict definition is:

$$\frac{\text{the percentage change in consumption}}{\text{the percentage change in national income.}}$$

The marginal propensity to consume is important in MACROECONOMICS because it determines the value of the MULTIPLIER.

The marginal propensity to save (MPS) can be considered as the opposite to the marginal propensity to consume, because all income which is not consumed is saved. The strict definition of the marginal propensity to save is, therefore, 1 minus the marginal propensity to consume; or to put it in a formula, $MPS = 1 - MPC$.

Occasionally in economic writings authors refer to the propensity to consume and the propensity to save. These are indications of the inclination to consume or save, but do not have a specific meaning unless qualified as average or marginal propensities.

Marginal propensity to save. ⊳MARGINAL PROPENSITY TO CONSUME.

Marginal rate of substitution. When an individual is moving along an indifference curve, he is giving up some of one good while obtaining more of another and keeping his satisfaction the same. The rate at which he has to give up one and have more of the other is known as the marginal rate of substitution. (⊳INDIFFERENCE ANALYSIS.)

Marginal revenue. When a businessman raises output by one unit his total revenue will increase. This increase in total revenue is known as marginal revenue.

Marginal revenue should be distinguished from price or average revenue. When a businessman is producing ten units he may expect to sell them for £10 each to make total revenue £100. If he raised output to eleven units the price might fall from £10 to £9.50 and the total revenue from eleven units would then be £104.50 In other words, the average revenue of ten units is £10, but the marginal revenue is only £104.50 minus £100, or £4.50.

Marginal revenue product. ⊳MARGINAL PRODUCT.

Marginal utility. When an individual consumes more of a good, his satisfaction or total utility will rise. This increase in total utility is known as marginal utility.

For example, suppose that someone is consuming 4 apples and is receiving 100 units of satisfaction. If he consumes 5 apples his return in these units may rise to 120. The marginal utility of 5 apples is, therefore, 20 units of satisfaction.

There has been a controversy in economics about whether or not utility should be a cardinal concept (one to which a number can be attached, as in the above example) or an ordinal concept (one which can be arranged so that you can say one good or collection of goods gives more utility than another).

Marginal utility, Law of diminishing. ⊳DEMAND (2).

Market. An institution in which goods and services are bought and sold. It need not be a specific geographic location. For example, the classified advertisement columns of newspapers and the subsequent telephone calls are a market in the same way that the Stock Exchange is a market, although the traders may be in many different places at the same time.

Market capitalization. ▷ CAPITALIZATION (3).

Market forces. The forces behind the laws of SUPPLY AND DEMAND. In essence they are tendencies enabling those prices to be established which maximize the utilities of consumers and the profits of producers, subject to the constraints of the consumers' incomes and the producers' possession of CAPITAL.

Market structure. The set of characteristics describing a market or industry. It is of interest to the economist because it is believed to affect economic behaviour. The characteristics which economists emphasize are the number of buyers and sellers, their relative size and the degree of collusion between them.

One example of market structure is PERFECT COMPETITION. Here a large number of buyers and sellers compete with one another and sellers are forced to bring prices down to the level of their costs, while buyers find it difficult to obtain their goods much cheaper than average. In other words, the structure of the market has affected people's behaviour.

Marketable securities. Marketable securities can be bought and sold on the Stock Exchange. They include equities with a QUOTATION and GILT-EDGED SECURITIES.

Mark-up. In setting prices businessmen often follow rules of thumb, of which the most common is that the price is the cost of an article plus a particular percentage. This percentage is known as the mark-up. For example, a furniture store may buy a chair for £10 and sell it for £15, with a mark-up of 50 per cent. When the factory raises the price to £20 the store charges £30, with the mark-up unchanged at 50 per cent.

Marshall Aid. After the Second World War most European countries were producing at beneath pre-war levels because of the destruction of capital equipment and buildings. The USA decided to give aid by means of the European Recovery Programme. This aid, which was known as Marshall Aid, after the US Secretary of State, General G. C. Marshall, came in the form of huge loans which went some way towards easing Europe's balance of payments problems. The programme was administered by the Organization for European Economic Cooperation (OEEC).

Marshall–Lerner criterion. The Marshall–Lerner criterion states the condition needed for a fall in a country's EXCHANGE RATE to improve its balance of trade. The condition is that the sum of the foreign elasticity of demand for its exports plus the home elasticity of demand for its imports be greater than one.

Marshallian. Certain types of economic analysis rely heavily on demand and supply curves and tend to be MICROECONOMIC in character. They are, therefore described as Marshallian, after Alfred Marshall (1842–1924), the great Cambridge economist who devised and perfected demand and supply curve analysis.

Marxian economics. The body of economic doctrine originating from Karl Marx (1818–83), the author of *Das Kapital* (1867), which has had enormous influence on the course of social and political history and provides the guiding principles on which the economies of the USSR, Eastern Europe and China are organized.

Marxian economics is, first and foremost, a theory of economic history. It predicts three main stages of development: feudalism, CAPITALISM and communism. In feudalism all property is owned communally, but society is organized hierarchically. In a capitalist society, property is owned by private individuals, but there tend to be great inequalities within the society and the middle classes, or bourgeoisie, are all powerful. With communism property is once more owned by the community as a whole, but society is organized in an egalitarian way, with the working classes, or proletariat, dominant. Marx said that feudalism inevitably gave way to capitalism and that capitalism would inevitably give way to communism.

Because of its emphasis on the eradication of inequality, Marxian economics rejects the traditional theories of income distribution and price determination. Incomes are not distributed according to productivity, as the marginal productivity theory of distribution insists, but according to power. The class which possesses the means of coercion, such as the aristocracy under feudalism, is the richest, and the most defenceless is the poorest. Prices are not determined by demand and supply, but by the amount of labour used up in production and by the rate of surplus value, which is equivalent to PROFIT in conventional theories and its treated rather like a MARK-UP. This theory is known as the labour theory of value.

The Marxian theory of distribution is not generally accepted by economists because it fails to explain, for example, changes in relative prices.

Marx also said that the price of labour was fixed by the socially necessary wage, usually equated with the subsistence level of wages.

But real wages have risen continuously in most capitalist countries for many decades and are now much higher than those needed for subsistence alone.

Marxian theory of distribution. ⟡MARXIAN ECONOMICS.

Matrix. A mathematical concept which enables a group of numbers to be manipulated together as if they were one number. A vector is a special kind of number group, which is arranged in rows of columns of single numbers. The operations of matrix algebra are a complicated branch of higher mathematics, but they are important for INPUT-OUTPUT ANALYSIS. The group of numbers in an input-output matrix is the set of COEFFICIENTS OF PRODUCTION which show how much of an input is required to produce a particular kind of output.

Maturity structure. When a financial institution borrows money, it agrees to make repayments at certain dates in the future, but it is unlikely to agree to repay all of its loans to all of its creditors on exactly the same day. Some repayments may fall due in a month's time, others in six months' time, and others in a year. The maturity structure is the term used to describe the pattern of these repayments. It is important because a bank which has 'lent long and borrowed short' – that is, one which will be repaid by its debtors more slowly than it has to repay its creditors – will be financially vulnerable if its depositors decide to withdraw their money in a rush.

Median. ⟡AVERAGE.

Medium of exchange. ⟡MONEY.

Mercantilism. A system of commerce adopted by governments almost universally in early modern times. It was based on the fallacy that money is wealth and that the accumulation of gold and silver was itself sufficient to achieve prosperity. It therefore encouraged governments to expand exports and restrict imports, which would lead to a favourable balance of payments and an inflow of money. The restriction of imports was accomplished by prohibitive tariffs. When countries in more modern times have raised tariffs their behaviour has often been described as mercantilist, although their objectives may not be to build up large reserves of gold.

Merchant banks. Financial institutions which are particularly active in commerce, rather than in lending to individuals or companies. Their other main characteristics is that the loans they give are usually more risky than loans given by the CLEARING BANKS. To avoid the danger of bankruptcy through excessive involvement in any one of a number of risky areas most merchant banks are engaged in several types of banking activity. In the City of London the leading merchant banks are members of the Accepting Houses Committee. An accepting house arranges the finance of exports and imports. For example, if a company is exporting a good and expecting payments in about three months' time, the accepting house pays the company a sum of money today in exchange for a piece of paper, known as a BILL OF EXCHANGE, which will entitle the house to the proceeds of the export deal when they become due. As the accepting house is, in effect, giving credit, it charges a rate of interest on the acceptance and a fee for the risk that the foreign customer will default.

Merger. When the activities of two companies are combined, a merger between them has taken place. A merger can take a variety of forms. It can mean that the products of two formerly separate companies are sold under the same name and by the same methods; or that the profits of two distinct concerns become available for distribution to only one group of shareholders. Another term for merger is amalgamation.

A merger should be distinguished from a TAKE-OVER as the two parties to a merger are normally both willing to enter the new arrangements, whereas a take-over is resisted by one of them.

Merry-go-round. ⧓ROUND-TRIPPING.

Microeconomics. That part of economic theory which deals with the behaviour of individual consumers and firms. It includes the theory of DEMAND (2) and the theory of the FIRM. It should be distinguished from MACROECONOMICS which is concerned with the behaviour of economic variables at the level of the economy as a whole. For example, whereas a macroeconomic problem might involve the company sector (or all the companies within an economy), a microeconomic problem would involve particular companies.

Minimand. A variable the value of which decision-takers are trying to keep as low as possible. For example, costs can be termed a minimand because companies try to keep them down.

Minimum lending rate (MLR). In all countries with an ordered financial structure there is a LENDER OF LAST RESORT or CENTRAL BANK. This lender of last resort has the power to issue currency which must be accepted in payment for goods and services. But when banks approach the lender of last resort for money they cannot expect to be lent it for nothing. On the contrary they will probably have to pay a rate of interest above the rate they have to pay to their ordinary depositors. The rate of interest charged by the central bank is known in the

United Kingdom as the minimum lending rate. It is an important barometer of MONETARY POLICY as a high minimum lending rate indicates that the BANK OF ENGLAND wants interest rates generally to be high and other financial institutions have to fall in line.

Mixed economy. One in which both the state and private individuals own property. In particular, NATIONALIZED INDUSTRIES and companies in private hands exist at the same time and often trade with one another.

The mixed economy is found throughout the world, but it takes many forms. In the USA and a few European countries, notably West Germany, most of industry is privately owned, whereas in others, notably the United Kingdom, France and Italy, the balance is much more nearly half and half. A typical situation is for essential services – such as railways and electricity – to be publicly owned, while manufacturing remains in private hands.

Model. Most of economic theory is abstract. It does not describe a particular situation, but contains elements common to a large number of specific situations.

The object of this approach is to make economic theory as general as possible. Its conclusions are valid not only for Unilever and ICI, but for all firms in the economy. But this means that analysis has to be by means of models, not by means of descriptions of actual experiences. Models are presented in terms like 'firms', 'businessmen', 'costs' and 'prices', not in terms like 'British Leyland', 'strikes at Cowley' and the price of a Mini is £1000'.

Monetarist. A term which entered political debate in Great Britain towards the end of 1974. In political circles it was usually taken to mean someone who favoured deflation to curb rising prices. The deflationary policies favoured included cuts in government spending and restraint on the MONEY SUPPLY which would cause increases in UNEMPLOY-MENT. The term was also associated with the school of thought in the Conservative party which believed that industrial policy should not involve selective assistance to particular industries or firms, particularly if these were in financial difficulties.

In economics a monetarist is someone who believes that 'money matters'. This belief is linked to a distrust of attempts to control the economy by FISCAL POLICY. A preference is given to managing the rate of growth of the money supply to bring it into line with the rate of growth by the economy's ability to produce goods. Monetarism has no necessary connection with a special attitude towards industrial problems, as the political usage suggested.

Monetarism is a development originating in the Chicago School (⟡QUANTITY THEORY OF MONEY).

Monetary policy. The set of techniques used by a government, usually through a CENTRAL BANK, to control the economy by adjusting the MONEY SUPPLY and the RATE OF INTEREST. The operation of the techniques is generally highly complicated, but the basic idea is that the central bank can increase the money supply by increasing its loans to other banks and can reduce the rate of interest by making these loans available on cheaper terms. MINIMUM LENDING RATE indicates how much the central bank will charge.

Classical monetary policy emphasizes control of the money supply, which is thought to have most effect on the economy. Ideally, the growth of the money supply in a year should be in line with the growth in real output. Keynesian monetary policy emphasizes control of interest rates. According to Keynes, the rate of interest matters because it affects the profitability of investment, except in a highly depressed economy (⟡LIQUIDITY TRAP). The authorities are successful if they keep interest rates stable.

Money. Money is a medium of exchange, which enables traders to deal with one another without resorting to BARTER. Although money by itself yields no utility, as it cannot be consumed or invested, it is helpful to the economy because it means that someone who is selling a good will accept a form of payment which is easy to carry round. It reduces TRANSACTIONS COSTS.

Money does not only consist of currency in the form of notes and coins. If someone pays for a good with a cheque, running down a deposit with a bank, this is also a means of payment, and the deposit is also money.

Money at call and short notice. The CLEARING BANKS often deposit money with the DISCOUNT HOUSES, where it earns a rate of interest. This return is low because the discount houses have to repay the clearing banks at short notice if the clearing banks need to lend it to their industrial or commercial customers instead. Consequently, the clearing banks' deposits with the discount houses are known as money at call and short notice.

Money illusion. When a worker receives a pay increase of 5 per cent in a year, he may consider himself to be 5 per cent better off. But the prices of the goods and services he buys may also have risen by 3 per cent, so that in REAL TERMS he is only 2 per cent better off. If the worker behaves as if he is really 5 per cent better off he is said to have money illusion.

Another good example of money illusion is for savers to invest in assets with a return of 5 per cent and think that the value of their savings will be 5 per cent higher in a year's time than it is now. Clearly, if the rise in prices is again 3 per cent, they are in fact only 2 per cent better off.

Money market. The market in the City of London where the DISCOUNT HOUSES lend to and borrow from the CLEARING BANKS and the CENTRAL BANK.

Money rate of interest. ⇨REAL RATE OF INTEREST.

Money supply. The community's spending power. It shows how much people can spend on goods and services without bankrupting themselves.

There are several components of the money supply, but the two main ones are notes and coins, and bank deposits. Notes and coins can be used to purchase goods because they are legal tender, while someone with a deposit in a bank can sign a cheque which will enable the person who receives it to transfer the amount specified into his deposits.

It has been suggested that certain other assets are equivalent to money because it is easy to convert them into notes and coins or bank deposits. This 'near money' consists of, for example, building society accounts and certificates of deposit. There are a number of definitions of the money supply, depending on the range of assets included.

Money has several characteristics. It is accepted as payment for goods and services throughout an economy. It does not yield a return in income, but there is a danger that its nominal value will change, as it is the standard of value for the remainder of the economic system. It is (usually) easy to carry about or to demonstrate that one possesses a particular amount of it. It is also the most liquid of assets.

The role of the money supply in the economy is much debated among economists. Some economists consider that the money supply exerts great influence over the behaviour of output, employment and prices, while others feel that it is not crucial and that the level of AGGREGATE DEMAND is determined by other factors.

Money terms. ⇨REAL TERMS.

Monopolies Commission. The Monopolies Commission, established in Britain in 1948, investigates companies and industries which the Secretary of State for Industry considers may be operating under monopolistic conditions against the public interest. It presents a report to the Secretary of State, who may then decide to prohibit certain practices if the report shows them to be undesirable. Since the Monopolies and Mergers Act of 1965 the Commission has also been able to examine proposals for mergers between firms in a monopoly situation or where the assets involved exceed £5 million.

Monopolistic competition. A MARKET STRUCTURE in which elements of PERFECT COMPETITION and MONOPOLY are blended. Firms are free to enter a monopolistically competitive industry, where a number of firms compete with similar but not identical products so that prices are brought down to the same level as average costs, as under perfect competition. But the price which any firm can receive for its output changes with the quantity it tries to sell, as under monopoly, with the result that prices are higher than MARGINAL COST. A monopolistically competitive industry is, therefore, less efficient than a perfectly competitive industry, but there is less profiteering than in a monopoly.

Monopoly. A company which is the sole supplier of a particular good. In its attempt to maximize profits it will keep prices above the cost of production and restrict output. Most governments therefore try to control monopolies by price control or by taking them into public ownership. A common example of government take-over is the natural monopoly where the provision of two or more sources of supply is wasteful. These tend to be public services, such as the telephones or postal system, where it would clearly be pointless to have more than one supplier. A monopoly can be as harmful if it dominates a market – with, say, 80 or 90 per cent control over supply – as if it is the sole supplier, with 100 per cent control. A firm with 100 per cent market share is said to be a pure monopoly.

Monopoly capital. A phrase used by some socialist economists to describe a stage in CAPITALISM's development. This stage, which has been reached, according to these economists, in most advanced industrial societies, is characterized by large companies dominating industries, influencing consumer choice and determining government policy. It is usually accompanied by the claim that these companies are insulated from competition by their size and are able to decide on their own PROFIT MARGINS. This claim is not consistent with the gradual decline in RATES OF RETURN in most advanced economies since the Second World War and few economists accept monopoly capitalism as an accurate description of the modern capitalist system.

Monopoly, Discriminating. ◇DISCRIMINATING MONOPOLY.

Monopsony. A single company or individual which buys the entire output of a product, even where this output is made by a large number of companies. The Post Office, which is the only buyer of telephone exchange equipment in the United Kingdom, is a good example.

'Most favoured nation'.   A phrase used in international trade negotiations. If the United Kingdom grants the USA 'most favoured nation' status, it means that the most favourable tariffs and quotas available to third nations, either now or at some time in the future after further negotiations, will also be available to the USA.

Moving average.   ◊AVERAGE.

Multilateralism.   ◊BILATERALISM; GENERAL AGREEMENT ON TARIFFS AND TRADE.

Multinational corporation.   A company which has manufacturing operations in a large number of countries. It may sometimes be involved in processing raw materials abroad for a plant in its home country or in maintaining distribution outlets in foreign countries. The main feature is that the company owns capital abroad and the profits from this capital are attributable to the shareholders in the home country Typical examples of multinationals are Unilever, IBM, and Ford.

Multinationals have become unpopular in many countries, particularly in the Third World, because of their excessive economic power. They also occasionally try to avoid high rates of taxation by selling goods to subsidiaries in countries with low rates of tax at unrealistically low prices. This practice is known as transfer pricing.

Multiple exchange rate.   ◊EXCHANGE RATE.

Multiple regression and correlation.   ◊CORRELATION; REGRESSION ANALYSIS.

Multiplier.   When the government decides to raise its expenditure permanently by £100 million it might seem that NATIONAL INCOME would increase by £100 million as well. However, this is not so because the recipients of the £100 million the first time it was spent will want to spend part of it as the second burst of spending takes place. This will make national income in the second period more than £100 million higher than it was at the start of the process.

Indeed, national income will only settle down again when it is higher by a multiple of the initial injection of extra government spending. The size of this multiple is known as the multiplier. It depends on the MARGINAL PROPENSITY TO CONSUME and is important to the determination of national income in KEYNESIAN ECONOMICS.

Although the example was presented in terms of government spending, the same reasoning applies to any increase in an exogenous component of demand. For example, if exports rise by £100 million, national income will probably rise by more than £100 million. However, some of the extra spending might in that case go on imports which will reduce the size of the eventual increase in national income. The export multiplier, or foreign trade multiplier, therefore, differs from the simple multiplier because it depends on the marginal propensity to import as well as the marginal propensity to consume.

Multi-product firm. A firm which produces a variety of goods and is active in more than one industry.

N

National accounts. GROSS NATIONAL PRODUCT.

National Board for Prices and Incomes (NBPI). The National Board for Prices and Incomes was set up in 1965 to investigate prices and incomes, as part of the British government's PRICES AND INCOMES POLICY. It had no statutory powers, but the government could decide to prevent or reduce a wage or price increase after considering its reports. The NBPI was abolished in 1971.

National debt. The total indebtedness of the government of a country. It includes GILT-EDGED SECURITIES and a number of short-term debts. The government pays interest on the national debt, a burden which is met from TAXATION.

In the eighteenth century, and at times in the nineteenth century, it was thought that the British national debt was so large that it would become an impossible strain on the country's finances and some Chancellors of the Exchequer set up sinking funds to try to eliminate it. Sums of money were set aside from the government's tax revenue to build up a total sufficient to repay the holders of gilt-edged securities. However, it was eventually realized that this idea was based on a fallacy. A nation can be in debt to other nations, but it cannot be in debt to itself.

National dividend. ▷GROSS NATIONAL PRODUCT.

National Economic Development Council (NEDC, Neddy). The National Economic Development Council was set up in 1962. Its first task was to consider the possibility that the United Kingdom could increase its growth rate to 4 per cent a year. It was envisaged as the first step in the more general use of national economic planning. It still survives, mainly as a forum for leaders of industry, the trade unions and the government, but it no longer frames large-scale economic plans.

National Enterprise Board (NEB). The National Enterprise Board, established in 1975, is a government-backed organization responsible for extending public ownership in manufacturing industry. It has powers to obtain a controlling stake in privately owned companies or to lend them money so that they can increase their INVESTMENT. The NEB is also intended as a complement to government plans to increase efficiency by planning agreements or the exchange of information between companies in order to coordinate investment strategies.

The NEB has been strongly criticized by industry and by the Conservative party because it uses public funds to help industry when industry should be seeking finance from private sources if its projects are worthwhile, and because it is an agent of government interference with the private sector.

National income. The sum of all income received in an economy in a particular period of time. It is, therefore, equal to the money value of the economy's output, although, as some output will have to be set aside to keep up the capital stock, only that part available after deduction of depreciation is truly income. The national income is equal to the gross national product minus depreciation.

National product. ⇨GROSS NATIONAL PRODUCT.

Nationalized industries. Enterprises either wholly owned by the state or where the state has a majority shareholding. The objective of nationalization is to maximize social benefit rather than to maximize the profits of private shareholders.

In the United Kingdom the main phase of nationalization was between 1945 and 1950 when the Labour government brought the electricity, gas, coal, iron and steel, and civil aviation industries into public ownership. (The Bank of England was also nationalized, although it had always accepted a responsibility to the state before 1945.) The programme was intended to achieve government control over 'the commanding heights of the economy'. More recently there have been signs that the Labour party would like to see large parts of manufacturing industry under government control and in government hands.

Natural monopoly. ⇨MONOPOLY.

Natural rate of growth. ⇨ECONOMIC GROWTH.

Near money. ⇨MONEY SUPPLY.

'Neddy'. ⇨NATIONAL ECONOMIC DEVELOPMENT COUNCIL.

Neo-classical. The term used to describe the major part of modern economics and, in particular, the examples of economic analysis which use its techniques. These techniques make much use of the marginal idea ($\Diamond$MARGINAL ANALYSIS). MODELS are thought out in which the main question being asked is 'If there were a small change in a particular direction would this be an improvement or a deterioration?' The models usually have to make a large number of assumptions – such as that all consumers and producers have perfect information about prices and production possibilities – and it has frequently been alleged that this detracts from their realism.

Net. Net is often used to describe economic variables where their value is difficult or misleading to interpret in gross terms. For example, a company may have gross assets of £10 000. This means that it either owns goods worth £10 000 or is owed money by other companies and individuals worth £10 000. But this may not be the value of the net assets of the company, because it may have bank borrowings of £4000. The net assets are gross assets minus bank borrowings (and other liabilities), i.e. £6000.

Another important meaning of net is net of depreciation. For example, gross investment in an economy may amount to £10 000 million, but half of this may be to replace machinery and equipment which is falling to pieces. The value of net investment is, therefore, £5000 million. Similar adjustments have to be made to arrive at the value of net domestic income, net income and net national product.

Net investment. $\Diamond$NET.

Net national product. $\Diamond$NET.

Net present value (NPV). $\Diamond$DISCOUNTED CASH FLOW.

Net profit. $\Diamond$PROFIT.

Net worth. The value of a company to its shareholders, according to the balance sheet. It is equal to the value of the total share capital when issued plus the estimated value of RETAINED EARNINGS plus CAPITAL GAINS. It is not equal to the market capitalization of the company, which is the valuation placed on it by the Stock Exchange.

Neutral technical progress. $\Diamond$TECHNICAL PROGRESS.

New Cambridge School. A school of thought, based on work in Cambridge, England, in the early 1970s, which proposed the doctrine that a country's balance of payments deficit is related to its public sector financial deficit. This relationship, which was derived from a study of FLOW OF FUNDS statistics in the 1960s, has not been properly explained and is not widely accepted. However, it became important for a brief period in the mid-1970s in the UK because of widespread concern over public sector finances and a large balance of payments deficit. (⟡CAMBRIDGE SCHOOL.)

New issue market. When companies wish to raise finance from the STOCK EXCHANGE they have to issue shares which entitle those who buy them to DIVIDENDS. The market in which these issues take place is known as the new issue market. (⟡ISSUING HOUSES.)

Nominal capital. ⟡EQUITY.

Nominal terms. ⟡REAL TERMS.

Nominal value. The face value of an asset, usually a share or bond, which is normally the value of the asset when it first appeared. For example, a GILT-EDGED SECURITY may have been issued at a PAR VALUE of £100. If someone wished to buy £100 of the security he would have to pay £100 on the date of issue. Subsequently the value of the security on the Stock Exchange might decline to £80. But the nominal value would still be £100.

Nominal yield. The return on a security expressed as a percentage of its NOMINAL VALUE.

Non-bank financial intermediaries (NBFI). ⟡FINANCE HOUSE.

Non-price competition. Rivalry between firms in which they try to outsell one another by providing better quality goods or better service, rather than by dropping prices. It is particularly characteristic of IMPERFECT COMPETITION.

Non-tariff trade distortions. Tariffs, or import duties, obstruct the free flow of international trade by making prices differ from those which producers would like to charge and which consumers would like to pay. There are other types of distortion caused by interference with the availability of imports and exports or by the use of the fiscal system to encourage exports and discourage imports. Two of the most common devices for promoting exports are the customs drawback and the export rebate. Customs drawbacks operate by the repayment of the government's proceeds from an import tariff on a good to a company which is re-exporting the good or using it to make into exports. An export rebate is a repayment of tax to a company which is exporting a high proportion of its output. All these devices are known as non-tariff trade distortions.

Normal profit. The level of profit which just makes it worthwhile for a company to stay in business and not to transfer to the most profitable alternative activity.

Normative. Normative statements are statements of opinion or value judgements. They are not statements of fact and someone else can express an opposite feeling or judgement without being wrong. For example, the statement 'the distribution of income is unfair' is normative.

O

Obsolescence. Machinery is taken out of service for one of two reasons – either it is falling to pieces or it is becoming too inefficient compared to more modern machinery to be worth operating. If it is taken out of service because it has become relatively inefficient it is said to have become obsolescent. Obsolesence is the value of capital written off for this reason.

Official settlement basis. ▷BALANCE OF PAYMENTS.

Offshore funds. Several small islands, such as the Cayman Islands, in different parts of the world have low rates of taxation on income from investments and no exchange controls. Banks and other financial institutions have in recent years moved to these islands in large numbers to obtain these advantages. They are known as offshore funds.

Oligopoly. A MARKET STRUCTURE in which there is a small number of firms competing for a share in the market for a product. It is unlike PERFECT COMPETITION or MONOPOLISTIC COMPETITION, where there is a large number of firms, and unlike MONOPOLY, where there is only one firm.

Economists have not decided on the most likely behaviour of oligopolistic industries. For example, they are not sure what the relationship between costs and prices will be in equilibrium. This is one of the biggest gaps in the theory of the firm because many industries today have an oligopolistic structure.

An important special case of oligopoly is price leadership. Here one firm decides the timing and size of price movements for other firms in the industry. They all follow its lead when it raises or lowers its price

Open economy (1). An economy which take part in international trade. This is in contrast to a closed economy which does not.

Open economy (2). An economy which a high proportion of its output sent abroad as exports and a high proportion of its expenditure spent abroad on imports.

Open economy (3). An economy with low or nonexistent tariffs and few EXCHANGE CONTROLS.

Open market operations. ▷BANK OF ENGLAND.

Open pricing. ▷RESTRICTIVE PRACTICE.

Opening prices. The prices ruling in a financial market as the start of a daily trading session.

Operating profit. The PROFIT a company earns before allowing for FIXED COSTS.

Opportunity cost. The concept of opportunity cost is one of the most fundamental ideas in economics. It is the cost of foregoing the nearest alternative to a course of action. For example, if someone has a choice between setting up a shirt factory or a rayon plant, the expected profits from the shirt factory are the opportunity cost of setting up the rayon plant. (▷COMPARATIVE ADVANTAGE.)

Optimal resource allocation. ▷ECONOMIC EFFICIENCY.

Optimum. The most desirable state of economic affairs. It is a frequently used in concept economic theory.
  The optimum is most commonly defined in terms of resource allocation and productive efficiency. A situation is optimal from the resource allocation viewpoint if it would not be possible to increase utility by increasing the production of one output and decreasing that of another. It is optimal from the viewpoint of productive efficiency if it is not possible to increase production by shifting FACTORS OF PRODUCTION from one industry to another or by altering the mix of different factors in any one industry.

Option. Someone may want to take advantage of an expected change in the price of a share on the Stock Exchange, but he may not want to buy it immediately. Instead he can buy an option, normally a small fraction of the share price. An option will enable him to buy or sell a share at some point in the future at a price agreed now. An option to buy is known as a call option; an option to sell as a put option; and an option to buy or sell as a double option.

Ordinal utility. When we analyse the well-being of a man by the goods that he possesses, there are two ways we can do it. The first is to say that when he has, for example, a five bedroomed-house and a motor car he had £1000 of UTILITY, but when he has a two-bedroomed house and a bicycle he has only £250 of utility. These are comparisons of cardinal utility. But some economists have felt that it is incorrect to use numbers to describe different levels of utility. They prefer the second method of expression, which is to say that when someone has a large house and a motor car he is better off than when he has a small house and a bicycle. These are comparisons of ordinal utility.

Ordinary shares. SHARES in a company which entitle their owner to receipts of income known as dividends. They are not certain to produce income, because if the company makes no profits it will probably not pay out any dividends. The great majority of shares traded on the Stock Exchange are ordinary shares. (◊ PREFERENCE SHARES; EQUITY.)

Organization for Economic Cooperation and Development (OECD). The Organization for Economic Cooperation and Development was established in 1961, taking over from its predecessor, the Organization for European Economic Cooperation (or OEEC). Its main functions are economic research and the compilation of statistics.

Its members are the richer nations of the world, including the USA, the UK, Austria, Belgium, Canada, Denmark, France, Greece, Iceland, Eire, Italy, Luxembourg, the Netherlands, Norway, Portugal, Spain, Sweden, Switzerland, Turkey, Australia, Finland and West Germany. The phrase OECD is often used, therefore, as a shorthand for the more affluent nations of the world as opposed to the Third World or less wealthy nations.

Organization for European Economic Cooperation (OEEC). ◊ ORGANIZATION FOR ECONOMIC COOPERATION AND DEVELOPMENT.

Organization of Petroleum Exporting Countries (OPEC). An organization comprising the most important oil-producing countries in the world, including Saudi Arabia, Iran and Venezuela. It is dominated by Arab members.

Established in 1960, it first attracted world-wide attention in October 1973 when its members, acting as a CARTEL, decided to increase the price of oil by about 70 per cent. Shortly afterwards they agreed on further, more massive increases which effectively quadrupled the price of oil in less than six months. This increased the price level in all oil importing countries and resulted in a world economic crisis, with most governments deciding to cut demand and eliminate the large balance of payments deficits caused by the higher price of a major import. (◊ PETRODOLLARS.)

Ottawa agreements. ◊ COMMONWEALTH PREFERENCE.

Overfull employment. A condition in which the proportion of the population of working age which is out of a job is smaller than is considered necessary for FULL EMPLOYMENT. One attempt at a definition is that it is that condition when the number of UNFILLED VACANCIES exceeds the number of unemployed.

Overheads. ⮑ FIXED COSTS

Overnight money. ⮑ INTERBANK MARKET.

Oversubscription. When a company wants to raise money for invest-ment, it may issue shares to the public. If it wants £1 million, it may issue 500 000 ordinary shares of £2 each. But the public may be so eager to invest in the company that 700 000 or 800 000 are subscribed for. The issue has, therefore, resulted in an oversubscription. Each investor receives 5/7 or 5/8 of his subscription unless he offered a price above £2.

Overvalued currency. ⮑ UNDERVALUED CURRENCY.

Own-price elasticity of demand. ⮑ ELASTICITY.

P

Paasche index. ▷INDEX NUMBERS.

Page Report. The Page Report was published in 1972 and was the result of the work of a Royal Commission on the National Savings Movement. It was extremely critical of the Movement's structure and called for a re-examination of the role of National Savings in a time of rapid inflation.

Paid-up capital. Paid-up capital is more or less equivalent to ISSUED CAPITAL and the two terms are usually regarded as synonyms.

Paper gold. ▷SPECIAL DRAWING RIGHTS.

Paper profit. A PROFIT which a company considers that it has earned, although it has not yet been realized by the sale of an output. The best example is when a financial company buys shares at, say, £1 each and the price on the Stock Exchange rises to £2 each. Even before the shares are sold the company may think that it has made £1 for each share. This is paper profit. If the share price fell it would turn out that including these paper profits in its annual accounts would have been misleading.

Par rate of exchange. ▷PARITY.

Par value. The price at which a security, particularly a government security with no default risk, is issued. This is normally £100. If the price then falls to, say, £80 it is said to have fallen beneath par or, if it rises to £120, to have risen above par.

Parameter. Something which is held constant in an economic MODEL, while other features are varying. For example, if an economist wants to find out the effect of a change in demand on price he may assume that supply conditions are unchanged. Supply is then a parameter of his model.

Pareto optimal. ▷ECONOMIC EFFICIENCY.

Parity; also known as par rate of exchange. In a world of FIXED

EXCHANGE RATES a country will declare the rate at which its CENTRAL BANK is willing to exchange its currency against the currencies of other countries. But it may allow some fluctuation either side of a central rate in response to supply and demand in the foreign exchange markets. The central rate is known as the parity.

Partial equilibrium analysis.　In an economy many things are happening at the same time. Because they interact it is difficult to analyse them together. Consequently, economists have developed a type of analysis called partial equilibrium analysis in which they examine the behaviour of two or three variables on the assumption that other variables in the system remain the same. (⟡EQUILIBRIUM.)

Participation ratio.　The proportion of the population of working age which is either employed or seeking employment.

Pay-back.　⟡INVESTMENT APPRAISAL.

Pay Board.　The Pay Board was established in 1972 to administer the provisions for the control of wages in the Conservative government's counter-inflation programme. It survived for more than two years until 1974 when it was abolished by the succeeding Labour government. Its main function was to ensure that workers and management abided by stages one, two and three of the counter-inflation programme.

Pay pause.　⟡PRICES AND INCOMES POLICY.

Peg.　⟡FIXED EXCHANGE RATES.

Per capita income.　The income of each person in an economy. It is not the same as the average wage, because it is equal to:

$$\frac{\text{national income}}{\text{total population}}$$

and, therefore, includes the income available for children and women who are not working. It is regarded as a good indication of the standard of living.

Perfect competition; also known as atomistic competition.　A MARKET STRUCTURE in which there is a large number of competitors. In such a situation a firm is not, therefore, able to manipulate buyers in its favour, because buyers will be able to retaliate by buying from its competitors.

Perfect competition is often associated with freedom of entry or the lack of restrictions on competition by new firms. But this idea is distinct from the idea of a large number of competitors and is occasionally given the name of pure competition.

Personal disposable income (PDI). ⇨ DISPOSABLE INCOME.

Personal taxation. Taxation of individuals based on an assessment of their income or wealth. It is roughly equivalent to direct taxation, except that direct taxation includes some taxes paid by companies.

The most important kind of personal tax in nearly all countries is income tax. In the United Kingdom this tax yields over £10 000 million a year to the government. The disadvantage of income taxes is that they can act as disincentives to effort. If a man has to pay part of any extra income he earns to the state he will possibly be less willing to work harder to achieve that extra income. A theoretical solution to this problem would be a lump-sum tax, a constant amount levied irrespective of earnings; but this is unpopular as it falls most heavily on the low paid.

In most countries the income tax system is progressive. The higher the income a man earns the higher the rate of tax he has to pay. The result of this system is that the disincentive to high-income groups is greater than that at the lower levels. However, as the state directs most of its spending towards the less well off, a progressive tax system redistributes income in favour of the poor, an attribute which is usually considered advantageous.

In most advanced industrial societies, the state pays certain benefits to individuals. These take a variety of forms, but generally the higher a man's income the fewer of these benefits are his as of right. This creates the 'poverty trap', the situation in which a low-paid worker has no inducement to improve his earning capacity because he loses his benefits.

The existence of the poverty trap has encouraged schemes for a reform of the income tax system whereby the state would give every income earner a sum of money regardless of the size of his income. This sum of money would then be added to his income to constitute his taxable income. If the tax assessed in this way exceeds the sum given him by the state he is on balance a taxpayer; if not, he is on balance a net recipient of benefits from the state.

This idea, known in the United Kingdom as the tax credit scheme – and in the USA as negative income tax – seems complicated, but it would leave the distribution of income unchanged while abolishing the poverty trap. It was supported by the Conservative government of 1970–74, but there was insufficient time to complete the reform.

The other main form of personal taxation is taxation of wealth and transfers of wealth between persons. A wealth tax is identical to an income tax except that it is assessed on wealth, not income. It is common in Europe as a substitute for the taxation of income from capital, and is at present under consideration in the United Kingdom with more comprehensive objectives, including the redistribution of wealth from rich to poor. A gift tax is a tax on the transfer of wealth between persons, designed largely to prevent avoidance of inheritance taxes by the practice of giving a gift to one's children. It is known as an accessions tax when it has to be paid by the person who is receiving the gift (the donee) rather than the donor.

A form of gift tax was introduced in the UK in 1975. Known as the capital transfer tax, it is levied on all gifts between individuals and should discourage rich parents from passing their wealth to their children before they die, formerly a common practice which avoided estate duty.

Petrodollar. The quadrupling of the price of oil in late 1973 and early 1974 caused a massive upheaval in international financial flows. The members of OPEC (ORGANIZATION OF PETROLEUM EXPORTING COUNTRIES) suddenly acquired huge balance of payments surpluses with their receipts from the exports of oil, mostly in the form of DOLLARS, greatly in excess of their imports. They had no choice but to invest the dollars in the financial markets of the advanced industrial countries. These dollars therefore became known as petrodollars. They were a great cause of concern to the industrial countries who feared that large sums of HOT MONEY might flow from one centre to another. These fears generally turned out to be groundless.

The problem of accommodating the flows of petrodollars was known as the recycling problem. It was widely thought that it would not be possible to provide sufficient investment outlets to meet the flows. In practice, several mechanisms were available. OPEC lent dollars to DEVELOPING COUNTRIES which then used the dollars to buy machinery and other goods from the industrial countries. Large sums were invested in US government securities and in a variety of financial assets in world financial centres, but particularly in London and New York.

Phillips curve. The Phillips curve is a relationship between the level of UNEMPLOYMENT and the rate of change of money wages. The higher is the level of unemployment, the lower is the rate of change of money wages (see Figure 11).

The relationship is of immense importance for economic policy because it suggests that one way of slowing down wage increases and, hence, INFLATION is to increase unemployment. The factual support for the relationship was provided by an economist, Professor A. W. Phillips (1914–1975), in the 1950s on the basis of historical experience stretching back to the nineteenth century. But some have claimed that the relationship broke down in the late 1960s because quite high levels of unemployment were associated with rapid inflation.

Physical controls. Official restrictions on economic behaviour which try to control production and prices directly by prohibiting them from differing from levels laid down by the government. They include such methods of economic policy as quotas on imports, price ceilings and rationing.

Pink Book. An official publication, prepared by the Central Statistical Office, the Treasury and the Department of Trade, which gives figures on the BALANCE OF PAYMENTS and its main components. It is published once a year.

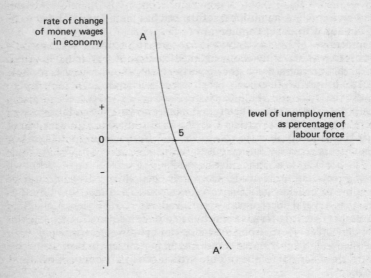

Figure 11. AA′ is a Phillips curve. When unemployment is less than 5 per cent money wages increase; when it stands at 5 per cent money wages are constant; when it is more than 5 per cent money wages fall.

Planned economy. One in which the government sets targets for economic attainment and encourages their fulfilment. For example, a government may decide that it would like production per head to rise by 5 per cent a year. This may involve a particular level of investment which the government will try to achieve.

There are two main types of planned economy – the command economy and the economy run by indicative planning.

In a command economy a central planning agency, which is usually a branch of the government and is, therefore, subject to political control, decides on the level of production which the economy should reach and also on the size of different industries compared to one another. The priority attached to different industries depends partly on consumer needs and partly on the requirements that sufficient resources be devoted to investment to achieve the planned rate of growth.

Different industries are interdependent, with the result that if one industry does not achieve its target other industries are unlikely to achieve theirs. The central bureaucrats are sometimes empowered to punish managers if targets are not met as they have the authority of the government behind them. A command economy is, therefore, dependent on a totalitarian political system and has, in practice, tended to be associated with either communism or fascism.

Indicative planning, however, is compatible with a democratic political system and has been adopted in France and India in recent decades. The government sets a growth rate for the economy as a whole and indicates what growth rate is required from each industry to achieve it. No compulsion is placed on firms or individuals to match the industry targets, but the government may encourage businessmen to take action in accordance with the plan rather than in accordance with demands from consumers and comparative profitability. For example, fiscal incentives may be given to producers of machine tools because this is thought to increase investment.

In the UK, the Labour government of 1964–70 formulated a national plan in 1965 which laid down a 4 per cent growth rate for the next five years. It was the culmination of earlier attempts at economic planning made by the Conservative government under Harold Macmillan in 1962 and 1963. In the event a much lower growth rate was achieved in the five years from 1965, and the only important institution to survive from that period is the NATIONAL ECONOMIC DEVELOPMENT COUNCIL.

Planning.   ▷PLANNED ECONOMY.

Ploughing back.   When a firm uses its profits to pay for its investment it is said to be ploughing back profits.

Point elasticity.   ▷ELASTICITY.

Portfolio.   A list of investments owned by an individual or company. For example, if a life insurance company owns shares in ICI and some government securities (or gilts), these shares and the gilts are said to be part of its portfolio.

Positive economics.   In economics two questions are constantly being asked. The first is 'If a particular action is taken what would the consequences be?' and the second is 'Should we take this action or another?'

In positive economics an answer is being given to the first question. The economist is, therefore, refraining from putting forward a policy recommendation, although he may be demonstrating the implications of following different policies. Positive economics involves describing reality and examining the way in which certain results flowed from certain courses of action in the past. However, it is not necessarily empirical, as much of theoretical economics is also designed to show, in abstract terms, how different economic variables interrelate.

NORMATIVE economics is intended to answer the second sort of question.

Precautionary motive. A reason for holding money. It exists when an individual wishes to have a certain amount of money available to meet unforeseen financial contingencies.

Preference shares. When a company is liquidated its shareholders are paid back some of the money they invested. Holders of preference shares are given better treatment than holders of ORDINARY SHARES. Consequently, these shares are less risky and receive a lower rate of dividend. Occasionally, companies do not pay dividends because they are going through a difficult year. Holders of cumulative preference shares are entitled to receive extra dividends when the company's position improves and the payment of dividends is resumed.

Premium (1). The difference between the actual price of a commodity or a security and the price paid for it in the first place. Its most usual context is the Stock Exchange, where a rise in the price of gilt-edged security above the price when it was issued is said to place the security at a premium.

Premium (2). A payment for an insurance policy, usually a regular monthly payment over a period of years.

Present value. When money is invested in a project or a security it is expected to yield a stream of incomes for several years. The value of this stream of future incomes, if assessed today, is known as a present value.

For example, someone may rent out a house and expect to receive in rents £100 for the next five years. If the year in which he receives the rents is unimportant to him, the present value of his house is £500.

In practice, most people do care about when they receive income. They would pay something to have the £100 due for the fifth year in the first year. Equally, they value £100 in five years' time lower than £100 now. Because of this the stream of future incomes has to be 'discounted'.

For example, the owner of the house may pay £2 to anyone who can arrange for him to have £100 now rather than in a year's time. Then, at the beginning of the five year period, the value of the second year's rents is £98 and of the third year's rents £96 and so on. The present value of the house is about £480, not £500.

Price Commission.   An official body set up in 1972 by the Conservative government under Edward Heath to administer the price provisions of the counter-inflation programme. It was unlike the NATIONAL BOARD FOR PRICES AND INCOMES, established in 1965 and abolished in 1971, because it was manned by civil servants and had powers to prevent price increases. The NBPI only had powers to refer excessive price increases to a minister.

Unlike the PAY BOARD, which was abolished in 1974 when the government decided that wage controls should be abandoned, the Price Commission still exists. It has been responsible for price control through successive stages of the counter-inflation programme.

Price discrimination.   The practice of charging a different price to different sets of customers or to a different market. It can be profitable to suppliers because demand conditions may vary from one market to another.

Price/earnings ratio (P/E ratio).   A technical idea used by Stock Exchange analysts to help them gauge the value of different shares. It is the ratio of the share price to earnings per share. Earnings per share are calculated by dividing a company's profits, minus interest payments and taxation, by the number of issued shares. It is not related to the yield to the shareholder from dividends. For example, a company may be paying out a dividend of 10p per share, although the earnings per share are 20p.

A rapidly expanding company, with good prospects and low risk, will normally have a higher price/earnings ratio than a declining company with poor profits and high risk.

Price elasticity.   ⟡ELASTICITY.

Price freeze.   ⟡PRICES AND INCOMES POLICY.

Price index.   ⟡INDEX NUMBERS.

Price leadership.   ⟡OLIGOPOLY.

Price mechanism.   ⟡PRICES AND INCOMES POLICY; LAISSEZ-FAIRE.

Price system.   In an economy, producers have to be given signals as to how much they should produce and consumers have to be given indications as to how much they can consume without exceeding income. An economy run according to the price system has the characteristic that prices are the signals of profitability and scarcity. The idea behind the system is that if prices are higher than costs, it will be profitable for a manufacturer to supply products in increasing amounts. A high price therefore encourages increased supply and meets consumers' demands.

Price theory. The branch of economic theory concerned with the determination of prices. It is closely connected with the theory of the firm. (◊ FIRM, THEORY OF; SUPPLY AND DEMAND.)

Prices and incomes policy. A programme to control wages and prices by the imposition of official limits on the rate at which they may increase. It has been widely adopted in advanced industrial countries as a method of curbing INFLATION. It is normally used in MIXED ECONOMIES in which the PRIVATE SECTOR traditionally has had the power to set its own prices without interference from the government.

The choice of a prices and incomes policy as the instrument of inflation control is a sign that conventional methods have failed or that they would risk consequences more serious than the unfavourable consequences of a prices and incomes policy.

The disadvantages of a prices and incomes policy are twofold. The first is that it disrupts the price mechanism. There might be a strong increase in the demand for a product which, if the market were free, would result in a sharp rise in the price to promote supply. But, with a prices and incomes policy, the government would prohibit suppliers from raising their prices as much as they would like. Although this may appear to favour consumers who will be paying a lower price, it tends to work against them. Suppliers will not want to put more of their product on the market if they cannot make a reasonable return. Hence, although consumers will be paying a low price, they will not be supplied with as many goods as they would like and there must be a loss of CONSUMER SURPLUS.

The second disadvantage is that, if the policy does not work, the government may be forced to abandon it. Afterwards a flood of price and wage increases may take place, undoing the work of the earlier period of restraint and increasing peoples' expectations of further inflation.

These disadvantages have to be weighed against the disadvantages of other techniques of controlling inflation. The main other technique is demand restraint by means of FISCAL and MONETARY POLICY. This usually causes UNEMPLOYMENT. Consequently, a fierce controversy has developed between those economists who believe that a prices and incomes policy can succeed and those who believe that the only answer must involve higher unemployment.

The most extreme form of a prices and incomes policy is a wages and prices freeze. Under this any increase in wages and prices is forbidden for a certain period of time. A freeze has been used in the United Kingdom on two occasions in recent years – in 1966 and in 1972–3. On both occasions it lasted six months.

There have been a number of prices and incomes policies in the UK in recent years. The first notable attempt was the Council on Prices, Productivity and Incomes, also known as the Cohen Committee, set up in 1957 under the chairmanship of Lord Cohen. It had only three members and did not investigate individual prices or wages, but only examined the overall problem of inflation.

In 1961, when inflation threatened to increase from low levels in 1959 and 1960, the government operated the pay pause. There was no direct intervention with wages in the private sector, but wages in the public sector were held back.

Powers to restrict price and wage increases in the private sector were taken by the Labour government of 1964–70. The NATIONAL BOARD FOR PRICES AND INCOMES functioned from 1965 to 1971 making recommendations to the government on the desirability of particular wage and price increases.

In 1972 the Conservative government was responsible for the counter-inflation programme under which the PAY BOARD and PRICE COMMISSION were set up, with even more extensive powers than the National Board for Prices and Incomes.

Primary commodities. Commodities which have not undergone any processing into finished goods. For example, copper and unrefined sugar are primary commodities.

Primary industry. ⟡SECONDARY INDUSTRY.

Primary market. ⟡SECONDARY MARKET.

Prime costs. Prime costs are more or less identical to VARIABLE COSTS, but unlike variable costs, they include certain costs which can be avoided if there is no output although the firm continues to remain in business.

Prime rate (USA). The COMMERCIAL BANKS in the USA charge different rate of interest on their loans, with a higher rate for their more risky customers. The most reliable customers are charged the lowest or prime rate. But, if the prime rate changes, all the other rates change and, consequently, changes in prime rates are indicative of credit conditions. In Britain, the equivalent term is base rate.

Principal. The sum lent or borrowed when a loan is arranged. The borrower usually has to repay the lender the principal and INTEREST. The calculation of interest is based on the size of the principal.

Private company. A company which does not offer its shares for sale to the public, but which nevertheless does have a restricted number of shareholders who have LIMITED LIABILITY.

Private sector. The sector of an economy owned by private individuals. It is normally also managed by private individuals, without government control over its operations. It is to be contrasted with the PUBLIC SECTOR which is owned and ultimately controlled by the government.

Producer surplus. Producer surplus is roughly equivalent to PROFIT, except that economists do not regard the opportunity cost of capital, or NORMAL PROFIT, as part of producer surplus. It is analogous to CONSUMER SURPLUS.

Product differentiation. The attempt by producers to make other similar products less substitutable for their products. This might be done by design differences, advertising or packaging. The more different a producer can make his product from all others the more he can act as a monopolist.

Production, Coefficients of. ▷COEFFICIENTS OF PRODUCTION.

Production function. A relationship which shows how much output can be obtained from different levels and combinations of inputs. It is an important idea in NEO-CLASSICAL economics, because the existence of certain types of production function implies the existence of measurable MARGINAL PRODUCTS. These are necessary to the marginal productivity theory of distribution, which has been opposed to the Marxian theory of distribution. (▷MARGINAL PRODUCTIVITY OF CAPITAL; MARXIAN ECONOMICS.)

Production possibility curve. ▷TRANSFORMATION CURVE.

Production, Theory of. The branch of economic theory concerned with the way in which inputs are used to make outputs. It is related to the theory of the FIRM, which concentrates more on the way in which output is sold.

Productive efficiency. ▷ECONOMIC EFFICIENCY.

Productive potential. In most economies there is usually a certain amount of unemployment of labour and under-utilization of machinery and buildings. As a result, the economy is not producing as much as might be possible if all resources were fully used. The output which the economy could achieve if all resources were fully used is known as productive potential.

Productivity.   A measure of how much output is being achieved from a given unit of input. If productivity is higher, more is being produced from each input.

One company may be producing 100 machines a year, whereas another is producing 50 machines. But this does not mean that productivity is higher in the first company because it may be employing 100 men while the second is only employing 25. In the first company a man makes one machine, and therefore, has lower productivity than in the second company where he makes two.

The measurement of productivity when there are two inputs is complicated because it is necessary to attribute part of the output to each input.

Profit.   Profit is popularly considered to be a company's reward for producing goods. It receives in sales revenue more than it spends on labour and CAPITAL and the difference is known as profit.

This notion is correct, but the economist has a special way of looking at profits. His idea is that owners of capital would not invest their money or businessmen put in energy and effort in a company unless they were going to receive something in return. The minimum amount, known as normal profit, that they would have to receive to make it worth their while to take part in a company is not part of true profit as an economist understands the term. True profit is calculated by deducting normal profit from the difference between sales revenue and expenditure.

The accountant's concept of profit corresponds to the popular one. But the accountant draws a distinction between gross profit and net profit. Gross profit is the difference between sales revenue and expenditure on VARIABLE COSTS. Net profit is gross profit minus DEPRECIATION and the payment of INTEREST on loans.

In the UK and the USA it is usual for net profit, expressed as a percentage of turnover, to be higher than in the European countries. The reason is that British and American companies rely less heavily on finance from loans than European companies and, therefore, the interest deduction is less. The higher net profit margins do not mean, therefore, that the companies are, in fact, trading more profitably.

There has been a dispute about the inclusion of stock appreciation in profit. Stock appreciation arises because the price of raw materials increases and, therefore, raises the value of the stocks of raw materials owned by companies. It has been claimed that, as companies will subsequently have to pay more to renew their stocks, they are not, in fact, better off. On the other hand, some economists have asserted that, if the companies are able to pay the higher prices, the value of their assets has increased.

Profit margin. The difference between the price of a good and its average total cost of production.

Profit taking. When the owner of some shares has made a profit because the price of his shares has risen on the Stock Exchange he may decide to sell the shares before the price goes down. This is known as profit taking. It also occurs in commodity markets.

Progressive tax. A tax where the rate of tax increases the more tax is paid. The best example is income tax, where the effect of progressivity is to cause rich people to pay a higher proportion of their income in tax than poor people. (⟡PERSONAL TAXATION.)

Project analysis. ⟡COST–BENEFIT ANALYSIS.

Project evaluation. ⟡COST–BENEFIT ANALYSIS.

Propensity to consume. ⟡MARGINAL PROPENSITY TO CONSUME.

Propensity to import. Some countries, such as the United Kingdom, are actively involved in foreign trade and import a high proportion of the goods they consume. They are said to have a high propensity to import.

The average propensity to import is the proportion of GROSS NATIONAL PRODUCT imported. For example, if gross national product is £10 000m and imports are £4000m, the average propensity to import is 0.4. The marginal propensity to import is the proportion of an increase in gross national product which is spent abroad on imports. For example, if gross national product increases from £10 000m to £11 000m and imports increase from £4000m to £4500m, the marginal propensity to import is 0.5 (gross national product has risen by £1000m and imports have risen by exactly half that, £500m).

Propensity to save. ⟡MARGINAL PROPENSITY TO CONSUME.

Proportional tax. A tax which has the same rate of tax whatever the amount of tax paid. The best example is value added tax. If the rate of VAT is 10 per cent, it is 10 per cent whatever the quantity sold. In contrast the lump-sum tax is a tax of a given amount which does not vary with the circumstances of the taxpayer. A poll tax, for example, is levied for the same fixed sum on all taxpayers regardless of their incomes.

Protection. The system of regulating a country's foreign trade to keep out imports, and, thereby, help domestic industry. The usual method is to place tariffs and quotas on imports, which either makes them more expensive so that fewer are brought or restricts the quantity which can be brought into a country.

Protective policies normally reduce a country's welfare because fewer resources are needed to produce the exports which would pay for the higher imports found in a FREE TRADE situation than are needed to produce at home the goods which are substituted for imports under protection. However, government have often shown great difficulty in understanding this argument and have defended protection because it is thought to increase employment and promote economic growth through the encouragement of infant industries. (⟡INFANT INDUSTRY ARGUMENT.)

Public company. A public company has a QUOTATION on the Stock Exchange. This means that any member of the public can buy SHARES in the company should he wish to do so. Most large companies in the UK are public companies.

When a company decides to offer shares to the public it is said to be 'going public'.

Public expenditure. Expenditure by central and local government on both CONSUMPTION and INVESTMENT. It sometimes includes and sometimes excludes expenditure by nationalized industries.

Public finance. A branch of applied economics and economic theory concerned with the economic policy of the government and, more particularly, of its taxation and expenditure policies. The theory of the effects on the economy of different forms and levels of taxation is a particularly important part of public finance.

Public goods. Public goods include a number of goods and services provided by public authorities in most countries, education, the legal system and defence being good examples. However, several of these goods and services could be supplied by private agencies so that the precise definition of a public good is still uncertain, with economists in dispute on the essential characteristics.

Public sector. The sector of the economy owned and controlled by the government. No single individual owns a share in a company or institution in the public sector, but every citizen has indirect control over the public sector through his votes for politicians in central and local governments.

Public sector financial deficit. Governments receive money from taxation and other sources and spend money on goods and services. Like companies or individuals they have to cover the gap between revenue and expenditure by borrowing. The gap is known in Britain as the central government borrowing requirement. Other public sector bodies have to undertake borrowing for the same reason. The public sector borrowing requirement consists of the central government borrowing requirements plus the borrowing requirements of local authorities and public corporations.

The public sector borrowing requirement is of considerable importance for the conduct of monetary policy. If the government borrows from banks, the liquidity of the banking system increases and causes a rise in the money supply. In due course this may fuel inflation. If, however, the government borrows from the public, for example, by selling gilts, the public will have to save more, putting up interest rates and discouraging borrowing by the private sector.

The public sector financial deficit is related to the borrowing requirement but is generally smaller. The reason is that the government lends money as well as borrowing it and any amount lent to the private sector has to be deducted from the borrowing requirement to arrive at the financial deficit.

'Pump-priming'. ⟡DEFICIT FINANCING.

Purchase tax. ⟡INDIRECT TAXATION.

Purchasing power parity. The name of a theorem in international economics. The idea is that the exchange rate between two countries should be such that the price of an internationally traded good should be the same in both. For example, if a book costs £1 in the UK and the exchange rate with the USA is £1:$2.40, the book should cost $2.40 in the USA.

Pure competition. ⟡PERFECT COMPETITION.

Pure monopoly. ⟡MONOPOLY.

Put option. ⟡OPTION.

Pyramiding. ⟡HOLDING COMPANY.

Q

Quantitative bank lending restrictions. When the government wants to reduce AGGREGATE DEMAND it may need the banks to slow down the growth of their lending, so that business and consumers have less to spend. Quantitative bank lending restrictions do this directly by laying down limits to the amount a bank may increase its advances. The alternative is for the CENTRAL BANK to raise the rate at which it lends money to other banks in the system, which obliges these banks to cut back on their commitments.

Quantity equation. ⟡QUANTITY THEORY OF MONEY.

Quantity theory of money. A school of economic thought which believes that control of the money supply is the best method of managing the economy. Quantity theorists or MONETARISTS are often opposed to the adoption of Keynesian techniques of demand regulation (⟡KEYNESIAN ECONOMICS).

Their starting point is the quantity equation, that

$$MV = PT,$$

where M is the money supply, V is the velocity of circulation, P is the price level and T is the volume of transactions. This equation is always true and no economist has ever disputed it.

The velocity of circulation is a measure of how quickly money is passing from hand to hand. What the equation says, therefore, is that what is being spent (i.e. MV – or the money supply multiplied by the velocity of circulation) is also being bought (i.e. PT – or the price level multiplied by the volume of transactions). The MV=PT equation is sometimes known as the Fisher equation.

However, the quantity theory of money has acquired a much more controversial character because some members of the school have claimed that the velocity of circulation is constant. Because it does not vary, any change in the money supply will also change the level of spending or PT. If there are unused resources because of unemployment, a higher money supply will cause an increase in output; if there is full employment it is not possible for a higher money supply to raise output further and the result must be an increase in prices. Believers in the quantity theory are, consequently, advocates of stricter control of the money supply to curb inflation.

In the 1970s, the most well-known advocates of the quantity theory have come from the University of Chicago in the USA. The Chicago School, led by Milton Friedman, has called for a policy of keeping the growth of the money supply in line with the growth of the economy's productive potential. The school has been critical of the use of prices and incomes policies to control inflation and has favoured greater freedom for market forces in the economy.

Quasi-rent. A form of profit. If a firm buys a piece of machinery superior to other machinery used in an industry, it will probably make profits above those of other companies. The difference between its profits and their profits is quasi-rent. Eventually, however, other companies will also purchase the better piece of machinery. They will compete more effectively and the higher profits of the innovator will be brought down to the average in the industry.

One important point about quasi-rent, therefore, is that it is a temporary profit.

Quotas. Restrictions, normally on imports. They lay down limits on the number of items of a certain product which may be purchased from abroad and should be distinguished from tariffs, which restrict imports by raising the price to domestic consumers.

The drawback of quotas is that fewer consumers are able to obtain foreign-produced goods than would like to have them. Consequently, any merchant who is given a quota by the government can charge a price much above the price he had to pay to import the goods. He is able to make a large profit.

Quotation. A quotation is given to a public company whose shares are traded on the Stock Exchange. The quotation shows the price of the shares to anyone who might buy them, and, therefore, makes them more marketable. Quoted companies are usually large and, because they have been acknowledged as justifying a quotation, they tend to be respectable and secure.

R

Radcliffe Report.   The Radcliffe Report was produced in 1959, after more than two years' work, by a Committee on the Working of the Monetary System under the chairmanship of Lord Radcliffe. The report was intended to outline the way in which the monetary system operated in order to provide better guidelines for policy. Its conclusion was that precise control of the MONEY SUPPLY was less important than measures to restrict LIQUIDITY, through curbs on consumer credit and control of capital issues (◊ISSUING HOUSES). It drew attention to the effect of non-bank financial intermediaries, such as hire-purchase companies, in enabling people to spend more money and increase demand, at the same time that the money supply was constant. (◊FINANCE HOUSE.)

Rate of interest.   The cost of borrowing money or the return on lending money expressed as a percentage. For example, if a bank lends £100 on 1 January 1975 and expects to be paid back on 1 January 1976 with £105, the rate of interest is 5 per cent a year. (◊INTEREST, THEORY OF.)

Rate of return.   A measure of profitability of capital. It is expressed as profit (after depreciation has been deducted) as a percentage of the capital used in a business. For example, suppose a company has purchased a machine for £100 which will last for five years. Then depreciation is £20 a year. If profits are £30 a year, net profit is £10 a year and the rate of return of 10 per cent.

Rate of technical substitution.   The same quantity of output can be produced with varying combinations of inputs. For example, it may be possible to make 100 brooms with 10 men and 10 machines or with 5 men and 15 machines. The rate of technical substitution measures how many of one input have to be substituted for the other to leave output unchanged. In the example, the rate of technical substitution is 1 because 100 brooms are still made when 1 man is substituted for 1 machine.

Rate of time preference. ⟡INTEREST, THEORY OF.

Rationing. ⟡DEMAND (2).

Real income. ⟡REAL TERMS.

Real rate of interest. When inflation is rapid the value of money decreases with time. If someone borrows money and has to repay it in the future inflation will make him better off unless he is obliged to pay a rate of interest which reflects the rise in prices. For example, when prices are rising by 10 per cent a year and the money rate of interest is 15 per cent (i.e. £115 has to be repaid at the end of each year that £100 is borrowed), then the real rate of interest is 5 per cent. In other words, the real rate of interest is the rate of interest that would be paid if prices were constant.

Real terms. Inflation distorts a number of economic relationships. For example, the price of cameras may rise by 10 per cent in a year and it would, therefore, seem that they were more expensive. But the price of clothes might rise by 20 per cent in the same year. Obviously, the same quantity of clothes could be exchanged for more cameras. In real terms cameras have become cheaper relative to clothes.

The object of expressing something in real terms is, then, to adjust for the effect of rising prices throughout the economic system. Normally the adjustment is made with a measure of the price level of all goods – such as the RETAIL PRICE INDEX. If no adjustment is made for inflation, prices are said to be left in nominal terms. In the above example, cameras are 10 per cent more expensive in nominal terms.

A common application of the idea is to determine whether people are better or worse off. If someone is being paid £2000 in 1975 compared to £1500 in 1974 he might seem to be 33 per cent better off. But prices might have risen by 50 per cent between the two years. His real wages, or real income, have fallen.

Real wages. ⟡REAL TERMS.

Recession. Recession is defined in the USA as a period of two or more quarters in which gross national product has declined. In the UK no precise definition has been adopted, but a recession is usually considered to be a mild economic downturn, with a small rise in unemployment and a slow rise in output. A slump or depression is more serious, with heavy unemployment and stagnant or falling output.

Reciprocal swap arrangements. ⟡'SWAPS'.

Reciprocity. The practice of lowering tariffs in response to a reduction in tariffs by a trading partner. It is a sign of economic good neighbourliness and has been an important idea in the removal of restrictions on trade in post-war commercial negotiation, particularly under the General Agreement on Tariffs and Trade. Reciprocity is sometimes also called a fair trade policy.

Recycling. ⇨PETRODOLLARS.

Redeemable securities. When a company or the government borrows money, it may issue SECURITIES which promise to repay the sum borrowed at some date in the future. Such securities are said to be redeemable securities. The owner of the securities will also receive interest payments until the redemption date.

Redemption date. The date on which the owner of a redeemable security is repaid his money.

Redemption yield. ⇨YIELD.

Re-exports. When goods are imported into a country by merchants who then export them to another country, they are known as re-exports.

Reflation. An increase in AGGREGATE DEMAND caused by government action. Reflation is, therefore, the opposite of deflation and should be distinguished from INFLATION which means rising prices.

Regional employment premium (REP). ⇨REGIONAL POLICY.

Regional policy. The set of measures taken by a government to improve economic conditions in regions where the standard of living is particularly low compared to the rest of the country or where the unemployment rate is above the national average. It has been part of economic policy in the UK since the 1930s.

At first the regions affected were known as the depressed areas. Aid was administered under the Distribution of Industry Act of 1945 for most of the 1950s, but there were a number of changes in regional policy in the early 1960s. In 1966 a new name, the development areas, was given to the regions and the scale of assistance was gradually increased.

In 1967 the regional employment premium was introduced. This was a subsidy to an employer in a development area amounting to 30s for each adult male manufacturing employee. (The rate has subsequently been increased to £3 for a male and £1.50 for a female.) Previous measures had included special grants for manufacturers investing in the regions and control over the location of industry by requiring companies who wished to expand in prosperous regions to obtain industrial development certificates.

The Hunt Committee, set up in 1967, examined the economic circumstances of regions which, although not far from the national average in terms of unemployment and income levels, were still behind the more prosperous regions, such as the South-East. The relatively poor regions have become known as the grey or intermediate areas. The Committee's report in 1969 recommended that investment and training grants should be available in these areas as well.

Regression analysis.   A statistical technique to determine the relationship between two or more economic variables. Its object is to answer questions of the form 'If X changes by so much, how much would we expect Y to change?'

When the relationship under consideration consists of two variables, simple regression is used. When there are more than two variables, multiple regression techniques are necessary.

Regression should be distinguished from CORRELATION. Correlation is concerned with how certain a relationship is. It tries to answer the question 'How confident can we be that Y will in fact change by x per cent when we know from regression analysis that an x per cent change is the most likely?'

Regressive tax.   A tax which is paid at a lower rate the more tax is paid, or, according to another definition of the term, a tax paid at a lower rate the higher the income of the tax-payer.

Regulator, The.   The power of the Chancellor of the Exchequer to alter rates of INDIRECT TAXATION without having a BUDGET. It is convenient in that it permits the government to alter economic policy more frequently than once a year. It was first introduced by Selwyn Lloyd in 1961.

Relation, The.   ⬦ACCELERATION PRINCIPLE.

Relativities.   ⬦DIFFERENTIALS.

Rent (1).   In everyday usage, rent means the payment for the use of property, particularly land and buildings.

Rent (2).   In economics, rent is the excess payment to the owner of a factor of production over that amount needed to keep the factor in its present employment. This idea stems from David Ricardo, an early nineteenth century English economist, who saw that the owners of high-class lands, receiving higher rents than the owners of low-class land, would still lease out their land if rents declined. There would be no alternative employment for their property. (⬦ECONOMIC RENT.)

Rentier.   An individual who lives off the dividends and interest payments from his capital.

Replacement cost. When a company buys equipment it will expect the equipment to fall to pieces eventually. It will then have to pay for a new piece of equipment. To make allowance for this it can either adjust for DEPRECIATION at historic cost or at replacement cost. Depreciation at historic cost assumes that the price of the equipment will be unchanged when replacement takes place. Depreciation at replacement cost takes account of the possible change in the price of the equipment as time goes by.

Repressed inflation. Prices are sometimes held down by government controls as part of official attempts to curb inflation. If the controls were taken off there would be a sharp rise in prices. When the price level is artificially held down in this way there is said to be repressed inflation.

Resale-price maintenance (RPM). The practice of a manufacturer requiring wholesalers and distributors to resell his products at a particular price or at a price not beneath a certain minimum level. Resale-price maintenance, which was common in the UK until the 1960s, was considered to be a RESTRICTIVE PRACTICE because it limited the freedom of retailers to compete.

In 1964 the Conservative government passed the Resale Prices Act. This prohibited the practice unless it could be proved in the public interest before the Restrictive Practices Court. The Act has subsequently been much acclaimed and it has been said to have been largely responsible for the rapid development of supermarkets in the late 1960s.

Reserve assets. ▷COMPETITION AND CREDIT CONTROL.

Reserve currency. A currency held by governments in their reserves of gold and foreign currency. It has to be widely used in international trade and to be fairly stable in value. Under the BRETTON WOODS Agreement of 1944 two reserve currencies – the US dollar and the pound sterling – were envisaged. Although these continue to be important, governments have recently increased their holdings of Deutschemarks and Swiss francs, because they have kept their value better than the American and British currencies. Reserve currencies are also known as key currencies.

Reserve ratio. ▷COMPETITION AND CREDIT CONTROL.

Reserves. ▷GOLD AND FOREIGN EXCHANGE RESERVES.

Resource allocation. ▷ECONOMIC EFFICIENCY.

Restrictive practices. A method of obtaining an unfair advantage over customers, suppliers, employers or employees. Restrictive practices are widespread in most economies, but the two main types are restrictive practices by companies, usually at the expense of the consumer, and restrictive practices by trade unions, intended to raise wages or protect employment.

Restrictive practices by companies also fall into two categories.

(a) Collusion, which involves an agreement between a number of companies to follow a course of action in their favour. Agreement on pricing and investment policies is the characteristic form of collusion. A large company in an industry may let other companies know if it is about to change its prices, giving them adequate warning to change their prices too. This practice, known as price leadership, discourages price competition and may mean that consumers have to pay more. A similar abuse, known as open pricing, can arise when companies circulate price lists to other companies even when there is no dominant company to ensure price uniformity.

(b) Restrictive practices pursued by a company acting on its own to the disadvantage of its customers. These are particularly common in relations between a manufacturer and wholesalers or between wholesalers and retailers.

Loyalty rebates are discounts given to a distributor if he buys goods from only one company for a long period of time. Because he has been loyal to the same company this company makes its goods available to him more cheaply.

Exclusive dealing is the restriction by a manufacturer of the number of his sales outlets. He will only allow his goods to be sold at the retail level if the retailer is considered suitable. This practice is found in the motor trade.

Full-line forcing obliges a distributor to take all the products made by a manufacturer even if the distributor does not want to buy the full line, but would prefer to have only one or two of the products.

Restrictive practices adopted by trade unions are of enormous variety, but the best known include 'the closed shop' and the apprenticeship system. Their object is usually to limit the number of people who can find employment with a company or industry, in order to raise the wages of those who are already in a job.

The Restrictive Practices Court was established by an Act of Parliament in 1956 to reduce the number of restrictive practices between companies. Trade union restrictive practices have on the whole resisted legislation.

Retail price index (RPI). A measure of the increase in prices in the shops. Most countries have a retail prices index, the UK's being compiled by the Department of Employment each month.

The retail price index is a cost-of-living index, which shows how much more (or less) an average family would have to spend to remain as well off after a rise (or fall) in prices as before. For example, if the retail price index rises by 10 per cent a year an average family which was spending £1000 at the beginning of a year would have to spend £1100 at the end to have the same standard of living.

The retail price index should be distinguished from the wholesale price index which is the price of goods as they leave the factory. Many such goods are intended for investment or exports and there is no necessary connection between wholesale prices and prices in the shops.

Retained earnings. When a company makes a profit it will have to pay part of the profit to the government as taxation and part to its shareholders in the form of dividends. The amount of profit remaining after these deductions is known as retained earnings. Retained earnings are important because they can be used to finance investment.

Returns to scale. When a company expands or contracts the number of inputs used in production it will expect output to expand and contract also. But it does not follow that output will change by the same proportional amount.

If a 10 per cent increase in the number of inputs is followed by an increase in output greater than 10 per cent, the company is said to have increasing returns or increasing returns to scale. If it is followed by a 10 per cent increase in output it is said to have constant returns to scale. If it is followed by an increase in output of less than 10 per cent, it has decreasing returns.

Returns to scale are, therefore, a measure of how output responds to inputs. It is important to be clear that reference to inputs in this context includes *all* inputs, not just fixed or variable inputs. There is often confusion in economics between decreasing returns to scale and the law of DIMINISHING RETURNS.

Revaluation. A revaluation occurs when an asset is valued more or less highly against other assets than before. The main example arises when a currency is increased in value compared to other currencies. For example, if the dollar can be exchanged for £2 on one date compared to £1 on a previous date, it is said to have been revalued. This makes US exports more expensive than before in terms of pounds.

Revealed preference. A technique of analysing DEMAND (2). It is based on comparisons of the quantities of different goods consumers buy at different price and income levels. The law of demand, and other propositions in consumer theory, can be demonstrated without measuring utility.

Revenue (1).   The sum of money a company receives from selling its production, also known as sales revenue.

Revenue (2).   The proceeds of taxation to a government, also known as tax revenue.

Revenue reserves.   ⟡ASSET.

Reverse take-over.   A take-over in which a private company acquires a public company. This is rather unusual because public companies are generally larger than private companies.

Reverse yield gap.   ⟡YIELD GAP.

Ricardian.   David Ricardo was an English economist who lived between 1772 and 1823. He discovered the law of DIMINISHING RETURNS and the principle of COMPARATIVE ADVANTAGE. His most famous book was *Principles of Political Economy and Taxation* (1817).
   Ricardian is an adjective used to describe certain economic attitudes and theories. For example, the belief that prices are determined by the cost of labour is Ricardian. There is a close resemblance between Ricardian and Marxist economic ideas.

Rights issue.   When a public company wants to raise more finance it may offer a new issue of its shares to the existing shareholders. The shareholders may, however, not want to invest more money with the company and they may sell the rights to the new issue to someone else. This type of issue is, therefore, known as a rights issue.

Rightward-shifting.   A term used to describe an increase in demand or supply. Demand conditions, for example, can be described by a demand curve (⟡DEMAND (2)) which shows how quantity demanded changes as price changes. If an economist needs to know whether demand has increased, he must be careful to distinguish between a situation in which quantity demanded has risen and a situation in which, for every price level, consumers want to buy more of a good. It is this second situation which is defined by an economist as a rightward-shifting of the demand curve.
   Leftward-shifting naturally refers to a decrease in demand or supply. 'Shifting' is said to occur whenever a demand or supply curve has changed position.

Risk.   When a number of different outcomes might flow from a particular course of action the action is said to be risky. The risk of loss – or the possibility that one outcome of an investment will be a loss – is the most important one in economic discussions. (⟡UNCERTAINTY.)

Risk capital. When funds are invested in a business and there is no certainty that the funds will yield a RATE OF RETURN or even that the money will be paid back, the funds are said to be risk capital. EQUITY is the most important form of risk capital.

'Roundabout' methods of production. 'Roundabout' methods of production require a number of processes before the final product is made. For example, tinned food is made with more 'roundabout' methods than fresh food, because an extra process (i.e. putting the food in tins) has been added.

Round-tripping. A method of making a profit by borrowing money from a bank on overdraft and investing it in certain financial markets in London, particularly in CERTIFICATES OF DEPOSIT. It was made possible by the new scheme of COMPETITION AND CREDIT CONTROL adopted in 1971 to improve competitiveness in the UK financial system, but was widely considered an abuse and came to an end in 1974. It was also known as the 'merry-go-round'.

Rule-of-thumb pricing. ⇨ BEHAVIOURAL THEORY OF THE FIRM.

S

Saving. That part of income not used for expenditure on goods and services or for consumption.

Saving is contrasted in economics with INVESTMENT, which does involve expenditure on capital goods. For example, the purchase of shares is not regarded as investment because no capital expenditure has taken place, but as saving. On the other hand, if someone builds a garage, this is an act of investment, not saving, because more goods have been created.

The distinction between saving and investment is important to KEYNESIAN ECONOMICS.

Savings banks. Banks, usually run by the government or on a non-profit basis, whose main object is to protect the deposits of small savers. In the UK, the most important savings bank is the Post Office Savings Bank. This takes deposits and then lends the money to the government. The other institutions for small savers are local Trustees Savings Banks, which generally offer higher interest rates than the POSB. The National Savings Movement encourages savers to put their money into these bodies, but it was much criticized by the Page Report in 1972 which argued that the savings banks had not protected small savers against inflation.

Say's law of markets. Say's law of markets, originated by the French economist, Jean-Bapiste Say (1767–1852), is that supply creates its own demand.

The law is best illustrated by an example. A manufacturer producing watches pays wages to his workmen, adding to the economy's spending power. When he wants to sell the watches, therefore, there should be a number of willing purchasers as a matching amount of spending power exists in the economy. It does not matter if his workmen want to spend their wages on other goods as long as the workmen in other industries want to spend some of their wages on watches. Everything should balance out, with all the goods produced also being sold.

If Say's law of markets were true there would never be a problem of unemployment. Unfortunately it is not because the workmen may decide not to spend part of their wages and this withdraws demand from the system.

Schumpeterian theory of the trade cycle. The Schumpeterian theory of the trade cycle argued that INNOVATION was crucial to an explanation of why business conditions fluctuated from year to year. If the economy became depressed, entrepreneurs would find new profitable investment opportunities as they made economic applications of scientific discoveries. The resulting increase in investment would cause the economy to boom.

Schumpeter, an Austrian economist who lived from 1883 to 1950 and spent most of his later years in the USA, also developed a theory of the trade cycle based on three time-periods. He claimed, from historical evidence, that there were three types of trade cycle – the Juglar (caused by changes in inventories over a eighteen month period), the Kitchin (caused by changes in investment and output over a three or four year period) and the Kondratieff (a long-run, fifty year pattern, with twenty-five years of prosperity and twenty-five years of slow growth and depression).

Scrip issue. An issue of new shares to existing shareholders for which they have to pay nothing extra. It does not raise new money for the business, but it sometimes improves the marketability of the shares.

Seasonal adjustment. When an economist interprets statistics, he will need to know if a rise or a fall from one period to another is significant. A rise in unemployment in the winter, for example, does not mean that conditions in the labour market have deteriorated since it is a normal seasonal movement. Seasonal adjustment is a method of adjusting economic statistics to remove these seasonal factors.

Seasonal unemployment. Unemployment caused by a seasonal fluctuation in demand: a decrease in construction activity because of winter weather, for example, or a lower demand for ice-cream salesmen in the winter than the summer.

Second best, Theory of. When economists develop theories they normally make assumptions about PARAMETERS of the MODELS. For example, when considering the best pricing policy for a nationalized industry, they assume that private firms are pursuing the best pricing policies for society by equating MARGINAL COST and price. However, private firms may not be doing this.

The theory of second best assumes that other features of the economy are not ideal and that, even if it were desirable, it is not possible to make them ideal. It then tries to work out the best policies in one particular part of the economy. It is called second best theory because the remainder of the economy is not working in the best way.

Secondary industry. Secondary industry processes raw materials and makes them into finished goods. It should be contrasted with primary industry which makes raw materials, by extracting them from the ground or by agriculture. For example, making leather into shoes is secondary industry, but raising cattle for their leather is primary industry.

Secondary market. Any market in which the first buyer of a commodity or security sells it to a second buyer without using it to the full. In other words, it is a second-hand market. It is used particularly to describe financial markets where securities are bought and sold many times.

The primary market is the market in which the security is first bought and sold.

Secular trend. A long-term trend in a series of economic statistics. It is usually contrasted with CYCLICAL or short-term changes.

Securities. Claims on assets or income. Their owners are entitled to certain payments from the institution which has issued them. A good example is a government security. When the government issues one it is borrowing money, which it will promise at some date in the future to repay. For the right of using the money now it pays a rate of interest to the owner of the security.

When the institution promises to repay the money, or redeem the security as it is known, at a date not far in the future it is termed a short-dated security. But if the redemption date is many years away it is called a long-dated security. In the case of government securities, the dividing line is five years: any security with a redemption in less than this is a 'short', anything with redemption in more is 'at the longer end'.

Selective employment tax (SET). ◊COMPANY TAXATION.

Separation of ownership from control. Before modern times the person who owned an asset also controlled its use. If a man inherited land or money it was his responsibility to ensure that they were utilized productively and efficiently.

In fact this was not completely true. It was possible to lend to someone else who would then have to repay the money, normally with some extra payments for interest or profit. But there were two problems with lending. The first was the borrower might not be able to repay the money in full. The second was that, if the borrower became bankrupt, the lender, who would of course be involved in the borrower's affairs, might be called upon to pay off all his debts, more even than had initially invested in the business. This situation arose because the investor's liability was unlimited.

Changes in company law which took place in Great Britain in the 1850s and 1860s prevented this possibility. The institution of limited liability was developed. This meant that if someone invested £100 in a 'limited company' and the company lost all of this – and more – the investor lost only £100 and the rest of the company's losses would not be his responsibility. This is the significance of 'Ltd' at the end of a company's name.

The emergence of limited liability caused a considerable increase in the separation of ownership from control. The people who controlled assets – the directors and managers of a company – were often not the same people as those who owned it – the shareholders or the banks. This is the characteristic form of business organization under CAPITAL-ISM today.

Normally shareholders do maintain some control over the company's affairs, through its annual meeting, where they can, if they wish, censure the board of directors or refuse to re-elect them, but this is unusual. At present, if a shareholder is dissatisfied with the way a company is being run, he can sell the shares and buy the shares of another company which he considers to be better managed. In this way the managers who control a company can be held responsible to the shareholders who own it.

Services. Services are productive activities not included in industrial production, agriculture or mining. Their main attribute is that there is no durable and tangible end product. They include, for example, teaching, banking, hairdressing and entertainment.

Servicing debt. ⟡DEBT-SERVICING.

Shadow wage. When an economist is conducting a COST–BENEFIT ANALYSIS of a project he will need to add up the SOCIAL COSTS before he can compare them with the benefits. It may, however, be difficult to determine the social cost of certain inputs because their cost in the market may vary from their cost to society.

The best example is found in developing countries where the government often lays down a minimum wage in the industrial sector much above the average wage in the country as a whole. If this wage is used to evaluate costs the result will be misleading because the real cost of labour is the reduction in output elsewhere as workers are transferred to the project and this will clearly be much less than the artificially high wage suggests.

The shadow wage is the social cost of labour. There are many ways of calculating it and economists have not decided on the best one.

Share. A piece of paper which entitles its owner to receive income in the form of dividends from a company. Because it yields income, money has to be paid before someone can own a share. The amount which has to be paid for each share is known as the share price and this is usually quoted, for each company, on the Stock Exchange.

Share option. ◊OPTION.

Shifting. ◊RIGHTWARD-SHIFTING.

Short-dated securities. ◊SECURITIES.

Short-run. ◊LONG-RUN.

Short-run cost curves. Short-run cost curves show how costs change with output while some inputs are held constant. The inputs held constant are usually land and capital. The increases or decreases in total cost are, consequently, accounted for entirely by changes in variable inputs, such as labour.

Siege economy. An economy where external trade is extensively regulated by the government. A good example of siege economy was the United Kingdom during the Second World War, where production was regulated to ensure maximum output of the required armaments and trade was regulated to ensure that scarce shipping space was utilized for the most essential imports and exports.

Simple correlation and regression. ◊CORRELATION; REGRESSION ANALYSIS.

Simple interest. A method of calculating interest payments. If the principal, or amount borrowed, is £100 and the rate of interest is 10 per cent per annum, the borrower has to repay £110 after the first year or £120 after the second year if the calculation is made according to simple interest. £10 is the interest due for every year of the loan. It never varies, being derived as a percentage of the principal

If, on the other hand, the alternative, compound interest is used, the calculation is performed differently. The borrower may not want to repay £110 after the first year and so the lender may consider that he is now giving £110 of credit. The interest payment for the second year is therefore, calculated as 10 per cent of £110 or £11. If the loan were repaid after two years the repayment would now amount to £121. In other words, the interest due under a compound interest system becomes progressively larger for each year of the loan.

Compound interest is much the most common method used when credit is given in business and commerce.

Sinking fund. A method of paying off debt. A company, realizing that repayment is to become due at some point in the future, sets aside sums in the sinking fund in order to have enough money available at the appointed time. This is a form of good housekeeping. (⟡ NATIONAL DEBT.)

Size distribution of firms. The size distribution of firms is an indicator of MARKET STRUCTURE. It shows how many firms account for a particular percentage of industry output. For example, two firms may account for 90 per cent of the total output of detergents, which would suggest that the market structure is a duopoly.

Slack. ⟡ AGGREGATE DEMAND AND SUPPLY.

Slump. ⟡ RECESSION.

Smithsonian Agreement. The Smithsonian Agreement of December 1971 was reached between the Finance Ministers of the Group of Ten to restore stability to the international monetary system. The dollar was devalued by 8.5 per cent, but the USA agreed to withdraw the 10 per cent surcharge on imports imposed by President Nixon in August 1971. Some European currencies were to be revalued, making the dollar's overall loss of value against them 10 per cent. But the USA refused to make dollars convertible into gold, as had been the case before 1971.

The return of FIXED EXCHANGE RATES heralded by the Smithsonian Agreement was short-lived. But the PARITIES established by Smithsonian now serve as a benchmark for a currency change in value against other currencies.

Smithsonian parities. ⟡ SMITHSONIAN AGREEMENT.

'Snake', The. The 'snake' is an agreement between certain North European countries to keep the exchange rates between one another's currencies fixed. It developed from the attempts of the European Economic Community to bring about a common currency for all its members, as envisaged in the Werner Report of 1970. The first stage of monetary unification was to be the elimination of exchange rate fluctuations between member states, which involved fixing parities. After one or two false starts in 1971 the 'snake' began in 1972, with all nine members of the EEC participating. However, the UK and Eire soon left and, by the end of 1973, both France and Italy had followed. The 'snake' survives, however, for several currencies, including the Deutschemark, the Dutch guilder, the Belgian franc and the Norwegian crown.

In May 1975, the French rejoined the 'snake' only to leave once more in March 1976.

Social accounting. The preparation of NATIONAL INCOME and GROSS NATIONAL PRODUCT statistics. Social accounts show how large the national income is, how much it has grown in recent periods and how large are the contributions of each sector of the economy. In the UK the statistics are prepared by the Central Statistical Office, with considerable help from other government departments.

Social benefits. When an individual or firm carries out some economic action it will have effects on other individuals within society. The economist needs to consider these effects on other individuals before it is possible to decide if the action was socially beneficial.

Social benefits include all the gains in social welfare from an economic action. They are particularly important in COST–BENEFIT ANALYSIS.

Social capital. Capital assets owned by the government. It is mainly composed of the INFRASTRUCTURE which includes, for example, roads, bridges and public parks.

Social cost. The social cost of an activity is the benefit society loses because the activity is being carried out. It may not be the same thing as the cost to the private individuals who are responsible for the activity. For example, if the entrepreneur opens a plastics factory he will cause workers to leave other factories. The reduction in output in these factories is a social cost. The new factory may also pollute the atmosphere – a further social cost.

Social cost is an important concept in COST–BENEFIT ANALYSIS

Social overhead capital. ◊INFRASTRUCTURE.

Social rate of time preference. The social rate of time preference measures how much society prefers CONSUMPTION today to consumption in the future. For example, if the rate were 5 per cent this would mean that the community is indifferent between £100 of consumption now and £105 in a year's time.

Social welfare function. An important idea in WELFARE ECONOMICS. It is assumed that, like an individual or a family, a community has needs or desires for several goods. Economists try to describe these desires by the social welfare function. No attempt has ever been made to calculate such a function in practice, largely because it would be difficult to weigh the relative importance of different people's desires. However, in certain theoretical exercises, the function is useful because it enables society's desires to be compared with society's ability to match those desires by production. It is a tool to help economists decide on the best policies for a community to pursue.

Soft currency. A currency which tends to lose value against other currencies. Since the Second World War the main soft currencies have been those of underdeveloped countries with high rates of inflation, although the pound sterling and the French franc might also be included.

Soft loan. A loan provided at favourable rates of interest to developing countries. It is a form of AID to stimulate their development. The main institution providing soft loans is the International Bank for Reconstruction and Development (◊ WORLD BANK).

Special deposits. Deposits placed by clearing banks with the BANK OF ENGLAND. Although the Bank of England has paid interest on these deposits occasionally, they have generally carried no interest. Consequently clearing banks do not want to place those deposits with the Bank and only do so when a special directive has been sent out to them. The Bank calls in special deposits as a way of tightening credit and holding down the money supply as, when the banks are forced to lend more to the Bank of England, they have to lend less to the public and industry. (◊ COMPETITION AND CREDIT CONTROL.)

Special drawing rights (SDRs). An international reserve asset. This means that, in transactions between central banks in different countries, SDRs are treated as money and are an acceptable way of settling international debts.

Agreement to use SDRs was made in 1969 between members of the Group of Ten. They are issued by the INTERNATIONAL MONETARY FUND, with each SDR equal in value to the DOLLAR before its devaluation in 1971. They can be used as alternatives to gold and RESERVE CURRENCIES and have been christened 'paper gold' as a result.

Specialization. ◊ DIVISION OF LABOUR.

Specific tax. ◊ AD VALOREM TAX.

Speculative motive. One of the reasons for holding money. Before John Maynard Keynes suggested the existence of the speculative motive in his book, *The General Theory of Employment, Interest and Money*, it had been thought that people kept money mainly in order to buy goods or, in other words, for transactions purposes. Keynes argued that people might hold money to wait for better savings opportunities. If they thought the rate of interest was too low and would be certain to rise, they would not want to buy government securities because a rise

191

in interest rates lowers their price. Following the speculative motive they would therefore keep most of their savings in the form of money which would reduce aggregate demand. (◊KEYNESIAN ECONOMICS.)

Spot market. A market in which a commodity is bought or sold for immediate delivery. (◊FUTURES.)

Spot sterling. The exchange rate for spot sterling shows how much foreign currency someone has to pay to obtain one pound sterling now. (He might have to pay a different price if he were ordering pounds for future delivery.)

Squeeze. ◊CREDIT SQUEEZE.

Stability. An economic VARIABLE is said to show stability if it does not change substantially in value from time to time or if it returns quickly to its original value after reaching a different value. For example, a country may have had an increase in its gross national product of 3½ per cent for five or six years, with no deviations to under 3 per cent or over 4 per cent. It is said to have had stable economic growth.

Stabilization policy. Stabilization policy describes government's attempts to control cyclical fluctuations in the economy. It consists of measures to smooth or eliminate sharp ups and downs in demand and output.

The three main targets of economic policy are full employment, price stability and maintaining a balance of payments with other countries. The difficulty is that full employment is usually associated with strong demand for labour, which drives up wages and prices. The government is faced, therefore, with a choice between making sure that there are large numbers of jobs available and increasing inflation. High or full employment policies are also often accompanied by strong demand for imports and this may result in a country buying more from other countries than it is selling to them. Curing the balance of payments deficit may cause unemployment. Again there is a choice between one aim of policy and another.

Stabilization policy is the government's decisions about which objectives should be given priority and its steps to implement those decisions. Its main instruments are the familiar ones of monetary and fiscal policy, although these are sometimes supplemented by more directly interventionist methods such as a prices and incomes policy.

Stabilization policy is concerned with short-term economic measures and is not designed to affect, for example, the growth of particular industries or the balance between different industries. Because it mainly operates by changing the level of AGGREGATE DEMAND the phrase is

often used synonymously with demand management. (◊KEYNESIAN
ECONOMICS.)

Stag. A speculator on the Stock Exchange who makes an offer for
part of a new issue of shares and then sells the shares at a higher price
when full trading in the issue has developed.

'Stagflation'. A situation in which an economy is simultaneously
suffering from stagnation (or slow growth of gross national product),
possibly accompanied by high and rising unemployment, and inflation.

Stagnation. A state of slow or zero growth in an economy or company.
It is a condition of few or no changes and little development. No new
products are introduced and the scale of output is not expanded.

Standard deviation. A measure of how much a set of numbers differs
from their AVERAGE. For example, it is obvious that the average of
both the set of numbers 1, 2 and 3 and the set 0, 2 and 4 is 2, but that
the second set includes 0 and 4, which differ from 2 more than the
first set. The standard deviation for the first set is, therefore, lower
than for the second. The variance is also a measure of dispersion around
an average, but has different mathematical properties from the standard
deviation.
  The standard error is a separate idea. When someone takes a sample
from a population he will not expect the characteristics of the sample
to correspond exactly with the characteristics of the population. The
standard error is a measure of how much a sample should be expected
to vary from the population.

Standard error. ◊STANDARD DEVIATION.

'Stand-by' arrangement. When a country's reserves of gold and foreign
currency are being depleted by a balance of payments deficit or by a
speculative attack on its currency, it may make an arrangement with
the International Monetary Fund whereby it can borrow other currencies from the Fund if need arises. As the country may not necessarily
draw on the Fund if the situation improves, the agreement is known as
a 'stand-by' arrangement.

State planning. ◊PLANNED ECONOMY.

Steady-state growth. A concept used in growth theory, steady-state
growth occurs in an economy growing through time as the same rate,
with all the variables in the same ratio to each other as at the beginning.
For example, although investment is raising the capital stock by, say,
5 per cent a year, population growth is raising the labour force by 5 per

cent a year as well, so that the ratio of capital to labour is unchanged and steady-state growth is achieved.

Sterling area.   The sterling area is now more or less extinct, but it was important for a long period after the Second World War during which a number of countries, particularly members of the British Commonwealth, held their reserves in London in the form of investments in British government securities and Treasury bills. These investments were known as sterling balances. The British government would have been unable to give members of the sterling area dollars or other currencies if they had decided to sell these balances because Britain's own reserves were so limited. Consequently, members of the sterling area adopted measures of exchange control and discriminated against, for example, the USA in trade in order to defend and improve Britain's reserve position.

The decline in the sterling area is mainly attributable to the pound's progressive loss of value in relation to other currencies. Central banks throughout the world have tried to avoid holding sterling in their reserves because each time the pound depreciates the value of their reserves falls. The process has been particularly rapid since the mid-1960s. In 1966 the pound sterling represented 31.9 per cent of world foreign exchange reserves. In 1973 it represented 6.3 per cent. (⟡DOLLAR.)

Sterling balances.   ⟡STERLING AREA.

Stock (1).   Companies usually find it impossible to predict demand and supply perfectly and therefore keep stocks both of finished goods to be sold to their customers and of raw materials to be used in production.

When prices are rising companies benefit from stock appreciation. For example, suppose that a newspaper company owns 100 tons of newsprint which it bought at £10 a ton. If the price of newsprint were to rise to £20 a ton the value of its stock would have increased and it would be better off. Stock appreciation is sometimes included in PROFITS, although there has been some dispute about the correctness of this.

When companies increase the quantity of stocks they hold they are said to be stockbuilding.

Stock (2).   The phrase 'stocks and shares' is commonly used to denote securities bought and sold on the Stock Exchange. Stocks in this phrase refers mainly to gilt-edged securities which are liabilities of the government, while shares refers to equity. Stocks give the same return to nvestors year after year because they are commonly fixed-interest securities. Shares give a variable return, depending on dividends.

Stock appreciation. ⟡STOCK (1).

Stock control. The set of methods used by management to control purchases and sales of stock. The object is to keep stock levels as low as possible while maintaining regularity of production and meeting customers' demands. In the USA stock control is known as inventory analysis.

Stock Exchange. The Stock Exchange is an institution where SHARES and GOVERNMENT SECURITIES are bought and sold. It is one of the characteristic institutions of CAPITALISM because it depends on the prevalence of private property.

There are stock exchanges in most capitalist countries, but the main ones are in New York and London. Their main function, apart from enabling owners of wealth to transfer ownership from asset to asset, is to raise money for industry. For example, a company may want to expand by building a factory and cannot find finance from its own profits or from the banks. By issuing shares – which entitle their owners to a share in the profits of the factory – the company can raise the money on the stock exchange.

To help the flow of business the London Stock Exchange has a system of account periods in which share transactions take place but no cheques pass hands. Account day comes at the end of this period when debts have to be settled.

Stockbroker. A dealer in a stock exchange who takes orders from members of the public to buy and sell shares. He may advise his clients on the wisdom of their purchases, but his main job is to execute the orders. The stockbroker does not himself own shares.

Stockbuilding. ⟡STOCK (1).

Stop-go. In the 1950s and 1960s the British economy grew in fits and starts. A year of growth would be followed by a year of slower growth and later by a year of no growth, a cycle which happened several times in succession. This pattern of economic expansion was known as stop-go.

The era of stop-go was generally considered to be one in which STABILIZATION POLICY failed to keep the economy in balance and made it difficult for businessmen to forecast ahead. For this reason it was sometimes blamed for Britain's poor rate of economic growth.

Stop-loss selling. ⟡TECHNICAL FACTORS.

Structural unemployment. Unemployment caused by a long-term decline in an industry due to a change in demand or to technical innovation. For example, unemployment in the shipbuilding industry in the UK has been caused by shipowners placing orders abroad. It is not due to a weakness of aggregate demand because it coincides with prosperity and high employment elsewhere in the economy. The main features of structural unemployment are, therefore, that it tends to be long-term, it has to be removed by specific measures aimed at the industry it affects, and that it co-exists with high employment in other industries.

Subsidies. Payments to a company, almost always by the government, which do not have to be met by the supply of goods or services. They typically cover a loss made by a company in its business operations and prevent the company becoming insolvent. Another important form of subsidy is to the agricultural industry, intended to encourage domestic output of food.

Economists are usually highly critical of subsidies. The reason is that they enable companies whose output is not in much demand to attract resources from other companies whose output is popular and easy to sell. Consequently, the popular companies are unable to produce as much as the public would like and resource allocation is distorted.

Subsistence theory of wages. Before the nineteenth century most economists assumed that wages could not rise much above subsistence level – or the minimum level required for survival. The reason was that, if any surplus above subsistence emerged, standards of nutrition and health would improve and the population would grow. But with the growth of population there would be fewer goods for each person and, sooner or later, wages would return to subsistence level. This doctrine, which has been proved wrong by the continuous improvement in living standards in the industrial countries since the beginning of the nineteenth century, is associated with MALTHUSIANISM.

Substitutes. Goods which are alternatives to each other in their main uses. If the supply of a good falls, the demand for its substitute rises. Complements, on the other hand, are goods which tend to be used together. If the supply of a good contracts the demand for its complement decreases.

There are more technical definitions of substitutes and complements which are expressed in terms of the MARGINAL RATE OF SUBSTITUTION.

Substitution effect. When the price of a good rises, consumers tend to buy less of it and more of something else. They are said to have substituted another good for the good which has increased in price. Another effect of the price rise will be that consumers are worse off – their incomes will buy less than before. Consequently they may cut down on their purchases of all goods, not only of the good which has increased in price.

The substitution effect is the effect of a price change on the consumption of two goods *as if income were unchanged*. It attempts to isolate the impact of a price rise on the quantities of goods consumed as if the price rise has not affected income. (◊INCOME EFFECT.)

Supplementary costs. A synonym for FIXED COSTS.

Supply. The quantity of a good which a firm or individual wishes to sell at a certain price. The conditions of supply are the conditions under which goods are produced, sold and distributed. In economics the analysis of supply is conducted with the help of the theory of the firm and the theory of production.

The main purpose of supply analysis is to determine the prices at which goods can be offered for sale and the quantities that should be produced. Normally it assumes that a businessman will want to maximize profits and then examines the effect of this on supply.

The two main technical tools of supply analysis are cost curves and supply curves.

Cost curves show how costs change as output changes. The businessman wants to maximize the difference between total sales receipts and total costs. He sets output at such a level that any change in output would not be worthwhile because the addition to total sales receipts would be less than the addition to total costs. This idea of 'the addition to total costs from changing output by one unit' is extremely important in discussing supply. It is known as MARGINAL COST.

The most valuable type of cost curve, therefore, is the marginal cost curve. The law of DIMINISHING RETURNS implies that marginal cost falls at certain levels of output, but then begins to rise. A typical marginal cost curve has the shape shown in Figure 12.

Supply curves show how the quantity of a good a businessman offers for sale depends on the price. The common-sense rule that the higher the price, the more will be produced and put on sale is roughly correct, but one of the achievements of economic theory is to show that the relationship does depend on MARKET STRUCTURE. In some circumstances the response of supply will be weaker than in others.

Under conditions of PERFECT COMPETITION the marginal cost curve is the supply curve. In other words, the businessman behaves in such a way that price is equated to marginal cost and any change in price, because of a change in demand, will cause him to move up or down the marginal cost curve. The reason for this is that the price a businessman can charge under perfect competition does not depend on his own output decision because he is only one of a large number of producers. The addition to total revenue from selling one more unit of output, or MARGINAL REVENUE, is, therefore, the same as the price. The businessman maximizes profits by setting marginal cost equal to marginal revenue, which in this case means setting marginal cost equal to price. This situation is shown in Figure 13.

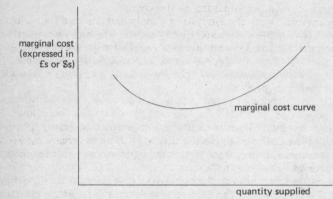

Figure 12. Typical marginal cost curve.

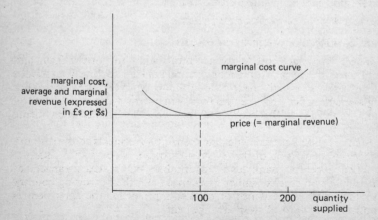

Figure 13. Determination of supply in perfectly competitive industry.

Many other price and output combinations are possible, depending on the number of sellers and the degree of collusion between them. Supply analysis uses cost curves and supply curves under varying assumptions to show which combinations are likely, possible or desirable.

Supply and demand. The forces which determine output and prices in the absence of government interference. They are often regarded as MARKET FORCES, although both the supply and demand for a good may be affected by RESTRICTIVE PRACTICES or artificial barriers to trade created by a manufacturer or merchant.

In economic theory the analysis of supply and demand is conducted by means of demand curves and supply curves, which show respectively how quantity demanded and quantity supplied respond to changes in price. The EQUILIBRIUM price–output combination is determined by the intersection of demand and supply curves. (♢SUPPLY; DEMAND (2).)

Supply curve. ♢SUPPLY.

Support facilities. When a central bank is running out of reserves because of a balance of payments deficit or because money is flowing out of a country, it may want to borrow from an international institution, such as the INTERNATIONAL MONETARY FUND, or from other countries. If it obtains the right to borrow money it is said to have support facilities, which can be used to defend or support the exchange rate. Support facilities are rather like an individual's overdraft facilities, except that they are available to countries.

Surplus, Trade. ♢BALANCE OF TRADE.

Surplus value. ♢MARXIAN ECONOMICS.

'Swaps'. Arrangements between central banks to borrow from and lend currencies to each other if one central bank is suffering from serious loss of reserves. Usually reserves are running down because of a balance of payments deficit and a central bank will borrow from another central bank, promising to pay back the money when the balance of payments has improved.

Some of these arrangements, the General Agreements to Borrow, are under the supervision of the INTERNATIONAL MONETARY FUND.

When a central bank lends to another, but makes arrangement whereby it will receive similar assistance from the borrowing country should it also face balance of payments problems, the agreement is known as a reciprocal swap arrangement.

Switching. The owner of an asset may want to own a different asset.

For example, the owner of equity may want to buy government securities. When he carried out the transfer, by selling his equities and buying the securities, he is said to have 'switched' from one to the other. Switching, rather than fresh buying, is the commonest form of transaction on most stock exchanges.

T

Take-off. ◊ECONOMIC GROWTH.

Take-over. The purchase of one company by another usually through buying up the majority of its issued capital on the Stock Exchange. A take-over is similar to a MERGER, but a take-over situation involves a conflict between one management and another for the support of shareholders, whereas a merger tends to occur after an amicable agreement between two companies that it is in their mutual interests to combine.

The most famous wave of take-over bids in Britain took place in the late 1960s. A number of large but ailing companies were taken over by companies which, if not much larger in terms of sales revenue, were much more profitable and better run. The principal examples were the acquisition of Associated Electrical Industries by the General Electric Company to form the company now known simply as the General Electrical Company or GEC, and the merging of several small firms in the British motor industry to create the British Leyland Motor Corporation (now British Leyland).

When one company buys another it can offer the shareholders of the acquired company cash or shares. Because shares can be a form of payment, take-over activity seems to depend very much on the level of the Stock Exchange.

Tap issue. When the British government is spending more than it is receiving in taxation, it has to borrow from the public. It can do so by selling government securities. However, rather than selling a large number of issues at the same time which would be cumbersome, the government sells a smaller number, usually three or four, which are known as tap issues.

Tariff, Import. ◊IMPORT TARIFF.

Tax, *Ad valorem*. ◊AD VALOREM TAX.

Tax avoidance. The attempt to reduce a tax bill by taking advantage of loopholes and concessions in the tax system. It is not illegal. In contrast, tax evasion – the refusal to notify the tax authorities of tax liability and the subsequent withholding of tax – is illegal.

Tax base. The value of an output or income on which tax is levied. For example, the tax base in the UK includes the incomes of all those earning more than about £700 a year and VALUE ADDED in industry and distribution, because the UK has both income tax and value added tax. But until recently it has not included wealth, because the UK has not operated a wealth tax. (◊PERSONAL TAXATION; INDIRECT TAXATION.)

Tax credit scheme. ◊PERSONAL TAXATION.

Tax evasion. ◊TAX AVOIDANCE.

Tax gathering season. The months of the fiscal year in which a number of important taxes are paid. In the UK the tax gathering season falls in December, January and February, when companies pay corporation tax. The bunching of tax payments in this period sometimes causes temporary liquidity strains to companies and the banking system. (◊COMPANY TAXATION.)

Tax incidence. The person or institution on whom the burden of paying a tax ultimately rests. For example, an indirect tax raises the price of a good, but it is not only the consumer who suffers. Less will be bought, reducing the incomes of retailers. The tax incidence is shared between the consumer and retailer. (◊INDIRECT TAXATION.)

Tax, Progressive. ◊PROGRESSIVE TAX.

Tax, Regressive. ◊REGRESSIVE TAX.

Tax reserve certificates. ◊COMPANY TAXATION.

Taxation. The raising of money from private individuals and institutions by the government to pay for services and goods provided by the the state. Taxation can be either direct or indirect. (◊INDIRECT TAXATION; COMPANY TAXATION; PERSONAL TAXATION.)

Technical factors. Influences on prices in markets not connected with changes in underlying supply and demand conditions. The phrase 'technical factors' is particularly common in reports on the Stock Exchange and is contrasted with changes in sentiment.

Two good examples are bear-closing and stop-loss selling. Bear-closing occurs when a speculator has promised to sell shares at a future date at a price similar to the current price. If he is lucky and the price falls, he then can buy them at the lower price to meet his obligation to sell. Because this adds to the demand for shares their price rises and the fall comes to a stop. Stop-loss selling arises because speculators want to sell their shares when the price is falling to prevent a possible small profit being converted into a loss.

Technical progress. Improvements in technique which allow fewer inputs to produce the same output. Another concept of technical progress is the invention of new products which are superior to old products, but are not easy to compare in terms of size or weight and cannot, therefore, be said to represent increased output.

If the same level of output is produced, the inputs saved can be either labour or capital. If the tendency of technical progress is to cause greater economies in the use of labour than capital it is said to be labour-saving. If it causes equal economies of labour and capital it is said to be neutral.

Terms of trade. A measure of how many exports have to be produced by a country to pay for a certain quantity of imports. If the terms of trade fall (or 'deteriorate'), more exports have to be sent abroad to obtain the same quantity of imports; if they rise (or 'improve') fewer exports are needed.

The terms of trade are usually expressed as a ratio between an INDEX NUMBER of the price of exports and an index number of the price of imports. The base of 100 relates to a starting point against which comparisons can be made. For example, the base of 100 may apply to 1970. If, by 1974, the terms of trade have risen to 133, this means that the same quantity of exports will obtain one-third more imports than in 1970.

Tertiary industry. Sometimes used as a synonym for the service sector of the economy. For example, school-teaching and hairdressing are tertiary industries.

Theory of distribution. ⇨INCOME DISTRIBUTION.

Theory of games. ⇨GAMES, THEORY OF.

Theory of income determination. ⇨INCOME DETERMINATION, THEORY OF.

Theory of second best. ⇨SECOND BEST, THEORY OF.

Theory of the firm. ⇨FIRM, THEORY OF.

Theory of value. ⇨DEMAND (2).

Third World. ⇨DEVELOPING COUNTRY.

Threshold agreements. A form of wage settlement. A flat percentage increase of the normal kind is given regardless of the rate of price inflation, but, should prices rise faster than a certain recognized level, or threshold, during the period covered by the agreement, workers are entitled to an extra rise for each 1 per cent increase above the threshold. Threshold agreements formed part of the British government's counter-inflation programme of 1972–4. Under stage three of the programme every worker with a threshold agreement was entitled to a 40p addition to his weekly pay for every 1 per cent increase in the RETAIL PRICE INDEX more than 6 per cent above the October 1973 level.

Tied aid. When an advanced country gives aid to a developing country its balance of payments deteriorates because it is sending money abroad. To minimize this effect advanced countries often insist that the money sent as aid should be spent on their exports. For example, if the UK arranged a tied loan with India, India has to spend part or all of the proceeds of the loan on UK exports.

Tied loan. ◊TIED AID.

Tight money. ◊CREDIT SQUEEZE.

Time deposit (USA). A term used in the USA for money deposited with a bank for a period of time. A time deposit corresponds to the British deposit account. A deposit which may be drawn on at any time is known as a charge account. This corresponds to the British current account.

Time preference. Most people place different valuations today on consumption they will be carrying out today and consumption they expect to carry out at some date in the future. For example, if someone offered an individual the choice between £100 of consumption this week and £100 of consumption in a year's time, he would probably prefer the £100 today. But he might be indifferent between £100 today and £110 in a year's time. To describe an individual's preference between present and future consumption is to describe his rate of time preference.

Time series. A run of statistics for several periods of time. For example a table showing investment in every year from 1960 to 1975 is a time series of investment figures. (◊CROSS-SECTION ANALYSIS.)

***Times* Share Index.** An index number of prices of securities traded on the London Stock Exchange published daily in *The Times* newspaper. Although superior in its method of compilation, it is less widely quoted than the *Financial Times* Industrial Ordinary Index. (◊FINANCIAL TIMES STOCK INDICES.)

Trade barrier. Any obstacle to the free flow of international trade between countries. Import tariffs and quotas are both trade barriers. (▷IMPORT TARIFF; IMPORT RESTRICTIONS.)

Trade bill. ▷BILL OF EXCHANGE.

Trade credit. When a merchant buys goods from a manufacturer, the manufacturer may not press for immediate payment because the buyer may be an old customer and there is no doubt about his ability to pay eventually. The manufacturer is said to have extended trade credit to his customer. It depends on goodwill and trust between buyer and seller.

Trade cycle. Business conditions vary over time, with years of high economic activity and employment being followed by years of low economic activity and UNEMPLOYMENT. A period of several years' length which includes an economic upswing and downturn is known as a trade cycle.

Since 1945 the adoption of Keynesian demand management techniques by governments has made the size of the change in conditions from the point of peak activity to the point of least activity – or the amplitude of the cycle – much smaller. Production has not risen by leaps and bounds and then collapsed dramatically, while employment levels have generally been well maintained. Consequently, the trade cycle as such is sometimes regarded as a phenomenon of the pre-Keynesian period.

The more mild trade cycle of recent years has occasionally been called the business cycle. The term inventory investment cycle is used to describe changes in activity caused by businessmen running down and building up stocks, although demand for their goods may not have changed significantly. (▷KEYNESIAN ECONOMICS.)

Trade diversion and trade creation. ▷CUSTOMS UNION.

Transactions costs. The buying and selling of goods involve the use of resources. For example, when someone buys a machine he has to inspect it in advance to check its reliability and a salesman has to demonstrate how it works. These costs, which may have nothing to do with the production of the good, are known as transactions costs.

Transactions demand. A motive for holding money, which arises solely from the need to finance future transactions, is known as the transactions demand. This may seem an obvious idea, but it is actually quite difficult to explain why people have money balances at all. As money does not in itself yield utility it would seem to be sensible for them to spend all their income as soon as it is received. In practice they cannot be certain of the time-pattern of their spending and they therefore hold money to make sure they can buy goods when they want them. The transactions demand for money depends mainly on INCOME.

Transfer income. ◊TRANSFER PAYMENTS.

Transfer payments. Numerous individuals receive income from the state or institutions for no productive activity. Such income is known as transfer income because it is transferred via government from those who make goods to others. Payments of transfer income are known as transfer payments.

They should be compared with payments of factor income which are rewards for producing goods and services. The principal forms of transfer income are pensions and social security benefits. Profits and dividends are factor incomes because they are rewards for enterprise, risk and saving.

Transfer pricing. ◊MULTINATIONAL CORPORATION.

Transformation curve. A concept in the theory of production and welfare economics.

A country is assumed to be able to produce two goods, say, X and Y. If it reduces production of X it is possible to release resources to the production of good Y. In other words the country has a choice between different combinations of good X and good Y. The transformation curve shows which combinations are possible given the country's factor endowments and its technology.

The transformation curve is also known as the production possibility curve. It normally has the shape shown in Figure 14 because of the law of DIMINISHING RETURNS.

Treasury bills. When the British government wants to borrow money for short-period it issues Treasury bills. These are promises to repay the holder £5000 ninety-one days from the date of issue. Normally, the buyer of a Treasury bill will have to pay on the date of issue a sum like £4900, the difference depending on the rate of interest he could have obtained if he had invested his money elsewhere. The Treasury bill issue, which is carried out through the discount houses, is, therefore, an important indicator of interest rate conditions.

Trend. Economic statistics are distorted by a great number of exceptional and non-recurring factors. The trend is the underlying behaviour of a variable shown by statistics which have been adjusted to exclude the effect of such factors.

Trust (1). An arrangement whereby assets owned by an individual or family are administered by another group of people, usually a financial institution. A trust is sometimes convenient to ensure continuity. For example, when a wealthy man dies his son may be too young to manage his inheritance and the job can be given to a trust until he has attained a mature age. Trusts have certain tax and legal privileges.

Trust (2).   In the USA, a very large company formed by the amalgamation of several small ones.

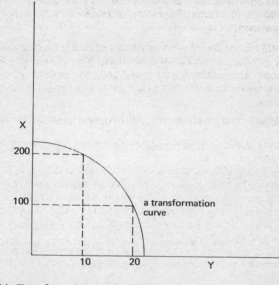

Figure 14. Transformation curve. With its resources of men and equipment, Ruritania can produce 200 cars and 10 ships. If it wants to increase production of ships from 10 to 20, it can do so, but it will only be able to produce 100 cars, because men and equipment have to be transferred to the shipyards from the car factories.

Turnover.   The total sales receipts of a company.

Turnover tax.   ▷INDIRECT TAXATION.

Two-tier exchange rate.   ▷EXCHANGE RATE.

Two-tier gold market.   In 1968 there were widespread expectations that the dollar would soon be devalued. This would have meant that the same quantity of gold could be exchanged for a larger number of dollars. As a result there was heavy pressure on the USA's gold reserves, held by the FEDERAL RESERVE, as speculators tried to switch from

207

dollars to gold before the devaluation took place. The USA was reluctant to devalue the dollar because it would have endangered the BRETTON WOODS system. To prevent the speculation, therefore, the US government decided not to give gold for dollars to private individuals in future, but only to deal at the official price of $35 per ounce of gold with central banks. The effect of this was to create a two-tier gold market in which the demand and supply for gold from private individuals in the free market established a different price from the $35 an ounce price which continued to prevail until 1971 in official transactions.

U

Uncertainty. Uncertainty has a precise meaning in economics and is to be distinguished from the related notion of RISK. An action may have a number of outcomes. For example, an investment in a factory may yield a return of 5, 10 or 15 per cent on capital. When it is possible to say that there is a 20 per cent likelihood of a 5 per cent return, a 50 per cent likelihood of a 10 per cent return and a 30 per cent likelihood of a 15 per cent return, risk is said to attach to the investment. But when it is impossible to make any precise judgement about the likely return the investment is said to be subject to uncertainty.

In many economic discussions uncertainty is used more loosely than this to indicate doubt about the future course of events.

Undated securities; also known as irredeemable securities. The money raised by the issue of most gilt-edged securities is eventually repaid (or redeemed, as it is known) by the government. But there is one category of gilts, undated securities, which the government never redeems. Instead it pays a rate of interest for ever. War Loan is a good example. For every £100 nominal value owned by an individual he receives £3.50 every year. But, if interest rates generally rise, the yield from War Loan has to rise in step. If the typical rate of interest on similar securities is 7 per cent, the market value of the holding has to fall to £50 and the yield on War Loan would then also be 7 per cent.

Underdeveloped country. ▷DEVELOPING COUNTRY.

Undervalued currency. When a country's exports are cheap compared to the exports of other countries, it is easy for the country to sell increasing amounts of its products abroad. This may cause a large balance of payments surplus. The cheapness of its exports may be due to the exchange rate it has chosen. It is possible to obtain too many units of its currency with a particular number of units of other currencies. Consequently the currency is said to be undervalued.

In the opposite case, when too few units of a country's currency can be obtained by exchanging them for units of other currencies and its exports are too expensive, the currency is said to be overvalued.

Unemployment. The level of unemployment can be considered as 'the total number of men and women of working age without a job'. High unemployment is universally considered a great social and economic evil, because it results in loss of production and deprives a large number of individuals of the chance to work and earn a living. Consequently, one of the principal objectives of economic policy is to minimize unemployment.

However, the idea of unemployment is more difficult to define than might at first appear. Most women of working age are housewives and, although they do not have a job, they cannot be considered unemployed. Furthermore, some men, for example, those with large personal fortunes who can live off the income from their capital, also do not seek employment, but cannot be regarded as workless. Other men, including the handicapped and the mentally unstable, are unemployable and, although they are part of the unemployment total, it would be wrong to raise AGGREGATE DEMAND in order to make jobs so abundant that employers are tempted to add them to their labour forces in default of a better alternative.

These difficulties make a clear-cut definition of the full employment level elusive. This is important because government in the United Kingdom, and in other countries, have accorded priority since the Second World War to maintaining full employment. Some economists have been critical of this commitment because, they claim, the full employment targets have been too ambitious.

If unemployment is held at low levels by Keynesian stabilization policy (◇KEYNESIAN ECONOMICS) it becomes increasingly difficult for employers to recruit new workers. As a result they tend to bid up wages. This causes an increase in costs and eventually prices. There is a relationship, therefore, between unemployment and INFLATION. This relationship is sometimes attributed to the effect of full employment on trade union bargaining power. It is said that, when the demand for labour is high, trade unions are less afraid to ask for substantial pay increases and these contribute to excessive price rises.

There are many reasons for unemployment. Some of the better known are changes in demand from season to season, or seasonal unemployment; unemployment caused by a downturn in demand due to the TRADE CYCLE, or cyclical unemployment; and unemployment due to a change in the structure of demand (for example, consumers changing their preferences for heating to oil or gas central heating and therefore buying less coal), or STRUCTURAL UNEMPLOYMENT.

The degree of unemployment is sometimes expressed as a percentage or proportion of the total labour force. It is then known as the unemployment rate. This shows how many in a typical sample of 100 workers are out of work. In the United Kingdom the unemployment rate for most of the 1950s and 1960s was under 3 per cent, but in the 1970s it has tended to rise much higher, to over 4 per cent.

Unemployment rate.   ◊UNEMPLOYMENT.

Unfilled vacancies.   In most countries there are always some employers who are looking for more workers. They may announce this through job advertisements in newspapers or by informing official employment agencies. When an employer is trying to increase his labour force in this way he is said to have vacancies or unfilled vacancies.

In most advanced industrial countries the government encourages labour mobility and attempts to keep UNEMPLOYMENT at a minimum by establishing an official employment agency. Here both unemployed workers and employers with unfilled vacancies can register.

In the United Kingdom the official employment agencies are known as Employment Offices. They were formerly called Labour Exchanges.

Unit of account (UA).   The standard of value of the EUROPEAN ECONOMIC COMMUNITY. Contracts between member countries are expressed in terms of the unit of account rather than in terms of any one currency. This is because currencies change value in relation to each other after devaluations and revaluations.

United Nations Conference on Trade and Development (Unctad).   In 1964 a conference was called where members of the United Nations discussed the problems of the DEVELOPING COUNTRIES and considered ways of easing them. The conference was named the United Nations Conference on Trade and Development. Further conferences were held in 1968 and 1972.

The main subjects of discussion have been the removal of trade barriers on industrial products made in the developing countries, the stabilization of commodity prices, the provision of sufficient INTERNATIONAL LIQUIDITY to the poorer countries and the best methods of giving international aid.

User cost.   The fall in the value of a machine or other item of capital resulting from its use. It is similar to DEPRECIATION, but differs slightly in that it is an economic rather than accountancy term and because user cost is not incurred if the machine is idle.

Utility.   The satisfaction derived from the CONSUMPTION of a good. All economic actions are motivated by the attempt to maximize utility and it is, therefore, an important concept in economic theory. Although there is a dispute about whether or not it is possible to measure utility, economists are agreed that a useful theory of choice can be built up from statements like 'Individual A buys two apples rather than two pears because the two apples give him more utility.' In this kind of statement there is no need to say exactly how much utility he derives from either choice.

V

Vacancies. ▷UNFILLED VACANCIES.

Value. Value is used in two senses in economics – as a synonym for price and as a measure of the worth of a good or service. An economist tends to be suspicious of the idea of absolute value. A good only has value relative to another good. For example, he might say that 'a diamond is valuable' but what he really means is 'one diamond is valuable compared to one unit of coal.'

Value added. There are often several stages in the making of a product. For example, a piece of furniture becomes available to the consumer only after wood has been cut, sold to a timber merchant and then put together by a furniture manufacturer. The total sales of the furniture manufacturer may amount to, say, £100 000 but it is clear that he alone is not responsible for all this production. The timber company which cut the trees and the timber merchant also contributed. If the furniture manufacturer paid £60 000 to the timber merchant, the manufacturer's value added (or net output) is £40 000. In other words, a company's or industry's value added is that part of total output for which it is responsible. The sum of all value added in an economy is equal to the economy's total output.

Value added tax (VAT). ▷INDIRECT TAXATION.

Variable. A statistic which can change its value. In economics, this statistic generally relates to a feature or TREND within an economic system. For example, both consumption and investment can change in value in response to changes in government spending. In a discussion on the economy, therefore, consumption and investment would be referred to as variables.

Variable costs; also known as direct costs. Costs which can vary in response to changes in output. For example, most companies can buy fewer raw materials and some can lay off workers with little delay. Costs such as these, which vary directly with output in the short-run, are known as variable costs.

Variable production coefficients. ⬦COEFFICIENTS OF PRODUCTION.

Variable proportions, Law of. ⬦DIMINISHING RETURNS, LAW OF.

Variance. ⬦STANDARD DEVIATION.

Vector. ⬦MATRIX.

Velocity of circulation. ⬦QUANTITY THEORY OF MONEY.

Vertical integration.   When a company is carrying out several stages of the production process in one factory or under one management, it is said to be vertically integrated. The most extreme case of vertical integration arises when a company is responsible for extracting a raw material, processing it and making it into a finished product. Large tobacco companies are good examples. They sometimes own tobacco plantations, as well as making and marketing cigarettes.

   The integration of a company has a wider meaning. It might involve combining the operations of several factories in one factory or it could refer to a MERGER

Visible balance. ⬦BALANCE OF TRADE.

Visible trade.   International trade in merchandise, such as finished manufactures or raw materials. It should be contrasted with invisible trade, which arises mainly from services provided by one country to another. (⬦INVISIBLES.)

W

Wage drift. The tendency for EARNINGS (1) to rise faster than wage rates. This tendency is particularly strong during periods of excess demand because employers find that they cannot recruit enough workers by paying the normal rates. They therefore pay more or raise overtime.

Wage freeze. ◊PRICES AND INCOMES POLICY.

Wage fund theory. A theory popular in the eighteenth and early nineteenth centuries that wages cannot be increased because employers only have a limited amount of money to pay workers. If wages are increased, consumption also increases and savings must fall. But, if savings fall, there will be less available to pay workers in the next period. The theory is fallacious and is now forgotten.

Wage–price spiral. A self-generating upward movement in wages and prices. If prices are rising, wages have to rise in step to preserve purchasing power. But, if wages rise, costs are increased and employers have again to raise prices to preserve profit margins. The further increase in prices gives added impetus to more wage increases and the process continues. (◊INFLATION.)

Wage rates. ◊EARNINGS (1).

Wall Street. The largest STOCK EXCHANGE in the world. It is situated in Wall Street, New York, and is the centre of American CAPITALISM.

Walrasian. ◊EQUILIBRIUM.

War Loan. ◊UNDATED SECURITIES.

Warehousing. A method of TAKE-OVER. It consists in the buying of a company's shares discreetly without letting the company know, for example, by making the purchases through several subsidiaries of the same financial institution. It is generally regarded as unfair and has been the subject of considerable disapproval.

Warranted growth rate. ⟡ECONOMIC GROWTH.

Ways and means advances. ⟡BANK OF ENGLAND.

Wealth. An individual's wealth is the total value of his assets. This is usually thought to consist of tangible objects, claims to tangible objects and claims to income from tangible objects. But there is also a view that an individual's ability to earn income over a period of years is part of his wealth. The reasoning behind this is that a professional man at the start of his career can expect to receive much higher incomes because of his training and education than a labourer, although the labourer may have more money in the bank. The professional man's expectations enable him to borrow money and to live in a better way than the labourer.

The main characteristic of wealth, therefore, is that it yields income or UTILITY in the future.

Wealth tax. ⟡PERSONAL TAXATION.

Weights. Measures of the importance attached to the different components in an economic statistic. For example, if an economist wants to say how much the retail price index has increased, he has to look at the prices of several goods in the shops. But bread is more important than tooth-paste and therefore is given a greater weight.

Welfare economics. The branch of economics which tries to derive rules for the best policy a country can adopt to maximize UTILITY. These rules relate to such economic variables as prices and investment. One of the most well known is the principle of marginal cost pricing (⟡MARGINAL COST).

Welfare economics is distinguished from other parts of economics by its emphasis on social benefits. The theory of the firm and similar branches of the subject, on the other hand, are concerned with the way businessmen behave to maximize benefits to themselves. Welfare economics is closely related to political and moral philosophy because of its concern with the advantages to the community as a whole of economic activity.

The notion of CONSUMER SURPLUS is central to welfare economics. It can be regarded as the benefit to the consumer from buying a particular quantity of a good rather than buying none at all.

Windfall gains and losses. Changes in asset values which make people better or worse off. They are called 'windfalls' because the individuals concerned may have done nothing to achieve them. For example, changes in Stock Exchange prices have a windfall character. They are believed to affect consumption patterns. If someone makes a capital gain he feels better off and spends a higher proportion of his income.

Window dressing.   A practice common among central banks and other financial institutions which conceals the underlying financial position by reclassifications and redefinitions of their holdings. For example, a central bank may have suffered a loss of reserves. It may not want to publish the figures showing how large the loss has been because it thinks this would affect confidence. It may, therefore, borrow reserves from other central banks and these borrowings then mask the deterioration which has actually taken place.

Working capital; also known as floating capital.   The part of the money used by a company to pay for recurring items of expenditure such as labour and raw materials. The most important form of working capital is bank deposits or overdrafts. Working capital is to be contrasted with fixed capital, that is plant, machinery and buildings.

World Bank; also known as the International Bank for Reconstruction and Development (or IBRD). It is an international institution for encouraging investment in the developing countries. It was set up in 1947 at the same time as the International Monetary Fund and the two institutions have a common membership. Its funds are provided by the members or obtained by borrowing on international financial markets.

X

X-efficiency. The measure of the extent to which the efficiency of production comes up to the highest possible levels. It may, for example, be possible to obtain 60, 80 or 100 units of output from the same combination of inputs. The manager who only succeeds in producing 60 units is plainly less efficient than the manager who produces 100 units. His level of X-efficiency is said to be lower.

X-efficiency is very similar to the less well-defined notion of productive efficiency found in popular discussions of managerial success or failure. (◇ECONOMIC EFFICIENCY.)

Y

Yield. The income from an asset expressed as a proportion or percentage of its current market price. Yields are most commonly used in reference to shares or gilts. On undated securities the investor is never repaid the money he has put in, but receives an interest income indefinitely. This interest income is said to be the flat yield. When the government does repay the money invested, the expectation of redemption affects the interest income which can be expected until the redemption date. The redemption yield includes both the interest received until then and the repayment of the capital sum.

The yield curve is an important concept in investment analysis, particularly for fixed-interest securities. It shows how yields increase on securities as the redemption date moves further into the future. A

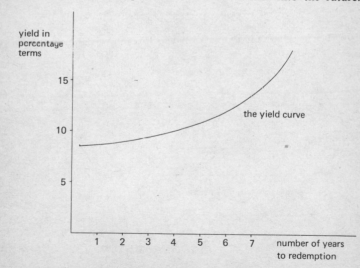

Figure 15. Yield curve.

security which will be redeemed in twenty years' time would probably show a higher yield than a security to be redeemed in a year's time (see Figure 15).

Yield curve. ⇨ YIELD.

Yield gap. Risky forms of investment normally show a higher yield than riskless. It used to be customary, therefore, for equities to show a higher yield than gilts. However, inflation has reduced the attractiveness of gilts and today gilts show a higher yield than equities.

When equities showed a higher yield than gilts the gap between them was known as the yield gap. Today, when the opposite applies, the gap is known as the reverse yield gap.

Z

Zero-sum game.   A concept in the theory of games. In certain types of economic activity, one person cannot be made better off without making someone else worse off. This type of activity is known as a zero-sum game. For example, if two companies are fighting for the control of a market, the increase of one firm's market share will always correspond exactly to the other firm's loss of market share.

Guide to Further Reading

There are many books on economics, but very few which explain the basic ideas simply. The two most important branches of the subject are microeconomics and macroeconomics.

Microeconomics

Microeconomics is mainly concerned with the determination of individual prices, like the prices of cars or meat, in the economic system. A good general textbook which is particularly strong on microeconomics is R. G. Lipsey, *An Introduction to Positive Economics*, Weidenfeld & Nicolson, 4th edition, 1975.

For readers who feel they would like to try something more difficult, W. J. L. Ryan, *Price Theory*, Macmillan, 3rd edition, 1976, is recommended.

K. Lancaster, *An Introduction to Modern Microeconomics*, Rand McNally, 1975.

Macroeconomics

P. Samuelson, *Economics*, McGraw Hill, 9th edition, 1973, is a justly famous textbook which has sold several million copies around the world. It is better on macroeconomics than on microeconomics, but covers both very well.

For an even easier guide, J. Pen, *Modern Economics,* Penguin Books, 1974, should be mentioned.

Recent Economic Developments

Many readable books are available, but S. Brittan, *Steering the Economy*, Macmillan; Penguin Books, 1971, should be singled out as the best single-volume account of post-1951 economic mismanagement in Britain.

Political Economy

For the larger implications of economics, two books must be mentioned:

S. Brittan, *Capitalism and the Permissive Society*, Macmillan, 1973.
J. Robinson, *Economic Philosophy*, Penguin Books, 1964.

More Specialized Reading

A number of short textbooks on particular aspects have been published. The Penguin Modern Economics series includes several useful texts, but most of the books are pitched at a high level and should not be treated as introductory reading.

The following books are suggested as additional and more advanced reading in specialized areas of economics.

THE THEORY OF THE FIRM

P. W. S. Andrews, *Manufacturing Business*, Macmillan, 2nd edition, 1976.
G. C. Archibald (ed.), *The Theory of the Firm*, Penguin Books, 1971.
E. H. Chamberlin, *The Theory of Monopolistic Competition*, Harvard University Press, 1933.
J. K. Galbraith, *American Capitalism*, Penguin Books, 1963.
J. Robinson, *The Economics of Imperfect Competition*, Macmillan, 2nd edition, 1969.

THE THEORY OF MONEY

A. Crocket, *Money: Theory, Policy and Institutions*, Nelson, 1973.
M. Friedman, *The Optimum Quantity of Money*, Macmillan, 1969
C. Goodhart, *Money, Information and Uncertainty*, Macmillan, 1975.
W. T. Newlyn, *The Theory of Money*, Oxford University Press, 1962.

GROWTH ECONOMICS

R. F. Harrod, *Towards a Dynamic Economics*, Macmillan, 1973.
S. Kuznets, *Economic Growth and Structure*, Norton, 1965.
R. C. O. Matthews, *The Trade Cycle*, Nisbet; Cambridge University Press, 1959.
J. E. Meade, *A Neo-Classical Theory of Economic Growth*, Allen & Unwin, 2nd edition, 1964.

INTERNATIONAL ECONOMICS

W. M. Clarke, *The City in the World Economy*, Penguin Books, 1967.

R. F. Harrod, *Reforming the World's Money*, Macmillan, 1965.

H. G. Johnson, *The World Economy at the Crossroads*, Oxford University Press, 1965.

C. P. Kindleberger, *International Economics*, Allen & Unwin, 1963.

B. Södersten, *International Economics*, Macmillan, 1970.

M. E. Kreinen, *International Economics: A Policy Approach*, Harcourt Brace Jovanovitch, 2nd edition, 1975.

WELFARE ECONOMICS

J. de V. Graaff, *Theoretical Welfare Economics*, Cambridge University Press, 1967.

I. M. D. Little, *A Critique of Welfare Economics*, Oxford University Press, 1950.

E. J. Mishan, *Cost–Benefit Analysis*, Allen & Unwin, 1971.

D. M. Winch, *Analytical Welfare Economics*, Penguin Books, 1971.